WALK
TO WIN

THE EASY 4-DAY
DIET & FITNESS
PLAN

OTHER BOOKS BY THE AUTHOR:

WALK, DON'T RUN. Philadelphia: Medical Manor Press, 1979.

THE DOCTOR'S WALKING BOOK. New York: Ballantine Books, 1980.

THE DOCTOR'S WALKING DIET. Philadelphia: Medical Manor Books®, 1982.

DIETWALK®: THE DOCTOR'S FAST 3-DAY SUPERDIET. Philadelphia: Medical Manor Books®, 1983. Pocket Books edition, New York, 1987.

WALK, DON'T DIE. Philadelphia: Medical Manor Books®, 1986. Bart Books edition, New York, 1988.

DIETSTEP®: The Working Woman's Easy Two-Step Diet & Fitness Plan. Philadelphia: Medical Manor Books®, 1990

WALK TO WIN

THE EASY 4-DAY DIET & FITNESS PLAN

BY

Fred A. Stutman, M.D.

MEDICAL MANOR BOOKS®

Philadelphia, PA

WALK TO WIN™
THE EASY 4 DAY DIET & FITNESS PLAN

MEDICAL MANOR BOOKS® is the registered trademark of Manor House Publications, Inc. REG. U.S. PAT.OFF.

DR. WALK® is the registered trademark of Dr. Stutman's Diet & Fitness Newsletter. REG. U.S. PAT.OFF.

DIETSTEP® is the registered trademark of Dr. Stutman's Walking Weight-Loss Program. REG. U.S. PAT.OFF.

FIT-STEP® is the registered trademark of Dr. Stutman's Fitness Walking Program. REG. U.S. PAT.OFF.

WIN-STEP™ is the trademark of Dr. Stutman's Life-Extension Program.

WALK TO WIN™ is the trademark of Dr. Stutman's Health, Fitness & Weight-Control Program.

Grateful acknowledgement to Dame Jean Conan Doyle for permission to use the Sherlock Holmes characters created by Sir Arthur Conan Doyle.

Library of Congress Cataloging-in-Publication Data

Stutman, Fred A.
    Walk to win.

    Includes index.
    1. Walking.   2. Physical fitness.   3. Reducing.
I. Title.
RA781.65.S89   1988   613.2′5   85-63311
ISBN 0-934232-08-3
ISBN 0-934232-07-5 (pbk.)

First Edition: June, 1989
Manufactured in the United States of America

To
Irene & George

And to:

The millions of potential walkers who have been sitting patiently along the side-lines waiting for the dead and disabled to be carried off the fitness-revolution battlefield. We have patiently watched as the jangled joggers, the aerobic acrobats, the calisthenic crazies, the wobbly weight-lifters, the raunchy race-walkers, and the wacky work-out nuts have all gone down for the final count. And now, fellow walkers, we are finally the rightful-rulers of the health and fitness revolution. We have won our cause by watchful waiting, patience and perseverance. Let's hold our heads up high and our tummies in and we can finally **Walk To Win!**

AUTHOR'S CAUTION

EVEN THOUGH WALKING IS ONE OF THE SAFEST AND LEAST STRENUOUS FORMS OF EXERCISE, IT IS STILL ESSENTIAL THAT YOU CONSULT YOUR OWN PHYSICIAN BEFORE BEGINNING THIS WALKING EXERCISE AND DIET PROGRAM.

Fred A. Stutman, M.D.

ACKNOWLEDGEMENTS

EDITOR: Dr. Suzanne T. Stutman

MANAGING EDITOR: Patricia McGarvey

ASSOCIATE EDITOR: Roni Bruskin

ASSISTANT EDITORS: Maryanne Johnston, Carol A. Verdi, M.D.

EDITORIAL STAFF: Sheryl Bartkus, Ann Birchler, Patricia Hartigan, Rose Schmidt, Mary Stutman, Linda Quinn

PERMISSIONS: Marvin Aronson, M.D.; ICI Americas, Inc.; J & J Snack Foods, Inc. (Superpretzel®); Alexander Leaf, M.D.; New England Journal of Medicine; Rorer Pharmaceuticals; Scholl, Inc.; Sons of The Copper Beeches.

SIR ARTHUR CONAN DOYLE: Grateful acknowledgement to Dame Jean Conan Doyle for permission to use the Sherlock Holmes characters created by Sir Arthur Conan Doyle.

CARTOONS: Reg Hider, Norm Rockwell.

WORD PROCESSING: Risa Sady, At Your Multiple Service, Co., Philadelphia, PA

TYPOGRAPHY: Graphic Arts Composition, Philadelphia, PA

BOOK PRODUCTION: R.R. Donnelley & Sons Company

PUBLISHER: Medical Manor Books®, Philadelphia, PA

TABLE OF CONTENTS

"For every **walk** is a sort of crusade, preached by some Peter the Hermit in us, to go forth and reconquer (**win**) this Holy Land from the hands of the Infidels."

"I think that I cannot preserve my health and spirits, unless I spend several hours a day at least — sauntering through the woods and over hills and fields, absolutely free from all worldly engagements."

Henry David Thoreau

"I like to walk about amidst the beautiful things that adorn the world."

George Santayana

"When you have worn out your shoes, the strength of the shoe leather has passed into the fiber of your body. I measure your health by the number of shoes you have worn out."

Ralph Waldo Emerson

INTRODUCTION

When I first started walking as a form of exercise over 25 years ago, I never realized that walking would become the major preoccupation of my life. Walking for me at first was just a way to lift my spirits—a form of meditation. After many long hours at the hospital, I needed a way to relax that was easy and convenient. In those days we didn't have fitness clubs or health spas. No one ever thought of adults exercising, unless they were on a bowling team or played golf or tennis.

Well, one night after two consecutive shifts at the hospital, I went out for a walk on a cold, crisp November night. I remember the moon was full and the air was filled with frost. I had felt physically fatigued and mentally exhausted that evening because of a particularly trying stint in the accident ward, where one emergency after another came in conveyor-belt style.

As I walked around the hospital grounds, the feeling of fatigue that so wracked my body seemed to dissipate. The mental lethargy that encompassed me began to lift. The cloudy thought processes that had hung over me like a nebulous cloud seemed clear. I actually felt refreshed, alert and alive as if I had never worked those 2 consecutive 12-hour shifts at all. My pace became faster and faster, my heartbeat quickened and my mind raced with wondrous thoughts. When I returned to the hospital, one of the other residents asked me if I was just coming on shift since I looked so alert and refreshed.

What had I done to feel this good? I was actually a different person than the one who had left the hospital a little more than an hour before. I tried to think if I had eaten or had drunk anything before I left the hospital that had acted as a stimulant. And then I realized, it could only have been that clear-crisp walk. Had I discovered a magic elixir? Did other people feel this good from walking? Was it only the unusual set of circumstances that surrounded my walk that made me feel so exhilarated? I would not learn until many years later and after much research that that little walk would be the start of something much bigger than I or the way that I felt. Walking was to become the major focus of my research along with the practice of medicine for the next 25 years and hopefully for the next 50 years.

This book which is now the seventh book that I have written on walking presents new irrefutable medical evidence that walking is by far the safest and most effective exercise for good health, physical fitness, weight control and longevity. Clinical research has now proven without a shadow of a doubt that strenuous exercise, fad diets and sedentary lifestyles all have the potential to cause serious disease, disability and even death.

In **WALK TO WIN**, you'll see how aerobic classes, fitness clubs, exercise clinics, and weight machines are responsible for a multitude of injuries and disabilities, ranging from simple muscle strain and fractured bones to strokes and heart attack. You'll also see how fad diet programs cause rapid rebound weight gain and potentially serious side-effects. And you'll see why sedentary people have a higher incidence of obesity, diabetes, hypertension, heart and vascular disease, and premature aging and death.

In **WALK TO WIN** you'll discover the secret of the *five frightening fitness fallacies*. You'll marvel at the *new 4-day step for fitness and pep and the easy 4-day diet plan*. You'll learn why *walking women win* and why *real walkers don't do windows*. You'll react with amazement to *Dr. Walk's fitness facts and diet tips*. You'll observe the miracle of a *figure supreme and a body that's lean*. You'll also realize why walking produces *body shaping not body breaking*. And finally you'll discover the secrets of *how to look younger and live longer*. And lastly you'll be spell-bound by the *Mystery of The Walking Men*.

Remember, walking every day is one of the only defenses that we have against the degenerative diseases of aging. Walking reduces stress and tension and lowers blood pressure, controls weight and fights obesity, prevents heart disease and strokes, retards certain forms of cancer and slows the aging process. If you want to live an additional 15, 20, even 25 years, then you'd better start walking as if your life depended on it—it does!

"A WALKING SHOE? THAT'S WONDERFUL! OUR LAST NEIGHBORS LIVED IN A JOGGING SHOE. THEY'RE DECEASED NOW!"

"ARE WE FIT AND HEALTHY YET?"

REG HIDER

I. FIT-STEP®: FITNESS WALKING PROGRAM

"Walking is the safest and most effective exercise known to man or woman. Walking is a moderate intensity, aerobic rhythmic exercise, which provides all of the health, fitness and cardiovascular benefits of strenuous exercises, without the dangers and hazards."

Fred A. Stutman, M.D.
WALK, DON'T DIE
Philadelphia: Medical Manor Books, 1986

"MY PULSE RATE HAS NOW REACHED ITS TARGET GOAL. IF THAT'S SUPPOSED TO BE SO GOOD FOR ME, THEN WHY DO I FEEL SO BAD?"

CHAPTER 1

FIVE FRIGHTENING FITNESS FALLACIES!

WHAT—ANOTHER WALKING BOOK?

When my editor asked me if I was planning a new book, I answered yes. She then said, "It's not a walking book is it?" And I again said, "yes."

"What more is there to write about walking," she asked in amazement.

"Until I have everyone in America walking," I stated, " I won't be satisfied."

She asked incredulously, "What else can you say about walking? In 1979 you first wrote about walking when the jogging craze was in vogue and walking was not even considered an exercise. You then wrote about walking when jogging was on the way out and aerobics was becoming the in-exercise. You also wrote about walking when fitness centers were in the forefront and walking wasn't even considered as a second rate contender. And now that walking is finally in as the number one exercise in America, you want to write about walking again. Everyone knows that you're the *'Father of the Walking Revolution'* and that they've nick-named you *Dr. Walk*®. What more could you possibly tell them?"

"Well for one thing, I want people to realize that walking isn't just for wimps. That's the tag that the exercise-nuts and the so-called fitness experts have tagged us with over the past two decades. Walking is an exercise for all seasons and for all reasons. Walking helps to relax not only the mind but the whole body as well. Just as music hath powers to soothe the savage beast, walking has the power to heal the ravages of time, inactivity, gluttony, obesity, sedentary life-styles, lethargy, slothfulness, anxiety, depression, disease, disability and even death. Yes walking is truly a real man's and woman's exercise. Walking is an exercise that's finally in. So lets all *Walk to Win!*"

WALK TO WIN is a unique book because it is not just an exercise, nor a diet, or a fitness program. WALK TO WIN is a unique concept in the way we live, breathe, eat, laugh, love, and survive this hostile world we live in. This total *body-mind-life plan* was designed to allow all of us to live happier, more fulfilling lives. *Walk To Win* can truly change the way that you live your life and the quality of that life that you live.

By applying a few simple concepts to your everyday lives, you will feel and look better, sleep and love better, play and work better, and live a better, happier, longer life. WALK TO WIN is not just a great diet and fitness program, it is a unique concept to follow for the rest of your life. It is actually a total body and mind commitment to a healthier, happier, more fulfilling way of life.

There's no doubt about it—if you follow the WALK TO WIN principles, your life will be longer, more rewarding, and it will be the best life you could possibly hope for. How can you believe that such a simple concept can produce all of these promises? Just follow the easy steps outlined in the book and you'll to become a believer. Walking is at the core of the moral fiber and biological structure of our minds and our bodies. In essence, it is at the very center of our existence.

The beauty of the WALK TO WIN program is that it's not really a program at all, not at least in the strict sense of the word. There are no hard and fast rules to follow. There are no strenuous calisthenics or exercises to endure, no rigid diets to adhere to, no special meals to prepare, no strict schedules to follow, and no difficult techniques or rules whatsoever, to master. In fact, there's nothing that you have to do that doesn't fit easily into your everyday lives. The walking and diet schedules are completely flexible and can be adjusted to suit your own needs and daily life-styles. As I have already stated, this plan which is really not a plan at all, is the WALK TO WIN WAY OF LIFE.

WALK TO WIN lets you really take charge of your life as never before. You'll excel at work, at play and at home. This is a program that lets you succeed at anything you set your mind to. You will overcome any obstacle that crosses your path, by simply applying the **WALK TO WIN** principles that will become an everyday part of your life. It's as easy and natural as breathing itself. Some say that winning is everything. Well if that's true, then walking to win is your own personal victory march.

You will be able to steer your life smoothly through any type of turbulent currents or troubled waters, with the efficiency of an experienced sea-captain. Just close your eyes and listen as the walking music of life permeates your whole being. Let the music of walking into your heart and the song of winning into your soul. Let the melody of **WALK TO WIN** release you from the bondage of mediocrity, anxiety, defeat, depression and failure. Inhale the cool, crisp, refreshing oxygen and blow-out the dirty polluted air and carbon dioxide. Let the good thoughts in and the bad feelings out. Let the inhaled oxygen unleash the pent-up energy in all of your body's tissues and cells. Yes, you will **WALK TO WIN** the war against obesity, disease, disability and even death. By *Walking To Win,* you will be winning back your life and that's a bet you can't afford to lose.

IN THE BEGINNING

I began my research into the health benefits of walking nearly twenty five years ago while I was still a young medical officer in the United States Air Force. My associates and I developed one of the first walking programs for cardiac rehabilitation in the nation. At that time, we were criticized for recommending any type of exercise for coronary patients, let alone such a strenuous exercise as walking. Coronary patients were put immediately to bed for six to eight weeks and were told to engage in little if any activity for the first six to nine months after their discharge from the hospital.

As you are all probably aware, the pendulum has swung full circle, and now patients with coronaries are out of bed within a week or two, depending on the severity of the heart attack. These patients are immediately started on a gradual walking program as soon as their EKGs and blood tests have returned to normal. Even patients who have had bypass surgery are up and around in a week to ten days and begin a gradual walking program as soon as they are discharged from the hospital. Walking has finally become an established part of the armamentarium of cardiac rehabilitation programs.

In the mid to late seventies, the country was engaged in its new masochistic exercise craze called jogging. For those of you who forget what that so-called form of exercise was—I'll give you a brief description of its characteristics:

1. First you must buy a designer running outfit and monogrammed running shoes.
2. Secondly, you must arise every day at 5:30 or 6:00 A.M. at the latest and don the above apparel without first bathing.
3. You must then descend onto the mist-filled streets in what appears to be your undergarments—no matter what the weather.
4. Next, you must engage in ritualistic stretching exercises which can only be described as a duckbill platypus cleaning its bill of lichen and debris.
5. Then, you must run through city or town like Paul Revere, grunting your groaning message to the sleeping populace.
6. You must not forget to pound the pavement with 4 to 5 times your body's weight to insure destruction of your ligaments, bones, and muscles, not to mention your internal organs.
7. Next, you must remember that no matter how much it hurts, no matter how fatigued or exhausted you are, and no matter what your body's pain is screaming at you—*you must never, never stop.*
8. And lastly, and above all else, *you must never smile.* No one living has ever seen a jogger smile, so make sure you're not the first. The only way we can tell that you are in pain is by the grimace on your face, and that is the characteristic trait unique to this truly American masochistic sport.

It was at the time of this jogging craze that I first published my little-known monograph entitled *Walk, Don't Run.* I was met with warm enthusiasm by the jogging American public—"buzz off,"—"get lost"—"go take a cold shower." What good can an exercise be if it doesn't hurt? What level of fitness can you attain without strenuous backbreaking, bone-shattering exercise? How can it possibly be worthwhile if it doesn't get your heart rate up to astronomical numbers? What god-fearing American would engage in a pansy type of sport that doesn't even work up a sweat? Who in his right mind is going to go in for a sport that doesn't have designer clothes or at least dues? And what self-respecting exercise nut is going to engage in a so-called sport that doesn't cause pain, disability, disease and even death? And besides, whoever saw a walker grimace—they're all smiling.

One editor liked my book at that time, probably because he was in such bad physical shape that he felt that walking might be his only hope. He called me into his office and said, "I'd really like to publish your book, but we have a problem with the title." He said that their bestselling book at that time was Jim Fixx's *Complete Book of Running*, and they weren't going to risk competing with it by putting a book in their catalogue called *Walk, Don't Run*. So they decided—or we did—on the bland title—*The Dr's Walking Book*, which incidentally, has gone into its fifth printing this spring, long after the jogging craze and unfortunately Jim Fixx met their respective demises.

Jim Fixx wasn't the only casualty of this death-defying exercise craze. Hundreds of thousands of Americans suffered either disease, disability or death during the dangerous, debilitating, decadent decade of the jogger. The casualties of this so-called jogging exercise craze can still be seen in hospitals and cemeteries across the nation. Never has a nation done so much for so little. The ultimate elusive physical fitness goal was a myth created by jogging and fitness entrepreneurs, in order to line their pockets with silver and gold. The fitness revolution spawned a whole host of gimmicks to part the exercise-seeker from his money. Designer clothes and monogrammed running shoes, health and fitness clubs, weight-loss and diet clinics, running and jogging associations, exercise and weight machines, are but a few of the many senseless costly ruins of the so-called fitness revolution.

FIVE FRIGHTENING FITNESS FALLACIES

I would like to present the five exercise and fitness myths or fallacies that will prove without a shadow of a doubt that strenuous exercise actually shortens rather than prolongs your life. Walking, on the other hand, is the safest, most effective exercise to provide good health, weight control, physical fitness, and longevity for people of all ages and all levels of physical fitness and all degrees of fatness.

1) THE MYTH OF THE MARATHON RUNNER

In the late 1970's, there was what I'd like to call the *First Exercise Myth* circulating throughout the nation. And that myth was that "**No Marathon Runner Ever Died of Heart Disease.**" Not only was that myth disproved during the last ten years, but in fact these runners may have actually precipitated heart attacks by their strenuous activity. The reason for that is that many people have undiagnosed coronary artery disease whether they are runners or sitters. This fact may stem from a multitude of factors—dietary, environmental, hereditary, obesity, hypertension, etc.

Many of the marathon runners including the late Jim Fixx, who had underlying coronary artery disease, duped themselves into believing that running would magically make them "**immune to heart attacks.**" And, unfortunately, many of these people might still be alive today had they had complete physical exams, stress EKG's and possibly coronary arteriograms, instead of believing the "hype" that running made you immune to heart disease.

2) THE MYTH OF THE JOGGER'S HIGH

The second exercise myth is that the "**Jogger's High**" or "**Jogger's Euphoria**" which comes from the group of brain chemicals known as endorphins is a healthy factor to be desired. The truth of the matter is that moderate to mild exercises like walking raise the level of endorphins to moderate levels, which have a mood-elevating and relaxing effect on the body. It gives you a feeling of calm and a sense of well-being. How many times have you noticed that after a walk you feel relaxed, refreshed, calm and more energetic? You are able to think clearly and concisely perhaps about a problem that had perplexed you previously. That is what I refer to as WALKING'S WITCHCRAFT—the calm, serene enchantment of walking leads you down the peaceful path of restful relaxation, fighting the voodoo of stress and tension.

Jogger's high, on the other hand, can make you die. The

extremely high levels of endorphins that occur with strenuous exercise, including jogging, have an analgesic, almost narcotic-like effect, as opposed to the relaxation effect of moderate levels of endorphins attained by walking. These abnormally high levels of endorphins make a jogger or exerciser completely numb to any type of pain. This is why so many runners and aerobics participants have injured themselves without feeling any pain. These injuries range from **simple strains and muscle pulls to severe tendon and ligament injuries and even broken bones**. It is not unusual for a runner or an aerobic exerciser to be completely unaware of the pain of a broken ankle or foot bone until some time after the exercise is over. Then, like in the cartoons, where they have the delayed effect after a bomb goes off in Daffy Duck's face—he lets out a delayed blood-curdling "**YOWL**."

Recent medical reports have also indicated that a condition known as "**silent ischemia**" may occur during strenuous exercise without the participant being aware of any pain whatsoever. This silent ischemia refers to the fact that the heart does not get enough blood supply either because of **diseased, narrowed arteries,** or because of the condition known as **coronary spasm**.

Both of these conditions are aggravated by strenuous exercise which narrows the arteries down even further, thus reducing the blood supply to the heart. If enough of the blood supply through the coronary arteries is restricted to the heart—the heart cries out in pain—a condition known as angina pectoris. But with high levels of brain endorphins, these cries are in vain, because they never reach the sensory part of the brain and subsequently the diminished blood supply to the heart may result in a heart attack with no feeling of pain at all. This pain may not occur until after the exercise is completed, providing that the person is lucky enough to still be alive. Many people unfortunately die of a heart attack during the actual exercise with no pain whatsoever.

There are some people who may be lucky enough to feel a little pain through this mask of analgesia and might stop and seek medical help. Others, unfortunately, who feel some pain, may think that it is "a good thing—a part of the exercise"—and will continue to "run through the pain" until they drop over. "I must keep up with my instructor, I'll be finished soon"—sooner unfortunately than many think.

3) **THE TARGET HEART RATE MYTH**

The third strenuous exercise myth, and by far the most popular one—even today—is what I call "**The High Pulse Rate Theory or the Target Heart Rate Fallacy.**" In other words, if you exercise hard enough and long enough you'll get your heart rate up to astronomically high numbers—the higher the better according to the so-called fitness experts. They even like to make it complicated so that it's more interesting when you calculate just how fast your heart rate is going. You take your pulse rate and multiply that by 220 and divide that by your grandmother's age and the number that you get is the number of minutes that you can hope to survive the exercise. The rule of thumb is that the higher the pulse rate for the longest number of minutes, equals the shortest possible life span that you can possibly hope to attain.

No one has ever proved that a rapid heart rate during exercise is beneficial to good health and cardiovascular fitness. On the contrary, medical studies have repeatedly shown that a rapid heart rate sustained for any significant length of time is a highly dangerous condition. For instance, at a **pulse rate of 120 beats per minute, your blood pressure starts to go up significantly**, and at a rate of **140 beats per minute, 95% of people develop a transient type of hypertension**. This temporary high blood pressure is not harmful unless the rapid pulse rate becomes sustained with repeated bouts of strenuous exercise. Then, a condition of permanent high blood pressure (hypertension) may develop.

With each of these bouts of a rapid heartbeat from strenuous exercise, small tears may occur in the artery walls. As the body repairs these tears, scar tissue forms, making the artery wall susceptible to the formation of cholesterol and calcium deposits. These deposits may cause the artery to narrow down. If it occurs in the brain, a **stroke** is likely to develop. If it occurs in the coronary arteries, then a **heart attack** is likely. And if it happens in the legs, then poor circulation may result, a condition known as **intermittent claudication**.

Also, some people may have a congenital weakness in an artery in the **brain (aneurysm)**. Strenuous exercise may elevate the blood pressure high enough to cause a brain hemorrhage—like a blow-out on a tire. Strenuous exercise may also cause **abnormal heart rhythms** ranging from simple palpitations to fatal arrhythmias (wild, erratic heart beats) leading to **heart failure** and **cardiac arrest**. This is especially likely if the patient has underlying coronary artery disease or high blood pressure.

Walking, on the other hand, raises the pulse rate only moderately. This is more than sufficient to accomplish the primary purpose of aerobic exercise, which is to **increase the maximum oxygen consumption** by aiding in the uptake and distribution of oxygen from the atmosphere and distributing it by way of the cardiovascular system to all of the body's cells. This is accomplished by walking without any fanfare or high pulse rate being necessary. The constant infusion of oxygen to the body cells is a gradual one, and this process which takes place at the cellular level (metabolism) is what **slows the aging process**. *The longer you walk, the longer you'll live.*

4) THE MYTH THAT STRENUOUS EXERCISE STRENGTHENS THE HEART

The fourth strenuous exercise fallacy is that "**Strenuous Exercises Strengthen the Heart and Cardiovascular System**." In other words—"**If you're fit, you're healthy— Right?— Wrong!**" Physical fitness is not the same as good health. ***Physical fitness*** by definition means that you have ***built up the capacity to do physical activity with less effort than when you were unfit.*** For example, you can lift heavier weights than when you first started your weight-lifting program.

Being ***healthy,*** on the other hand, means one thing only—to be ***free of disease.*** You can be the most physically fit person in America and still be filled with arthritis, cancer, or heart disease. And doesn't running and strenuous exercises make the heart healthy? Definitely not! Doesn't jogging strengthen the arteries and the heart and lungs? Not in a million years! So what's all this talk about running and strenuous exercise being so good for you? Sorry, but you've been handed another pile of cow manure.

Strenuous exercises do nothing but condition the actual muscles engaged in the exercise. For instance—the legs, arms, back, chest wall, and respiratory muscles. These are the muscles getting the workout, and they are the only ones that are getting the extra oxygen. Initially, strenuous exercise starts as if it were a moderate exercise like walking which is an **aerobic exercise**. This means that the *oxygen demand to the large muscles doesn't exceed the oxygen supply.* Even though the exercising muscles are getting more than their share of oxygen, there is still enough to go around to the rest of the cells in your body (liver, spleen, intestines, etc.) that are not actually engaged in the exercise itself.

As this strenuous exercise progresses at a faster clip, the exercising muscles begin to demand more and more oxygen until a point is reached where the *oxygen demand exceeds the supply of oxygen* that we can breathe in. This is now known as **anaerobic exercise** or anaerobic metabolism (without oxygen). At this point blood begins to be diverted away from our little friendly body cells (liver, spleen, kidneys, GI tract, etc.) and shunted towards the exercising muscles. If this anaerobic exercise continues for too long of a period of time then these cells can become temporarily or permanently damaged — bloody diarrhea, blood in urine, intestinal cramps, etc.— which has occurred in marathon runners and in some individuals after strenuous exercise.

There eventually comes a point, however, when the exercising muscles can no longer get enough oxygen from the air we breathe or cannot steal any more oxygen from the cells of the body. At this point, the body goes into a condition known as **OXYGEN DEBT**. The body then begins to break down muscle starch (**glycogen**) in order to squeeze out a little extra energy without using oxygen. This breakdown of glycogen causes the formation of a chemical called **lactic acid** which produces muscle cramps, weakness and fatigue, and causes you to stop exercising.

When you stop exercising you still owe oxygen (oxygen debt) to these muscle pigs who have been gobbling up all of your oxygen. And you must get rid of the accumulated lactic acid. As soon as you stop exercising you automatically begin to **pant** (breathing deeply and rapidly). The extra oxygen that you now take in goes to the muscles that were unable to get enough oxygen during exercise and you are actually paying off their oxygen debt. The additional oxygen is also used to *remove the lactic acid* from the muscles and to *replenish the stored packets of energy (ATP)* that the exercising muscles stole during oxygen debt.

Do you remember that the exercising muscles gluttons

stole extra oxygen from our body's cells—the non-exercising ones. Well, then wouldn't it be fair to say that they should be first in line to get their extra supply of oxygen when the oxygen debt is paid off. Right? Wrong again! The little body cells get stood up for the second time in a row—while they watch patiently with their little mouths open ready to drink in the extra oxygen—the exercising muscle pigs gobble it all up again to pay off their oxygen debt. Whoever said life was fair.

These cells now run a second risk from a lack of blood supply, better known as **ischemia**. This may result in damage to your kidneys, intestinal tract, spleen, pancreas and adrenal glands. For example, marathon runners can develop a severe form of kidney damage known as **tubular necrosis** (death of kidney tissue) caused by a combination of dehydration and a loss of blood supply. **Intestinal infarcts** (hemorrhages) may also occur causing not only bloody diarrhea but even death of a segment of the colon. Any vital organ in the body could conceivably be damaged by a prolonged lack of oxygen rich blood.

5) NO PAIN, NO GAIN MYTH

There can be no doubt whatsoever that strenuous exercises including jogging, race-walking, aerobics and weight-machines among others have one thing in common. They are all dangerous to your health. These death-defying masochistic, strenuous exercises all have the potential to cause disease, disability and even death.

The only positive thing that resulted from this so-called fitness revolution, is that it underscored what I have been saying for the past 25 years. And that is that an exercise doesn't have to be painful or stressful to be beneficial. In other words, the **NO PAIN, NO GAIN**, principle is another one of *the fitness myths*. It is not necessary to feel pain or discomfort to become fit and healthy. On the contrary the truth of the matter is—"MUCH PAIN, NO GAIN"—"NO PAIN, MUCH GAIN."

Walking, without even looking like an exercise, produces the same physical fitness and health and weight-control benefits as the more strenuous exercises, without the dangers and hazards. There can be no doubt that strenuous exercises are harmful and dangerous to life, limb and the pursuit of fitness. Why engage in an exercise that could actually shorten rather than prolong your life. You can now exercise safely without fear of loss of life or limb, because *Walk to Win is finally in.*

AND SO, "ENTER THE WALKERS"!

Remember that old expression "go take a hike!" Well fortunately a lot of people are now taking that bit of advice literally and are actually going outside every day to take a nice refreshing walk. Yes, even in the dead of winter, men and women are actually leaving their warm houses and television sets and taking healthful walks. What's going on? It just used to be those nutty joggers who braved the elements for the sake of running. Well the trend has finally come full circle and now it's time for the new improved exercisers—"enter the walkers."

Well it's about time! The most beneficial, safest, and healthiest exercise has lain dormant for centuries. Not since the days of the ancient Egyptians have people begun to take walking seriously as a formidable exercise. The fact that it was "too easy" and "just too obvious" like Poe's purloined letter, was one fact that kept its secret hidden. Also the fact that the exercise promoters filled the media with their hype that "an exercise had to be painful and stressful in order to be beneficial." These so-called fitness experts filled their pockets with gold by promoting the fallacy that "no pain, no gain" was the only way to achieve physical fitness.

And so the potential walkers sat patiently, as the hundreds of thousands of health clubs, fitness clinics and diet centers sprang up like weeds across the country. The so-called fitness experts continued to drum into their brains that these dues-paying clubs were the only way to remain fit and healthy. So the walkers remained sitters and watched with wondrous eyes as millions of Americans became injured and disabled in the name of fitness.

Then the physicians entered the fitness arenas to heal the injured sports enthusiasts, and the whole new field of "sports-medicine" was founded. Now these sports physicians, instead of simply telling these injured patients to stop exercising, began to mend and splint them, so that they could return to the battlefield of fitness and re-injure themselves. And then these able-bodied physicians attempted to re-heal them again, so that they might once again fight for their country in the name of Life, Liberty, and the pursuit of Health and Fitness. And this army of the limping lame gallantly re-entered the fitness battlefield and re-injured themselves over and over again, all in the name of God, Country and Fitness.

And the potential walkers who were still sitting at home, sat and stared with wondrous eyes at the fitness revolution. These sitters also watched with astonishment as the fitness-soldiers were injured and as their doctors mended and bandaged them, so that they might return to fight the good fight in the fitness revolution.

When once the revolution was over, and the dead lay strewn across the battlefield, then the sitters slowly got up and walked cautiously out onto the battlefield and looked with amazement at the dead and disabled. They looked also at one another and finally a light shone in their eyes. They had come all this way to find out what they already knew deep in their hearts—that they and only they were the "chosen ones"! That these good people who had sat quietly all these years, now would have their place in the sun. That they would once again resume their places as the rightful rulers of the fitness world. These sitters who for so long were potential walkers, would now be able to leave their chairs without fear of reprisal from fitness buffs, and walk into their role as the undisputed winners (even if by default) of the fitness revolution.

And so—*"ENTER THE WALKERS"!* May you reign forever more and may you be beneficient gods to the masses. May you never require that these huddled masses sweat and strain for the sake of fitness. May you never make them engage in back-breaking exercises in the name of health and fitness. And may you never set stringent diet restrictions on the dieting masses, or require that they take liquid or powdered protein drinks, or diet pills for weight control.

We as a people know that you will be kind and provide weight control, health and fitness benefits without strict controls or guidelines. Nor will you make us pay exorbitant dues to join your walking clubs and associations. We hope that you will not fleece our coiffures of gold to make us buy designer clothes and shoes so that we may worship your walking ways. Please be kind and good rulers, and help us to derive health, fitness and weight control benefits, free-of-charge and free-of-injury, disease, death and persecution. O' Thank you "almighty walkers of the world!"

No longer do we have to feel inferior to the joggers and runners, aerobic dancers and jumpers, weight-lifters and the mangle-machine enthusiasts. We can now hold our heads up high for the very first time in history. And who do we have to thank for this new feeling of energy, vitality and exhilaration? Why no other than our good friend and ally Dr. Stutman, who single-handedly started the walking revolution back in 1979. It took him 10 years to fight for our cause, but in the end we won! We now are the rightful-rulers of the health, fitness and weight control revolution. We have won our cause by watchful waiting, patience and perseverance. And so now fellow walkers, we can hold our heads up high and *WALK TO WIN!*

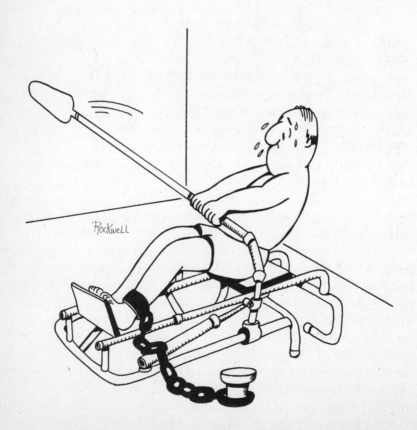

"NO PAIN, NO GAIN—I MUST BE INSANE!"

CHAPTER 2

4-DAY STEP FOR FITNESS AND PEP

TAKE THAT FIRST STEP FOR ENERGY, FITNESS AND PEP

With the advent of modern technology, man is forced by design to do less and less physical labor, since he has invented machines which do these jobs for him. It would seem that this would result in more energy available for other activities. How many times have you noticed that the less you do, the more tired you feel, whereas the more active you are, the more energy you have for other activities? Exercise improves the efficiency of the lungs, the heart and the circulatory system in their ability to take in and deliver *oxygen* throughout the entire body. This oxygen is the catalyst which burns the fuel (food) we take in to produce energy. Consequently, the more oxygen we take in, the more *energy* we have for all of our activities.

Oxygen is the vital ingredient which is necessary for our survival. Since oxygen can't be stored, our cells need a continuous supply in order to remain healthy. Walking increases your body's ability to extract oxygen from the air, so that increased amounts of oxygen are available for every organ, tissue and cell in the body. Walking actually increases the *total volume of blood,* making more red blood cells available to carry oxygen and nutrition to the tissues, and to remove carbon dioxide and waste products from the body's cells. This increased saturation of the tissues with oxygen is also aided by the opening of *small blood vessels,* which is another direct result of walking.

So let's take that first step for energy, fitness and pep. Walking every day will keep a fresh supply of oxygen surging through your blood vessels to all of your body's hungry cells. Don't disappoint these little fellows because you depend on them as much as they depend on you. If you short-change them on their daily oxygen supply, they'll take it out on you in the form of illness and disease. A Fit-Step® a day keeps the doctor away.

ON YOUR MARK, GET SET, DO THE FIT-STEP®

When you first start your Fit-Step® walking program, pick a level terrain, since hills place too much strain and stress on your legs, hips and back muscles. Concentrate on maintaining **erect posture** while walking. Walk with your shoulders relaxed and your arms carried in a relatively low position with natural motion at the elbow. Don't hold your arms too high when you walk, otherwise you will develop muscle spasms and pain in your neck, back and shoulder muscles.

Make sure you walk at a **brisk pace** (approximately 3 to 3½ mph) for maximum efficiency. When you begin walking your respiration and heart rate will automatically become faster; however, if you feel short of breath or tired, then you're probably walking too fast. Remember to stop whenever you are tired or fatigued and then resume walking after resting.

Concentrate on walking naturally, putting **energy** into each step. Soon you will begin to feel relaxed and comfortable as your **stride** becomes smooth and effortless. Walk with an even steady **gait** and your own rhythm of walking will automatically develop into an unconscious synchronous movement.

Your Fit-Step® walking program should be planned to meet your individual schedule; however, when you begin it's a good idea to walk at a specific time every day to ensure regularity and consistency. You will be able to vary your schedule once you have started the program. Lunchtime, for example, is an ideal time to plan a half-hour walk since it combines both calorie burning and calorie reduction. If you have less time for lunch, you'll eat less. Better yet, take an hour walk on your break and carry your lunch (example: an apple and a fruit drink or a small carton of skim milk).

FIT-STEP®:
4-WEEKS IS ALL YOU NEED

To get the most benefit from your Fit-Step® walking program, you should walk **one hour every other day** or ½ **hour daily** after you have completed the 4-week Fit-Step® conditioning program (Table I). The following table includes the slow, brisk and fast pace schedules for the first four weeks of your Fit-Step® program. It is not important which pace you choose as long as you are comfortable with it and consistent in the **TIME** that you walk every other day. In fact, you may find that your pace (miles per hour) falls somewhere in between any of these walking speeds. This is perfectly acceptable, since this program of walking is based on *regularity* and *consistency*—**NOT SPEED**. Remember, the Fit-Step® program is for good health and fitness, not for speed records.

Once you have completed this 4-week conditioning program, you are ready to begin walking ½ **hour daily** or **1 hour every other day of the week**. How far should you walk in this hour? Don't worry. It's the **time**, and not the distance, which is the most important factor. Whether you walk 2½, 3, 3½ or even 4 miles in *one hour,* you will still gain the same fitness, health and weight loss benefits from your Fit-Step® walking program. You will be *walking 4 days each week to keep your fitness and energy level at its peak*.

Remember, the speed of walking is not important, unless you are walking too slowly (under 2 mph). The most important factor is that you walk regularly at a relatively brisk pace. If you become tired easily or get short of breath or develop pain anywhere then you are probably walking too fast (a speed over 4 mph is usually too strenuous for most of us). If these symptoms persist or any other unusual symptoms occur, check with your physician immediately. See Medical Precautions at the end of this chapter.

TABLE I

YOUR 4-WEEK FIT-STEP®
CONDITIONING PROGRAM

WEEK/DAY	TIME	SLOW PACE (2 mph) DISTANCE	BRISK PACE (3 mph) DISTANCE	FAST PACE (4 mph) DISTANCE
1st Mon.	15 min.	½ mile	¾ mile	1 mile
1st Wed.	15 min.	½ mile	¾ mile	1 mile
1st Fri.	15 min.	½ mile	¾ mile	1 mile
1st Sun.	15 min.	½ mile	¾ mile	1 mile
2nd Mon.	30 min.	1 mile	1½ miles	2 miles
2nd Wed.	30 min.	1 mile	1½ miles	2 miles
2nd Fri.	30 min.	1 mile	1½ miles	2 miles
2nd Sun.	30 min.	1 mile	1½ miles	2 miles
3rd Mon.	45 min.	1½ miles	2¼ miles	3 miles
3rd. Wed.	45 min.	1½ miles	2¼ miles	3 miles
3rd. Fri.	45 min.	1½ miles	2¼ miles	3 miles
3rd. Sun.	45 min.	1½ miles	2¼ miles	3 miles
4th Mon.	60 min.	2 miles	3 miles	4 miles
4th Wed.	60 min.	2 miles	3 miles	4 miles
4th Fri.	60 min.	2 miles	3 miles	4 miles
4th Sun.	60 min.	2 miles	3 miles	4 miles

4-DAYS A WEEK IS REALLY NEAT

Remember, it's the amount of **TIME** that you walk every day that is more important than the distance or even the speed. If you walk **1 hour every other day** or ½ **hour every day**, it doesn't make any difference whether you are walking 2, 2½, 3, 3½ or 4 miles per hour. You are still burning calories, losing weight, and developing physical fitness. In other words, **it doesn't matter how far you walk as long as you walk regularly.**

If you would like to measure how far you've walked, the simplest way is to use the odometer on your car. Drive along the course you intend to walk and the odometer will record the distance you traveled in miles. Once having done this a few times you will be able to measure similar distances in the same neighborhood or area by yourself. Ten to twelve city blocks usually equals one mile, so that if you walk around one square block approximately three times, you will have walked approximately one mile. All you have to do is walk 4 **days a week**—one hour every other day or ½ hour daily and you'll be *fit, trim, and healthy for the rest of your life!*

There are other more specific methods of measuring distance which we will now discuss. Remember, however, that these methods are for your own information and pleasure in walking. They are not a necessary part of your Fit-Step® walking program since it is only the **TIME** that you walk each day, and not the distance which is really important. Some people like to know how far or how fast they've gone, so we've included these charts for them. The rest of us can just go out for a nice refreshing walk!

1. FIT-STEP® PEDOMETER

By far the easiest method for measuring distance is using a pedometer. For a nominal fee, you can purchase a reliable pedometer at any sporting goods store. It is a small instrument resembling a watch, which attaches to your belt or pocket, and measures how far you walk in any given time period. Its mechanism depends upon an oscillating weight which causes the dial to advance a certain distance with each step. All you have to do is set the stride-length adjustment on the pedometer and walk at a steady even pace. The distance you walk in any given time period is then recorded on the dial.

2. FIT-STEP® WALKING SPEEDS (mph)

Another easy method you can use for estimating the distance that you walk, is to actually time your walk. This method is based on the most common walking speeds (measured in miles per hour): slow (2 mph), brisk (3 mph), and fast (4 mph).

DISTANCE	SLOW SPEED (2 mph)	BRISK SPEED (3 mph)	FAST SPEED (4 mph)
½ mile	15 minutes	10 minutes	7½ minutes
1 mile	30 minutes	20 minutes	15 minutes
1½ miles	45 minutes	30 minutes	22½ minutes
2 miles	60 minutes	40 minutes	30 minutes
2½ miles	75 minutes	50 minutes	37½ minutes
3 miles	90 minutes	60 minutes	45 minutes

Example: Take a 30 minute walk in an area that is familiar to you. Consult the chart. If you have walked 1 mile, then you walk at a speed of 2 mph. If you've covered a distance of 1½ miles, then your walking speed is 3 mph. And if you've walked a distance of 2 miles in 30 minutes, your walking speed is 4 mph. After you become sure of your walking speed (Ex.: 3 mph), you can estimate how far you've walked in areas where you are unfamiliar with distances. Time your walk, consult the chart under the column of your walking speed and you'll see approximately how far you've walked.

3. FIT-STEP® STEPS

You can also determine the time it takes you to walk one mile by counting the number of steps that you take in one minute at your normal walking speed. The following chart is based upon the average stride, which is approximately *two feet per step*. Since there are 5,280 feet in one mile, and you divide that by 2 feet, then it will take 2,640 steps to walk one mile. Refer to the step/min. column in the following chart, and find the number closest to the number of steps you take per minute. You will then have the approximate time it will take you to walk one mile. For example, if you take about 132 steps per minute, then it will take you approximately 20 minutes to walk a mile or 60 minutes to walk 3 miles; therefore you walk at a speed of 3 mph. Sound complicated? It is!

STEPS/MILE (2 foot stride)	STEPS/MINUTE	DISTANCE WALKED	TIME
2,640	44	1 mile	60 minutes
2,640	48	1 mile	55 minutes
2,640	53	1 mile	50 minutes
2,640	59	1 mile	45 minutes
2,640	66	1 mile	40 minutes
2,640	75	1 mile	35 minutes
2,640	88	1 mile	30 minutes
2,640	106	1 mile	25 minutes
2,640	132	1 mile	20 minutes
2,640	176	1 mile	15 minutes

Note: This chart will vary slightly depending upon the length of your foot and the length of your stride. To determine your stride length in feet, measure the distance from toe to toe or heel to heel that you take with each step. If your stride is considerably more or less than two feet, then you have to divide that number into 5,280 feet and make up a new chart. If you want my advice, you'll forget this chart entirely and go out and take a nice refreshing Fit-Step® walk.

TAKE THE NEXT STEP FOR VIGOR, VIM AND PEP

At the end of your 4-week Fit-Step® conditioning program you will begin to notice the many changes brought about by your improved **aerobic fitness and maximum oxygen capacity** (the uptake and distribution of oxygen through your body). You will have lots of pep and energy, a trim figure, improved breathing capacity and muscle tone, improved exercise tolerance, a better night's sleep, a feeling of peace and relaxation, and a lessening of tension. Once you have completed this 4-week conditioning program, you will have taken the first steps towards improved cardiovascular fitness, good health and a long, happy life.

The great part about walking as an exercise is that you aren't limited to a particular time or location. Walking doesn't require special clothes, shoes or equipment. You can walk before or after work or if you drive to work, you can park your car a block or two from the office, and walk the rest of the way. If you take the bus or train, get off a stop before your station and walk. An enclosed mall could be the perfect place for your walk in bad weather. Remember to take that half-hour from your lunch break and walk, or just walk for the whole hour. Just think of how good that fresh air will feel.

Each city usually has a guide book containing historical sites, restaurants, shops of interest, cultural centers and interesting walking tours. If you live near a park, the country or the seashore, a walking trip will be a refreshing change. Take the time to walk everywhere. Each new area has its own natural beauty. The wonderful world of walking is literally at your feet. For more information about the highways and by-ways of walking check the Fit-Step® Walking and Hiking Organizations in chapter 13. Just take that next step for *vigor, vim and pep.*

LET'S DO THE INDOOR FIT-STEP®

Don't wait until the "weather is better" to go out and walk. There's no excuse for not exercising at home on any day when the weather is too bad to go outdoors. Be careful about walking when the weather is too cold or windy. Also take precautions against exercising when it's very hot or humid outdoors. Heat exhaustion and occasionally heat stroke are complications frequently found in those crazy screwball jogging nuts that you see running on hot humid days. Remember it's not necessary to walk outdoors if the weather is extremely cold, windy, wet, hot or humid. For more information on *weather warnings* see chapter 13. Here are a few ways to stay on your **FIT-STEP® PROGRAM:**

1. STATIONARY FIT-STEP®:

This is a combination of walking and running in place. Walk in place for 5 minutes lifting your foot approximately 4 inches off the floor and taking approximately 60 steps a minute (count only when right foot hits floor).

Alternate this with 5 minutes of running in place lifting your foot approximately 8 inches off the floor and taking approximately 90 steps a minute (again only count when the right foot hits the floor).

Use a padded exercise mat or a thick rug. Wear a padded

sneaker or walking shoe. Bare feet will cause foot and leg injuries. Repeat this walk-run cycle (10 minutes total) 2 or 3 times daily. If you tire easily, stop and rest.

2. TV FIT-STEP®:

If you have a large family room or a basement recreation room, you can set up 2 TV sets at opposite ends of the room. You can walk for ¼ hour twice a day while watching your favorite shows. You can even watch two different shows at the same time as you walk in one direction and then the other. If you only have one TV, then you can watch when walking towards the TV and listen when walking away from the set. It may look silly, but so are the programs on TV.

3. SKIPPING FIT-STEP®:

If you're coordinated enough to use a rope, skipping can be a fun indoor exercise. Skip over the rope alternating one foot at a time for 5 minutes and then skip using both feet together for 5 minutes. Use a mat or padded rug with a padded low sneaker or walking shoe.

This 10-minute session can be repeated 3 times daily. If you feel you are not coordinated enough for rope skipping, then *skip it!*

4. STAIR FIT-STEP®:

A rather boring but effective method for aerobic fitness is walking up and down the stairs—not running. Wear a padded sneaker or a padded walking shoe and hold on to the rail on your way up and down. This is the only indoor exercise so far with which you can't watch TV.

Five minutes 3 times daily should be more than enough if you can stand it or rather step it. Walk at a speed that is comfortable for you.

5. STATIONARY BIKE FIT-STEP®:

One of the easiest ways to continue your indoor Fit-Step® program is by using a stationary exercise bicycle. This is the only one-time investment you'll ever need to make as you travel the road towards fitness and good health. No other type of exercise equipment is necessary for your Fit-Step® program.

The most important features to look for in a stationary

bicycle are a comfortable seat with good support, adjustable handle bars, a chain guard, a quiet pedal and chain, and a solid front wheel. Most come with speedometers to tell the rate that you are pedaling and odometers to tell the mileage that you pedal. An inexpensive stationary bike works just as well as an expensive one.

Stationary bikes with moving handle bars are worthless. They claim to exercise the upper half of your body. In reality, they move your arms and back muscles passively, which can result in pulled muscles and strained ligaments.

The stationary bike is the safest and most efficient type of indoor exercise equipment that can be used in place of your outdoor walking program. You can listen to music, watch TV, talk on the telephone, or even read (a bookstand attachment can easily be clamped onto the handle bars) while riding your stationary bike. If the bike comes with a tension dial, leave it on zero or minimal tension. Remember, it is not necessary to strain yourself to develop aerobic fitness. Exercises like walking and the stationary bike can be fun, without being painful or stressful.

You should pedal at a comfortable rate of approximately **12 miles/hour.** This will complete your daily exercise requirements in **30 minutes** (divide into three 10-minute sessions to avoid fatigue). Consult the following table for the 4-week stationary Fit-Step® bike-conditioning program before you begin (Table II).

* * * *

Caution: If any of these Fit-Step® indoor exercises cause excessive fatigue, weakness, shortness of breath, dizziness, headaches, chest pain, pain anywhere in the body or any other unusual symptoms or signs, stop immediately and consult your physician. See Medical Precautions—at the end of this chapter.

TABLE II

4 WEEK FIT-STEP® CONDITIONING PROGRAM FOR STATIONARY BIKES WITH SPEEDOMETERS AND ODOMETERS

WEEKS	TOTAL PER DAY (MIN/SEC)	DIVIDED INTO 3 SESSIONS (MIN/SEC)	DISTANCE (MILES)	SPEED (MPH)	FREQUENCY (DAYS) (PER WEEK)
1	10:00	3:20	2	12	4
2	15:00	5:00	3	12	4
3	20:00	6:40	4	12	4
4	25:00	8:20	5	12	4

MAINTENANCE SCHEDULE

5+	30:00 Min	10:00 Min	6 Miles	12 Mph	4 Days/wk

NOTES:

1. Get a complete physical exam from your physician before using the stationary bike. Check Medical Precautions at the end of this chapter.
2. Time pedaled and miles per hour are only approximate. If 12 miles per hour is too fast—slow down.
3. Stop at the first indication of palpitations, weakness, fatigue, shortness of breath, dizziness or pain and/or discomfort anywhere. Always check with your doctor if any unusual symptoms occur.
4. Follow conditioning chart for good health and physical fitness. Do not attempt to set endurance or speed records.
5. The above table can be used to supplement or replace your outdoor Fit-Step® walking program, depending on the weather.
6. If you are already finished with your 4-week outdoor Fit-Step® conditioning walking program (TABLE I), you may be able to follow the daily maintenance schedule without going through the stationary bike conditioning program. If you get tired, move back a week or two.
7. If you have not completed your 4-week outdoor Fit-Step® conditioning program, use common sense and your own level of physical fitness to determine which week you will

begin with on the above table. It's best to start at the beginning.

8. You may alternate days or outdoor walking and indoor cycling or you may even divide each day into half outdoor and half indoor exercise. The choice is yours.

9. Wear a walking shoe or sneaker (never pedal barefoot). A chain guard prevents clothing from getting caught in the bike chain; otherwise roll up trousers.

10. Don't exercise immediately after a meal, before bedtime or when you are feeling ill. Always make sure the room has proper ventilation.

GET A CHECK-UP BEFORE YOU FIT-STEP®

Even though walking is the safest and most hazard-free exercise known to man or woman, it is still essential that you have a complete physical examination by your family physician before starting your walking program. A thorough examination will usually include a complete physical examination, your personal and family medical history, a resting electrocardiogram, a chest X-ray, complete blood testing, a urinalysis and perhaps a pulmonary function or breathing test.

An exercise electrocardiogram may also be recommended for those over 35 years of age and for anyone younger if your physician thinks that it is indicated. This type of electrocardiogram is taken while you are walking on a treadmill and measures your heart's response to stress while you are exerting yourself. Sometimes this test is combined with an injection of dye (Thallium scan) for a more detailed evaluation of your heart's condition. A normal exercise electrocardiogram, however, does not always completely rule out the possibility of heart disease. Your physician may feel that other heart tests, like a coronary arteriogram or an echocardiogram, may be needed if he suspects that you could have heart disease.

It is essential that you follow your own individual doctor's recommendations before beginning any exercise program including walking. Follow your doctor's recommendations after he checks you out and in. And remember, *Walk, To Win!*

MEDICAL PRECAUTIONS FOR YOUR WALKING FIT-STEP® PROGRAM

1. It is essential that you consult your own physician before embarking upon a walking program or any other form of exercise plan whatsoever.
2. If you have a medical disorder that requires that you take medicine or treatment of any kind (e.g., high blood pressure, arthritis, diabetes, etc.), check with your physician before starting upon your walking program.
3. If you develop chest pain, excessive fatigue, dizziness, shortness of breath, pain or discomfort anywhere in the body, stop your walking program and see your doctor immediately.
4. Avoid any exercise, including walking, immediately after eating. Time is necessary for digestion to occur.
5. Never walk if you are ill or injured. The body needs time to repair or heal itself.
6. Avoid walking outdoors in extremely cold or hot weather, or when the humidity is above 60%. Use the **FIT-STEP® INDOOR PLAN** as described in this chapter.
7. Do not smoke. Carbon monoxide from smoking decreases the blood's supply of oxygen to the body's cells and tissues. Nicotine narrows the blood vessels, which impairs the circulation. Also, don't forget about the risks of heart disease, cancer and lung disease, which are the direct result of smoking.
8. Alcohol should be restricted since it has an adverse effect on the heart's ability to respond to exercise. Many cases of abnormal heart rhythms have been reported from the combination of alcohol and exercise.
9. Anytime you become tired, stop and rest. It is important to remember that (2) thirty minute sessions or (3) twenty minute sessions spaced throughout the day are just as effective as a walk for one continuous sixty minute period. Don't push yourself—walking should be fun, not work.
10. Your heart rate usually will not exceed 85-100 beats per minute when you are walking. A rapid heart rate is not necessary for physical fitness and good health. If you

become short of breath or tired or feel your heart pounding, stop and rest; you're probably walking too fast. Remember, a walking program at any speed is beneficial for
fitness and good health.

**"DO YOU THINK WE COULD ATTACH A TV DINNER
TRAY TO THE HANDLEBARS, HARRY?"**

CHAPTER 3

REAL WALKER'S DON'T DO WINDOWS!

WALK-AT-WORK WALKERS, WIN!

A recent study conducted by the Scholl Company of the activity level of various occupations in New York, Chicago and Seattle produced some startling findings. The study was to determine which type of occupation walked the most and the least at work each day. Hospital nurses, sales people and security officers won the top prizes, walking approximately 1500 miles per year at work. Dentists, teachers and secretaries took the booby prizes for walking less than 500 miles per year at work.

Let's look at the following list and see which of us has to get out and walk every day after work, and which of us can lighten up a little on leisure walking. Don't take this study too seriously, but then again don't take it too lightly either. Remember, even if your job profile doesn't appear here you can get an approximation of how much you walk at work each day by comparing your occupation to one that's similar to the activity level listed below. Also remember that walking at work while beneficial, is not the same as taking a brisk refreshing walk in the fresh-air outdoors, excluding perhaps smog-polluted big industrialized city streets.

OCCUPATION	MILES WALKED AT WORK EACH DAY
RETAIL SALESPEOPLE	5.2
SECURITY OFFICERS	5.1
HOSPITAL NURSES	4.9
FOOD SERVERS	4.9
HOTEL EMPLOYEES	3.8
REAL ESTATE AGENTS	3.6
BANKERS	2.8
DOCTORS*	2.5
HOUSEWIVES	2.4
REPORTERS	2.4
SECRETARIES	2.3
LAWYERS	1.7
TEACHERS*	1.7
DENTISTS	1.3

*Surveyed in New York Only

Source: Dr. Scholl's Workday Study, Scholl Inc., Memphis
　　　　Tennessee

START SIMPLY, NOT SIMPLE-MINDEDLY

Why is walking so great? It's the best and safest cardio-vascular fitness conditioner. It's a superior figure trimmer because walking burns calories while it firms and trims thighs, buttocks, and abdominal muscles. And best of all, walking is easy to do and requires no special training or equipment. Walking is kind to your joints, ligaments and bones since you're not pounding the ground with 3-4 times your body's weight as you would in running. Efficient walking causes an impact of approximately 1½ times your body's weight—not enough to do any real damage but enough to exercise you completely.

I'm often asked at walking clinics what types of stretching exercises should you engage in before walking? "Should I do a calf stretch or a hamstring or quadriceps stretch?" The answer I invariably give is that no stretching exercises are necessary before you start to walk. I suggest that you start slowly, getting your blood circulating gently, and gradually build up your momentum until your arms and legs feel limber. Walking is the body's natural muscle and ligament stretcher, so why take the time and trouble to go through a set of silly stretching gyrations before you start to walk. Walking does all of that for you naturally, without the risk of pulling muscles or tearing tendons by so-called stretching exercises. Many an exerciser has had to give up his/her exercise program even before they begin, because of a muscle or ligament injury sustained in pre-exercising stretching rituals. Let your body limber up naturally, as you gently walk down the path to fitness and good health.

The next most frequent question is, "Should I time my pulse by pressing my finger against the carotid artery in my neck?" If you have to ask that now, you may as well throw this book away. I'll say it once more, *"If you have to time your pulse to see how fast you're getting fit, then you shouldn't be walking at all."* Fitness is not a measure of how fast your pulse is going. It's dependent on the maximum oxygen consumption, which by definition is a measure of the body's ability to extract oxygen from the air, distribute it throughout the blood stream from the lungs and deliver it to all of your body's cells, tissues and organs. And that's it! It's not how fast your pulse is going, but it's how steady and regular the oxygen delivery system is functioning. Moderate walking at a pace of 3 miles per hour is the ideal speed (not too fast and not too slow) to enable this oxygen delivery mailman to make all of his appointed rounds without undo fatigue or danger to the mailman himself.

Another frequent question I get at these walking clinics is "Should I carry hand-held weights or wear ankle weights for maximum fitness conditioning?" The answer is unequivocally—NO! Hand or ankle weights defeat the entire purpose of walking. They make walking strenuous. They increase the likelihood of injury. They cause early fatigue and decrease rather than increase the benefits of aerobic exercise. And they have no place in a walking program for fitness and good health, nor in any other exercise program for that matter.

When you start your walking program, start simply. Walk approximately 15 minutes every other day for the first two weeks. Then increase your walking time to 30 minutes every other day for the next two weeks. After that you should begin walking 45 minutes every other day for the 5th and 6th weeks. Now you are ready for the **one-hour walk every other day** for your maintenance program. If one hour every other day isn't convenient for you, then walk ½ **hour daily** which affords you exactly the same health, fitness and weight control benefits.

Always start simply. Don't start your first few weeks of walking on hilly areas or areas with street inclines. Walk on relatively flat surfaces until you have built up your exercise tolerance level. Never be afraid to stop walking and rest if you're tired. If you're short of breath or your heart is beating too fast, then you're probably walking too fast. Always remember to have a complete physical examination by your physician before starting your walking program.

Remember, walking is a *gradual fitness conditioner*. It is not necessary to push yourself to the point of exhaustion. Walking is not a punishment, it is supposed to be fun. And isn't that what we've been talking about all along. We're all looking for fitness, good health, weight control, and longevity. Well, walking fits the bill perfectly. It is the only activity that provides all of these things without killing yourself in the process. Don't let the so-called exercise experts fool you. *Exercise doesn't have to be painful or stressful to be beneficial.* Walking provides all of the essential ingredients in an exercise and fitness program without the hazards.

Disease, disability and **death** don't have to be part of your fitness program. Leave those goodies for the joggers, the racewalkers, the aerobics nuts, the weight lifters, and all the rest of the terrible torture-type exercises that society keeps dumping on us. Remember to begin your walking program simply, and keep it simple thereafter. The *exercise nuts* don't keep their fitness programs easy and simple. That's because they're *simple-minded*.

A MODERATE PACE WINS THE RACE

The key to a successful walking program is to start slowly. Walk around the block once a day for a week or take a 15 minute to one half hour walk in a nearby shopping mall if the weather's bad. Spend a half hour walking during your lunch break or walk a short distance to a local store for a few items—don't carry a heavy bag home. Start to smell the fresh air each day and stop on your walks to rest if you tire easily. Remember, you don't have to walk briskly like a marionette when you first start your walking program. You're just tuning your body up as you gradually improve your cardiovascular fitness. There's no need to shock your system with strenuous activity when you first start a walking program.

Don't forget, walking is a moderate-type of activity, one that you'll stay with for a lifetime. So take your time! Fitness doesn't come overnight. It is a gradual process and one you can't rush. And besides, walking is more than just an exercise. *It's a way of life and a life of ways!*

It's the way to fitness and good health. It's the way to happiness and a feeling of well being. It's the way to increased energy and vitality. And it's the way to a long healthful life. *A moderate pace wins the race! The race of life!*

TOO TIRED TO MOP? TRY A WALK AROUND THE BLOCK!

Are you too tired to do the housework? Are you too fatigued to work out in the garden? Do you feel that you're not able to do any type of leisure activity, let alone exercise? Well it's actually this lack of activity that leaves you feeling chronically fatigued. Recent studies at a major university revealed that people who exhibited chronic fatigue had considerably less stamina and were less fit than a similar group of people who never complained of being fatigued at all.

When both groups were tested on a treadmill and on an exercise bike, the group that complained of chronic fatigue did poorly in all categories of fitness; whereas the group that had no complaints scored high marks in cardiovascular fitness. Their study went one step further to prove a point. The people in the chronic fatigue group who started an exercise program were tested again two years later. The results were that these individuals scored considerably higher on the cardiovascular fitness testing and no longer complained of chronic fatigue. The people who hadn't exercised during this two year period still complained of chronic tiredness and they again scored poorly on the fitness testing.

It was determined that it was actually the lack of activity itself that perpetuated this vicious cycle of fatigue and tiredness, which in turn inhibited the people from exercising.

The main point is that you must make yourself break the *fatigue/lack of exercise cycle!* You must will yourself to start a walking program if you are chronically fatigued. Of course you should first check with your physician to make sure that the fatigue is not a medical problem. Once he clears you medically and it is determined that your tiredness is due to a lack of exercise, then you're ready to start a limited walking program. Remember, I said limited! No one should go from doing no exercise at all, to starting a gung-ho exercise program all at once. This will lead to additional fatigue and exhaustion and you'll give up your exercise program before you even start it. *Too tired to mop? Try a walk around the block.*

RUNNERS BEWARE, SAID THE TORTOISE TO THE HARE

Walkers take anywhere from 15-20 minutes to cover one mile. Runners on the other hand go at speeds two to three times as fast. Does this mean that runners get more protection against heart attacks than walkers? Not on your life!

A recent medical study from Toronto, Canada compared the blood cholesterol levels of two groups of exercisers. One group consisted of runners averaging 7 to 10 minutes per mile and the other group of walkers averaging 16-20 minutes per mile. Both groups lowered their total cholesterol and increased their HDL cholesterol (high density lipo-protein or "good" cholesterol) which has a protective effort on the heart. The theory behind this improvement in the level of blood fats is that the exercise burns calories, causing weight-loss. This weight loss helps to lower the cholesterol and increase the HDL levels. *You burn approximately the same number of calories whether you walk or run a mile,* so that the weight-loss factor is nearly the same for each exercise.

These results depended on the distance covered and not the speed. The runners and walkers who covered 10-12 or more miles per week had the lowest cholesterol and highest HDL levels. Walking ½ hour daily or one hour every other day at a brisk pace of approximately 3 miles per hour seems to fit the bill perfectly.

Runners and strenuous exercisers, on the other hand, who usually engaged in infrequent short bursts of activity, rarely maintain a high level of HDL cholesterol for long periods of time, because they usually don't keep up with their exercise program on a regular basis. Also, these short bursts of activity result in partial anaerobic activity, which unlike aerobic exercise does not lower cholesterol nor raise HDL levels. The reason for this is that in anaerobic exercise the body spends most of its time supplying oxygen to the exercising muscles only and very little time supplying oxygen to the rest of the body. This results from the condition known as oxygen-debt as we have previously discussed. When the body is busy paying off its oxygen-debt it has very little energy to contribute to the body's metabolism and thus cannot effectively lower blood cholesterol and raise the HDL cholesterol levels.

So again we have another example of the tortoise and the hare. Slow and steady wins the fitness race and in this particular case—the cholesterol race. Walkers have the lowest total cholesterol and highest HDL levels of almost any type of athletes and/or exercisers because of their moderate, regular walking programs. Like the mailman, neither rain nor snow nor dark of night will slow the walker's appointed rounds. Walkers are committed to a life-style that includes walking as a regular part of their daily lives and walking will improve the quality and quantity of each one of their lives. *Runners beware, said the tortoise to the hare.*

FAST FEET ARE NOT DISCREET

The so called sport "fitness-walking" may be just that, a so-called sport. Advocates of fast-walking or race-walking have coined the term "fitness-walking" as being the desired type of walking program for fitness development. Not so! As we have previously seen, the faster we walk the more likely we are to change the exercise from a beneficial aerobic type of exercise to a potentially dangerous anaerobic exercise which is lacking in the vital life-giving element, oxygen.

Now, the American Academy of Podiatric Sports Medicine has reported a 70% increase in the amount of injuries of the foot and ankle related to fast-walking types of activities. The faster you walk the more likely you are to sustain an injury of your foot, ankle, knee or hip. This was the consensus of opinion of two-thirds of the podiatrists surveyed. Rapid walking puts an excessive strain on the ligaments of the foot, ankle and knee. In particular, hill-walking, which many of these hot-shot, racewalking enthusiasts advocate, is extremely hazardous to the lower extremity.

Not only does climbing hills at a face pace raise the heart rate and blood pressure to potentially dangerous levels, but it also puts considerable strain on the ligaments, tendons and bones of the foot, ankle, knee and hip. Even more dangerous to the foot and leg is the rapid descent that these exercise masochists take as they literally run down these hills. Down-hill walking or in this case down-hill running, is actually much tougher on the muscles and joints, since the heel hits the ground with a significantly greater force than level or up-hill walking. Since the leg is extended at the knee when the heel lands, in order to allow the foot to reach the ground, the knee is less able to flex and absorb the tremendous shock of the heel strike. The result: torn cartilages and ligaments which support the knee.

Stick to level ground most of the time to reduce or minimize foot, ankle, knee and hip injuries. If you must go up inclines or hills, take them gently. Remember moderate walking is for fun and physical fitness. If you start to make it like work, then you might as well be at work or doing some activity that you really hate, like cleaning out the basement or the garage. Let walking remain the get-away-from-work-and-tension-activity that it was meant to be. Let the fast walking nuts spin. We'll all just *Walk to Win*.

STEAMY SHOWER — NOT FOR AN HOUR!

Exercise, particularly strenuous exercise, increases the blood flow to the exercising muscles. The faster you exercise the more you perspire to maintain your body's temperature. If you take a hot shower immediately after exercising you increase the blood circulation to the skin. The combination of the increased blood flow to the muscles and the increased circulation to the skin can be a dangerous combination. The blood supply to the body's vital organs may become dangerously diminished, because of this shunting of blood away from the internal organs to the muscles and skin.

This may result in a feeling of light-headedness or can

actually cause a person to faint. Cases of heart attacks have also occurred in hot, sweaty athletes who take hot showers immediately after exercising. It is recommended that you cool-off just before you shower, so your body temperature returns to normal. It's safer if you wait for at least an hour. It is recommended that if you must shower right after exercise, the water should be cool to luke warm rather than hot. This allows the body temperature and heart rate to return to normal. Walkers don't usually have this problem since it is not necessary to work-up a sweat while walking for fitness. But if you do perspire, then heed this precaution.

RACE-WALKERS ARE FAST-TALKERS

Race walking enthusiasts are trying to make you believe that race walking is better for you then regular old walking. Don't believe them! They're fast-talkers, that's all. Race-walking is a poor-man's type of jogging and is equally fraught with injuries and disabilities. The only difference between race-walking and jogging is that different ligaments and joints are injured in each so-called sport.

What distinguishes race-walking from regular walking is its exaggerated motions. Race walkers take a much longer stride than walkers, to the point that their legs straighten fully. This hyperextension of the leg can lead to knee injuries. They reach out with a straight leg, landing on their heels with a high-impact ratio. Then they roll forward onto their toes and push off again. Sound complicated? It certainly is! And if you think it sounds complicated you should see how it looks. I can only describe it as a cross somewhere between a fat duck waddling and a gorilla walking hunched forward on all fours. If you think jogging is painful, you should watch a race walker's face—it looks as though someone put glass in his shoes and burrs in his shorts, and he's trying to walk very carefully so that you won't know that he's in pain.

Race walkers also keep their arms close to their bodies at a 90 degree angle. Rather than swinging their arms freely as in regular walking, they use exaggerated short choppy upper arm and shoulder motions to accomplish their ridiculous set of gyrations. They claim that this is what helps them to walk faster. So what! What's the purpose of walking faster? None at all! Studies show that the faster you walk the more likely you are to be injured, and there's no evidence that faster walkers are fitter than moderate-paced walkers. In fact much to the contrary, the moderate-type of exercise provides better fitness development because of the continuous infusion of oxygen to the body's cells and tissues. Faster exercises, as we have seen, spend too much time supplying the exercising muscles with oxygen and not enough time sending this precious cargo of oxygen to our inner body cells.

Another serious hazard of race-walking, not to mention its silly appearance, is the exaggerated hip-motion that race-walkers must have in order to produce their daffy duck gyrations. Because of their very long stride and short choppy upper arm motions, the hips have to waddle in order to prevent the walker from falling on his face. One runner told me that he no longer had any leg pains when he gave up jogging for race-walking. Now he said, "Only my low-back and hips hurt whenever I sit down or try to stand up." Low back and hip injuries are very common in race-walkers and can be extremely debilitating.

The last but not least, often overlooked injuries in race-walkers are those involving the heel, ankle, and the forefoot. With the intense heel-strike and rolling forward motion on the outer sole of the forefoot, fractures of the small bones of the feet and ankle ligament injuries are being seen with increasing frequency. And don't forget, race walking is designed to be a competitive, not a healthful and relaxing activity. So here again, we're faced with competition, not fun for fitness. Who needs the hassle anyway? Not real walkers. *Real walkers are just walkers, not fast talkers!*

Our bodies were made for natural walking, not exaggerated race-walking. Not only is it an unnatural activity, but it is a potentially dangerous type of sport. It seemed that just when Americans were getting it through their thick skulls that jogging was dangerous to their health, along came another fitness guru with his new and better exercise for the modern man. If God had intended us to be race-walkers he would have given us tiny little stubby legs and arms, and a rear-end designed for rolling on the ground, not walking.

Why do people have to tamper with a good thing? Why can't they leave well enough alone? Probably because the promoters can't make enough money from you if you're just a walker. So they have to come up with exotic exercises and contraptions to help you unload your wallet, so that you'll be lighter and better able to walk faster. *Race-walkers are fast-talkers—they're not really walkers at all!*

REAL WALKERS DON'T DO WINDOWS!

Let's take a fun walk for fitness. That's what walking's all about—**fun**! Don't let anyone tell you that the only type of walk that's good for you is the new so-called "fitness walking." There's no such thing! It's just another gimmicky term coined by some exercise enthusiasts who don't even know the difference between physical fitness or the back side of a mule.

Any walk, no matter what the speed, distance, or time, is a walk for fitness. Walking at any speed is beneficial to your health. Cardiovascular fitness, contrary to popular belief, is not dependent on the speed of your heart rate or how fast you're walking. In fact, the faster you walk, the faster your heart beats, and the less likely you are to gain any benefits whatsoever, let alone cardiovascular fitness. Recent medical studies show that walking at a moderate pace of 3 miles/hour produces maximum cardiovascular fitness. This is because all of the body's cells and tissues are constantly infused by a continuous supply of oxygen. This produces a lowering of blood pressure, a decrease in blood fats, an improvement in the efficiency of the heart's pumping action, an increased flexibility of the blood vessels throughout the body, a lessening of the chance for blood clot formation and an overall improvement in the body's metabolic processes.

Rapid walking over 4-5 miles per hour like jogging, race walking and other strenuous sports actually results in a decrease in the cardiovascular conditioning process. First, as we have previously seen, the rapid heart rate causes a transient, often permanent rise in blood pressure. Secondly, the rapid heart rate and increased blood pressure can cause microscopic tears in the walls of the arteries in the body. These small tears are repaired by scar tissue, making them likely spots for cholesterol and blood clots to form. Thirdly, the elevated blood pressure can possibly cause strokes to occur if you happen to be unlucky enough to have inherited a weakened blood vessel in the brain. This elevated blood pressure can cause a weakened artery to blow out like a tire. Fourthly, rapid heart rates during exercise can occasionally cause erratic heart beats to occur (arrhythmias). If these abnormal heart beats persist, they could conceivably lead to heart failure and/or sudden death, if you happen to have underlying heart disease or hypertension.

And lastly, rapid heart beats during strenuous exercises can cause the internal organs of the body to suffer. As we have previously seen, when the body is doing strenuous exercise, the only parts of the body that can be supplied with oxygen fast enough are the exercising muscles themselves (legs, arms, chest wall, back and respiratory muscles). And when these muscle gluttons can't get enough of the oxygen on their own, they steal it from our internal organs by making the arteries shunt the blood away from these organs to their hungry muscle mouths. And even when these muscles have spent every last cent of oxygen, they beg, borrow and steal energy from their own muscle fibers, by breaking down a chemical called glycogen in the muscles to lactic acid and small amounts of energy (anaerobic metabolism—without oxygen). Then these muscles actually go into "oxygen debt." They owe everybody! They owe oxygen to the body's organs, to the body's muscles and to the body's blood supply.

So what do these muscle robbers do? Well like any dyed-in-the-wool gambler, they try to pay off their gambling debts! When the body is too pooped to pop, the exerciser must stop exercising and pant like mad to breathe in extra oxygen to pay off its gambling debts. So who gets paid off first? Not our starved internal organs who loaned their hard-earned oxygen to the muscle gamblers. No, it's the muscle-goons themselves that gobble up all of this extra oxygen to pay-off the lactic acid and muscle mob, to get themselves out of oxygen debt. The last on the list to get their allotment of oxygen are your trusty internal organs. Who ever said life was fair?

Well, what happened in the meantime to these trusting internal organs who believed that this was a short-term oxygen loan anyway? When any organ is deprived of oxygen-rich blood for too long a period of time, a condition known as *ischemia* sets in. This condition results in damage to the organ or tissue which is deprived of blood. In the case of your intestinal tract, bloody diarrhea or vomiting may occur. And if the blood supply isn't returned promptly, then ischemia or death of sections of tissue (in this case, stomach or intestinal tract) may occur, which would require surgery (resection) to remove the dead areas.

In the case of your kidneys, small hemorrhages (infarcts), may occur. If dehydration is combined with this lack of blood supply, then this could result in permanent kidney damage (a type of nephrosis). All of the other internal organs including the spleen, liver, pancreas, adrenal glands, ovaries, testicles, etc. could be similarly affected by a decrease in their respective blood supplies. *So let's give our organs a nice refreshing walk—they'd thank you if they could talk!*

So when someone tells you to take your pulse while you're exercising so that you can reach your maximum training heart rate, (by subtracting your age in years from 220 and multiplying the result by 0.6 and 0.9 in order to get the bottom and top of your target heart rate for aerobic training),—tell them to go and multiply the hairs on their feet by those on their head and stuff the answer in their shoes and walk on it! *Real Walkers don't do windows or time their pulses for that matter!*

ODE TO A MALL WALKER!

Neither rain, nor sleet, nor dark of night will keep the mall-walkers from their appointed rounds. This hardy new breed of walkers have been hitting the cement floors in malls across the country in increasing numbers. In fact, mall walkers are among the largest organized groups of walkers in the United States.

While conducting walking clinics across the country, I was especially impressed with the growing number of mall walkers. In fact, many of the seminars that I have given on the health and fitness benefits of walking have been conducted in numerous malls across the nation. These groups of mall-walkers are more organized than any group of walkers that I have seen anywhere in the country. And for the most part, the majority of these mall walkers are senior citizens. You would never know it to look at these enthusiastic young-looking walkers, since most of them look and act 10-15 years younger then their chronological ages. These walkers love what they're doing and walking loves them back—*taking years off their lives with every step that they take.*

I was amazed to discover during my walking clinic tour that the management of many of these malls are opening their doors ½ to 1½ hours earlier than the stores actually open, in order to accommodate these dedicated walkers.

An obvious benefit to the mall walkers is the controlled climate in these enclosed malls. No longer hindered by rain, snow, heat, humidity or any type of inclement weather, these walkers stroll comfortably each and every day. Another plus is that the mall walkers no longer need to fear stray dogs, cars, muggers, bikes or children playing ball in their paths. No longer hampered by an uneven terrain where injuries may occur or where too much stress is exerted on hills, the mall walker can walk with a regular stride and pace on the even, level mall floor.

Many people have complained of boredom when they walk daily around the same city blocks. Mall walkers, on the other hand, have a constantly changing scenery with new sights, sounds and aromas each day they walk. Many displays in the store-windows change from week to week offering a panorama of different visual effects. Don't get the wrong idea, these mall walkers don't do window-shopping walking. Not on your life—or theirs either for that matter. These walkers walk briskly and catch these sights on the walk, so to speak. Of course if anything strikes their fancy they can always return to a display after they've finished their walk.

Many walkers like the companionship of people when they walk, and mall walkers certainly have a monopoly on fellow walkers. Many of these walkers have found new friends and have formed long-lasting relationships outside the malls with their fellow walkers. If they prefer, they can certainly walk alone and enjoy the exhilarating-high of walking, without the need to be with other walkers. Walking alone or with others is an individual matter and whatever makes you feel good is the right choice for you.

Many malls have formed walking clubs sponsored in co-operation with area hospitals or local health organizations like the American Heart Association. Many of these organizations provide the mall-walkers with mileage records to keep track of their progress. Some mall sponsors have even posted mileage markers on the mall walls in order to mark off distances for the mall walkers.

With the growing number of senior citizens in the United

States there is an ever increasing growth in mall-walking across the nation. And as more senior citizens take up walking, there will in turn be more and more seniors around because of the health benefits of walking. I think we can all drink to that. Let's hold our glasses high and toast the mall-walkers of America.

AN ODE TO A MALL WALKER

Long live our country's mall walkers
We know they're not just big talkers
They're the heart of our American pride
All across the nation's countryside
Keep your chest out, tummy in and walk tall
In every town, city and country mall
Hip, Hip, Hooray, when we see your dust
You're an inspiration to every one of us
We're all very proud of what you do
Mall walkers of America, we salute you!

"I'LL CROSS YOU OVER AS SOON AS THE MALL WALKERS PASS."

"NOW WHAT DID DR. STUTMAN SAY? WAS IT—EAT MORE AND WALK LESS OR WALK MORE AND EAT LESS?"

II. DIETSTEP®:

WALKING WEIGHT-LOSS PROGRAM

"There are only two ways to lose weight effectively. One is to eat less and the other is to walk more. If you want to stay fit, trim and healthy — follow a low-fat, low cholesterol, high fiber diet, combined with a regular walking program."

Fred A. Stutman, M.D.
DIETWALK®
Philadelphia: Medical Manor Books, 1983

"CAN YOU BELIEVE THAT I ACTUALLY FEEL THIN-
NER ALREADY AND WE'VE ONLY BEEN WALKING
FOR AN HOUR?"

CHAPTER 4

WALKERS WIN BY STAYING THIN!

DON'T BE OBESE, GET OFF YOUR BUTT AND ON YOUR FEET!

Women are more likely to perceive themselves as fat, whereas in reality, men are more likely to be overweight. In a recent Harris pole of over 1,200 men and women nationwide, the findings were are as follows:

- Over 50% of women considered themselves overweight compared to 38% of men.
- 65% of the men were actually overweight compared with 62% of the women.
- Almost 40% of those people surveyed stated that they were on a diet.
- 60% of those surveyed were overweight, which was exactly the same percentage as last year's survey.
- More than 50% of those surveyed felt they weren't getting enough exercise.

It doesn't appear that we're getting any thinner despite all of the diet books, health clubs, fitness centers and diet promoters! So what's the answer? *Walking, of course!* Walkers by and large are the least overweight segment of any population group. This fact has been verified in one medical study after another.

One 25-state study in particular showed that the proportion of overweight residents varied from 14% in Utah and Hawaii to 24% in West Virginia. Utah has young, health-conscious people, Hawaii has many outdoor activities, and West Virginia has many poor unemployed residents who are inactive.

If you don't want to be obese, get off your butt and on your feet!

THE FAT FORMULA

The latest report from the National Institute of Health meeting in Bethesda, MD (Feb., 1985) again confirmed that obesity is a *major health risk*. The evidence is strong that obesity not only shortens life, but actually affects the quality of life also.

Almost 20 percent of Americans are overweight. How can you tell if you're one of them? It's simple—just follow the **fat formula**:

Females—100 lbs. for the first 5 feet in height, plus 5 lbs. for each additional inch. Example: 5'2" = 110 lbs.

Males—106 lbs. for the first 5 feet in height, plus 6 lbs. for each additional inch. Example 5'9" = 160 lbs.

The increased medical risks for being overweight are: *hypertension, heart attack, stroke, diabetes, arthritis, cancer of all types, and increased surgical risks* if you happen to need an operation. These risks seem to be even worse if most of your weight is carried in the upper body (chest, hips and abdomen) rather than in the buttocks and legs.

If you flunk the fat formula, just Walk-Off-Weight using the **Dietstep® Plan**. Let's put felonious fat where it belongs— off the street and behind bars.

"I DON'T REALLY EAT THAT MUCH!"

The question I get asked most often from patients about being overweight is— "How come I keep gaining weight?" I don't really eat that much." Well, the truth of the matter is that we get fatter as we get older because our physical activity tends to decrease even though our food intake stays the same. The only way to beat the battle of the bulge is to burn those unwanted pounds away. Walking actually **burns calories**. The following table will give you an idea as to the energy expended in walking, which is actually the number of calories burned per minute or per hour (**TABLE III**).

TABLE III

WALKING SPEEDS	CALORIES BURNED/ MINUTE	CALORIES BURNED/ 30 MINUTES	CALORIES BURNED/ HOUR
Slow Speed (2 mph)	4-5	130-160	260-320
Brisk Speed (3 mph)	5-6	160-190	320-380
Fast Speed (4 mph)	6-7	190-220	380-440
Race Walking (5 mph)	7-8	220-260	440-520

A *pound of body fat* contains approximately *3,500 calories*. When you eat 3,500 more calories than your body actually needs, it stores up that pound as body fat. If you reduce your intake by 3,500 calories, you will lose a pound. It doesn't make any difference how long it takes your body to store or burn these 3,500 calories. The result is always the same. You either gain or lose one pound of body fat, depending on how long it takes you to accumulate or burn up 3,500 calories.

You can then actually lose weight by just walking. When you walk at a speed of 3 mph for *one hour every day,* you will burn up *350 calories* each day. Therefore, if you walk *one hour a day for 10 days,* then you will burn up to a total *3,400 calories*. Since there are 3,500 calories in each pound of fat, when you burn up 3,500 calories by walking, you will lose a pound of body fat. You will *continue* to lose one pound of body fat every time you complete 10 hours of walking at a speed of 3 mph. It works every time!

WON'T EXERCISE MAKE ME HUNGRY?

Another myth regarding diet and exercise, is that exercise stimulates the appetite. So after exercise you're hungry, you eat more, and you cancel out any calories you burned during exercise. **Right?—Wrong!**

Contrary to popular belief, walking actually decreases your appetite. It does this by several mechanisms which are described as follows:

1. Walking regulates the brain's appetite control center (appestat) which controls your hunger pangs. Too little exercise causes your appetite to increase by stimulat-

ing the appestat to make you hungry. Walking on the other hand slows the appestat down, thus decreasing your hunger pangs.

2. Walking re-directs the blood supply away from your stomach, towards the exercising muscles. With less blood supplied to the stomach, your appetite is reduced.

3. Walking burns fat rather than carbohydrates and therefore does not drop the blood sugar precipitously. Strenuous exercises and calorie-reduction diets both drop the blood sugar rapidly, and it is this low blood sugar that stimulates your appetite and makes you hungry. Walking on the other hand is a more moderate long-term exercise and consequently burns fats slowly rather than carbohydrates quickly. This results in the blood sugar remaining constant. And when the blood sugar remains level, you do not feel hungry.

4. Walking also helps to keep up the resting basal metabolic rate (BMR). This basal metabolic rate refers to the calories your body burns at rest in order to produce energy. When you go on a calorie restriction diet, your BMR slows up. This is because your body assumes that the reduction in calories is the result of starvation and your body wants to burn fewer calories so that you won't starve to death. The body has no way of knowing that you're on a diet. This is also one of the reasons that you don't continue to lose weight on a calorie reduction diet. The body prevents this excess weight loss by lowering its BMR, so that you stop losing weight, even though you are eating the same number of calories that you ate in the beginning of your diet. If, however, you are combining walking with your diet, then the walking keeps the BMR elevated even though you are dieting. So, in effect, it prevents the BMR from dropping and burning fewer calories, as when you are dieting alone. The result: less hunger and more calories burned when you walk every day, especially if you are also on a diet.

So, you can clearly see that walking, rather than increasing your appetite, actually decreases it! And if you only want to maintain your present weight or just lose a few pounds, you can just add walking to your regular daily activities and *walk off those unwanted pounds!*

However, if you really want to take off a significant amount of weight, then you can cut down approximately 500 calories a day to lose an additional 1 pound per week or just reduce your daily intake by 250 calories to lose an extra pound every 2 weeks. Combined with walking, just a slight reduction in your daily calorie intake is all that you need for permanent, safe weight reduction.

PEOPLE WHO SAT, DIDN'T BURN FAT

If you just count calories, your chances of losing weight are minimal. *Walking,* however, is the only certain way towards permanent weight reduction. The majority of fat people are much less active than the majority of thin people. It is their sedentary life style that accounts for their excess weight and not their overeating. If they just took a brisk walk for one hour every day they could lose 18 pounds in 6 months, or 36 pounds in one year without any change in their diets.

If you want to lose weight permanently, then the energy burned during your exercise should come from *fats* and not from carbohydrates. During the first 20 minutes of moderate exercise, ⅔ of the energy burned comes from carbohydrates while only ⅓ comes from body fats. During the next 40 minutes of exercise, ⅔ of the energy burned comes from body fats and only ⅓ from carbohydrates. It stands to reason, then, that longer periods of a continuous exercise like walking is better for permanent weight reduction than short spurts of strenuous exercise (examples: jogging, calisthenics, racquetball, etc.).

If you increase the duration of your exercise from 20 minutes to 30-60 minutes you will burn more energy from body fats than you will burn from carbohydrates, resulting in weight-loss that really stays lost. Once you've lost your weight, you will maintain your weight-loss better by **walking** 60 minutes every other day or 30 minutes every day than by doing calisthenics or jogging for 15-20 minutes. This occurs because you will be burning a higher proportion of body fats rather than carbohydrates. Remember, *people who sat, didn't burn fat.*

After a large meal, especially around the holidays, many people say—"It doesn't matter how much I eat, I work it off after dinner by shoveling the walk, or jogging, or playing football with the kids." Heavy exercise immediately after a meal is one of the leading causes of heart attacks in middle-aged and older people. The accident ward in all of the hospitals throughout the country are stacked up with coronaries, immediately after the big Thanksgiving and Christmas dinners. Strenuous exercise after a large meal causes the increased supply of blood in the stomach and intestinal tract to be diverted to the exercising muscles. This puts a strain on the cardiovascular system especially in anyone who has a heart or circulatory problem. This is often the first time that many of these people become aware that they have a heart condition, and unfortunately in many cases the last.

A calm *walk,* on the other hand, approximately 1½ hours after eating, does not stress the cardiovascular system and burns many of the excess calories that you should not have eaten in the first place. It's far better to get up and walk away from that big meal before you overstuff your face. When you physically walk away from the table you are removing yourself from temptation, but even more importantly, you are allowing the fullness control center in your brain to catch up to what's really going on in your stomach. You are actually full, but you don't know it yet. Remember, *eating less* and *walking more* are the only two ways to lose weight effectively.

W.O.W.!—WHAT A DIET!

Many studies have clearly documented the *weight-loss effects* of exercise. Even more important is that the weight loss caused by walking is almost all due to the *burning of body fat,* not protein. The only exceptions are a small amount of initial water loss and the burning of carbohydrates during the first 20 minutes of exercise. This weight loss or weight maintenance can be continued indefinitely as long as you walk regularly. You are literally **walking off weight (W.O.W.).**

Not only does walking *before meals* decrease your appetite, but recent studies show that walking approximately 60-90 minutes *after eating* increases the metabolic body rate to burn away calories at a faster rate. It appears, then, that walking after eating is an effective way to lose additional pounds. Never walk however, after a large meal is ingested.

This burning of calories at a faster rate has been explained as a combination of the energy expended from walking and the calories burned from the actual ingestion of food itself. This is called the **Thermic Effect of Food** or the **Specific Dynamic Action**. We actually burn more calories as we eat because the energy metabolism of the body actually increases 5-10 percent. This doesn't mean that the more you eat the more calories you'll burn. But it is a good reason for *walking 60-90 minutes after small meals* for additional weight loss.

Remember, never strenuously exercise after eating, and for that matter, never exercise strenuously at all. And remember, you were told never to even walk after a meal. Well, we are now modifying that rule to read—never walk immediately after eating; however, if you want to lose weight at a faster rate, then walk before meals to cut down your appetite and walk approximately 60-90 minutes after small meals to burn more calories. Sounds good to me! W.O.W.!—What a diet!

DON'T WAIT TO LOSE WEIGHT!

THE DIETSTEP® PROGRAM is based on walking at a brisk pace (3 mph)—provided that there is *no change* in your daily food intake. This weight-loss program is based upon *calories burned by walking only*. By following **The DIETSTEP® PROGRAM**, you will lose weight by actually Walking-Off-Weight!

Three miles per hour is a speed that can be maintained for a long duration without causing stress, strain or fatigue. We are not talking about window-shopping walking which is much too slow (1 to 2 miles/hr) and which is not at all useful in burning calories. Nor are we suggesting fast walking (4-5 miles/hr.) which is too fast to be continued for long periods of time without tiring. And we certainly are not recommending race walking (5 to 6 miles/hr) which is worthless as a permanent weight reduction plan, and has all of the same hazards and dangers that jogging has.

The following walking plans have been designed for either weight loss or weight maintenance. You can walk anywhere, any time, any place, as long as you make the time. Remember, you can always take the time to fit a walk into your schedule. And if you don't have the time—make it! Don't *wait* to lose *weight*, when just walking will make your figure look *great*.

DIETSTEP®
WALKING-OFF-WEIGHT
PLANS

1. DIETSTEP® PLAN #1 (LOSE ONE POUND EVERY 20 DAYS)

On this Dietstep® plan you will walk for **one hour every other day** or ½ **hour every day.** Walking at a brisk pace of 3 mph, you will burn up approximately **350 calories every hour** that you walk. Let's see how much weight you'll lose by this plan.

1) Walk ½ hour daily × 350 calories/hour = 175 calories burned per day.
2) Walk 3½ hours per week × 350 calories/hour = 1,225 calories burned per week.
3) Walk 10 hours every 20 days × 350 calories/hour = 3,500 calories burned or **one pound lost every 20 days** (or 175 cal. burned per day × 20 days = 3,500 calories).

On this walking-off weight Dietstep® plan you will lose one pound every 20 days or 18 pounds in one year. You can actually **walk off 18 pounds in one year without dieting!**

2. DIETSTEP® PLAN #2 (LOSE ONE POUND EVERY 10 DAYS)

On this Dietstep® plan you can lose **one pound every 10 days** just walking **one hour every day of the week.** The only difference in this plan is that you are now walking an hour every day. You will still be burning up 350 **calories** every hour that you walk briskly (3 mph).

Remember, this Dietstep® plan also works without any change in your diet. Since it takes 10 hours of walking at 3 mph to burn up 3,500 calories or one pound, if you walk for an hour every day, you will lose **one pound every 10 days.** By following this plan you can actually lose **3 pounds every month** or **36 pounds in one year.** Not bad, for just walking.

3. DIETSTEP® PLAN #3 (LOSE ONE POUND EVERY WEEK)

For those of you who want to lose weight a little faster, you can walk for **45 minutes twice daily.** By walking a total of **1½ hours every day** of the week you will be able to speed up the walking-off-weight Dietstep® plan. When you walk 1½ hours every day, you will burn up 525 calories each day or 3,675 calories per week. You can see that you will lose a pound a week on this plan with a few extra (175 calories) to spare. You may divide your 1½ hours of walking into **three 30 minute sessions** daily if that's more convenient for you. The weight-loss results will be the same.

This plan will enable you to lose **one pound every 7 days,** or **4½ pounds a month,** or approximately **52 pounds in a year.** Again, all this weight loss occurs without your changing one thing in your diet.

4. DIETSTEP® PLAN #4 (STAY THE SAME WEIGHT)

When you have walked off as much weight as you want to lose and are now satisfied with your present weight, then you are ready for the Dietstep® maintenance plan. You can maintain your present weight on this plan and have an **extra 175-calorie snack every day** as a bonus. Remember, you must continue walking **one hour every other day** or ½ **hour daily** as indicated on the **Dietstep® Plan #1**. You will continue to burn up an extra 1,225 calories every week or 175 calories daily which is where your 175 calorie bonus snack comes from.

By following the Dietstep® Maintenance Plan your weight stays the same while you enjoy your 175 calorie snack every day. All you have to do is walk an hour every other day or ½ hour every day! Sound easy? It is!

5. DIETSTEP® PLAN #5 (FOR CHEATERS ONLY)

Let's say your weight is just where you'd like it to be, but you don't want to gain another ounce. Or say your weight is nowhere near what you would like it to be, but you really can't afford to gain another pound without splitting your seams. Each of you would like to be able to cheat and at least stay the same weight. Well fear no more, the **DIETSTEP® CHEATER'S PLAN** is just for you.

How about a piece of candy, a slice of cake, french fries, a cone of ice cream, a slice of pizza or a cold beer? With **THE DIETSTEP® CHEATER'S PLAN** you have the perfect method that allows you to **cheat** without paying the price. Eat your favorite snack food, consult the following table (**TABLE IV**) and walk the number of minutes listed in order to burn up the extra calories you've cheated on. The following table shows how many minutes of walking at a brisk pace (3 mph) are necessary to burn up the caloric value of those foods listed.

If your favorite snack food is not listed on the following table, you can easily figure out the time you have to burn off your snack's calories. Look in the **Appendix** at the end of this book for the number of calories of your favorite snack food and divide by the number 6. This answer will give you the number of minutes it takes to walk off your snack. The number 6 comes from the fact that walking at a brisk pace (3 mph) burns approximately 6 calories per minute. Example: Frankfurter and roll = 300 calories. Divide 6 into 300 and you get 50. It will take you 50 minutes to walk off this snack—"Hot Dog!"

* * *

TABLE IV
DIETSTEP® CHEATER'S PLAN
BRISK WALKING (3 MPH) BURNS SNACKS

American cheese (1 sl.)	16 minutes
apple (medium)	15 minutes
apple juice (6 oz.)	17 minutes
bagel (1)	23 minutes
banana (medium)	16 minutes
beer (12 oz.)	30 minutes
bologna sandwich	50 minutes
candy bar (1 oz.)	45 minutes
cake (1 slice pound)	63 minutes
chocolate bar/nuts (1 oz.)	28 minutes
cheese crackers (6)	35 minutes
cheese steak (med.)	55 minutes
chicken, fried (3 pieces)	50 minutes
chocolate cookies (3)	25 minutes
corn chips (small pack)	33 minutes
doughnut (jelly)	40 minutes
frankfurter & roll	50 minutes
french fries (2 oz.)	50 minutes
hamburger (4 oz.) and roll	73 minutes
ice cream cone	30 minutes
ice cream sandwich	35 minutes
ice cream sundae	75 minutes
milk shake, choc. (8 oz.)	42 minutes
muffin, blueberry	25 minutes
orange juice (6 oz.)	16 minutes
peanut butter crackers (6)	50 minutes
peanuts, in shell (2 oz.)	37 minutes
pie, apple (1 slice)	46 minutes
pizza (1 slice)	40 minutes
potato chips (small pack)	33 minutes
pretzels (hard—3 small)	30 minutes
pretzels (soft—1 Superpretzel®)	30 minutes
shrimp cocktail (6 small)	18 minutes
soda—cola (12 oz.)	24 minutes
tunafish sandwich	41 minutes
wine, chablis (4 oz.)	14 minutes
Whiskey, rye (1 oz.)	17 minutes

By following any of these five Dietstep® plans you can either lose weight or maintain weight, or just cheat by walking only. **Remember, it's easy to lose weight and look your best. Just do the Dietstep®.**

* * * * * *

6. DIETSTEP®—WALKING & CALORIE REDUCING PLAN #6 (FOR THOSE WHO CAN'T WAIT TO LOSE WEIGHT)

Now by combining the **Dietstep® Walking Weight Loss Plans** (either **½ hour daily** or **1 hour daily**) with the simple reduction of calories, you can lose weight faster than by just dieting alone. See **Table V.**

HOW TO USE TABLE V

1. The 1st column is the **distance** you walk each day.
2. The 2nd column is the number of **calories burned walking** each day.
3. The 3rd column is the number of **calories you must subtract** each day from your present diet, in order to lose 1, 5, 10, 15, or 20 lbs.
4. The 4th column is the **total calories** expended daily (calories burned walking and calories subtracted from diet).
5. The last columns indicate the **number of days** needed to lose 1, 5, 10, 15 or 20 lbs.
6. Consult **Appendix** for caloric values of different foods.

THOSE THAT SAT, DID GET FAT!

Walking is the ideal weight control and fitness program. Studies in human physiology have proven that walking acts as a weight reduction plan without actually dieting and a fitness program without strenuous exercises. Too often today we allow a sedentary lifestyle to dominate our daily living. We sit at our desks all day and in front of the TV set in the evenings. We drive to our destination, no matter how close or

TABLE V

DIETSTEP® — WALKING & CALORIE REDUCING PLAN

(½ HOUR DAILY WALK)

MILES WALKED DAILY	CALORIES BURNED WALKING	MINUS CALORIES IN DAILY DIET	TOTAL CALORIES EXPENDED DAILY	DAYS NEEDED TO LOSE				
				1	5	10	15	20 LBS.
1½ miles	175 cal.	0 cal.	175 cal.	20	100	200	300	400 days
1½ miles	175 cal.	175 cal.	350 cal.	10	50	100	150	200 days
1½ miles	175 cal.	325 cal.	500 cal.	7	35	70	105	140 days
1½ miles	175 cal.	525 cal.	700 cal.	5	25	50	75	100 days
1½ miles	175 cal.	700 cal.	875 cal.	4	20	40	60	80 days

(ONE HOUR DAILY WALK)

MILES WALKED DAILY	CALORIES BURNED WALKING	MINUS CALORIES IN DAILY DIET	TOTAL CALORIES EXPENDED DAILY	DAYS NEEDED TO LOSE				
				1	5	10	15	20 LBS.
3 miles	350 cal.	0 cal.	350 cal.	10	50	100	150	200 days
3 miles	350 cal.	150 cal.	500 cal.	7	35	70	105	140 days
3 miles	350 cal.	350 cal.	700 cal.	5	25	50	75	100 days
3 miles	350 cal.	525 cal.	875 cal.	4	20	40	60	80 days
3 miles	350 cal.	825 cal.	1,175 cal.	3	15	30	45	60 days

how far, instead of doing what's easy, natural and healthful—walking.

Most of us would rather spend 15 minutes in our cars waiting at the drive-in window of a bank, rather than getting out and walking the length of the parking lot. Even at golf we follow the easy path. Instead of using and enjoying this healthful and relaxing sport in a positive way for fitness and exercise, we allow ourselves to be "driven" in little motorized carts around the course. You might as well stay home and watch golf on TV.

In order to lose and control weight effectively, the energy burned during exercise should come from body fats rather than from carbohydrates. As we have previously seen, we burn more body fat after longer periods of a sustained activity (walking) than we do after brief bouts of strenuous exercise (jogging). It is therefore apparent that walking is far superior to brief flurries of exercise for a complete and effective weight reduction and weight control program. Remember—**those that sat, did get fat!**

WALKERS WIN BY STAYING THIN!

The question always comes up as to when you should exercise. Is it before or after eating? How long before? How long after? Many professional athletes schedule their day's activities around their meals. Also, many fitness-enthusiasts actually become fanatical and inflexible about the time sequence of exercise and meals. Although walkers don't have to be as particular about timing their walking in relation to mealtime, it's still essential to become familiar, at least in part, with the physiology of digestion.

As food enters your stomach, the heart pumps a significant quantity of blood into the stomach to aid digestion. This does not pose a problem when you are at rest, but if you decide to exercise immediately after eating, then there is a conflict of interests. The stomach now has to compete with the exercising muscles for the blood it needs for digestion. If the exercise gets vigorous then digestion is arrested and you begin to feel bloated and develop abdominal cramps. Exercise should therefore begin after a meal has passed through the stomach and small intestines. This takes approximately 2-3 hours after ingesting a large meal and from 1-1½ hours after eating a smaller meal.

Foods high in fat and protein are digested slowly and tend to remain in the digestive tract for a longer time than a meal that is higher in complex carbohydrates (pasta, vegetables and whole grain cereals and breads). Foods that are high in refined sugar like cakes, candy and pies can trigger an excess insulin response if they are eaten immediately before exercise. This means that the excess insulin produced as a result of the high sugar content of food, combined with the exertion of exercise, could drop the blood sugar rapidly. This could result in weakness, muscle cramps and even fainting.

On the other hand, fasting for long periods prior to exercise is in itself counter productive. In order to replenish the stores of liver and muscle glycogen needed for energy, it is necessary to eat several hours before exercising. With fasting you are depleting these energy stores, and exercise then becomes difficult and tiring without adequate fuel storage depots for energy.

So what does this all have to do with walking and eating? Very little, if anything. Most of these rules of digestion apply to strenuous and vigorous exercise with relation to mealtime. They do, however, affect us somewhat with regards to our walking program. The most important fact to be learned from this discussion on digestive physiology is that it is essential that you don't walk immediately after eating, especially if you've consumed a relatively large meal (which you shouldn't be eating in the first place). This puts a strain on the cardiovascular system and can even deprive the heart of its own essential blood supply, particularly, if you exercise vigorously immediately after eating (which you shouldn't be doing in the second place).

Walking, however, 1-2 hours after a small to moderate meal can actually aid in digestion, by nudging the foodstuffs gently along the digestive tract. This in no way competes for the blood in the digestive tract, since the walking muscles are gentlemen and gentlewomen, who do not pig-out for every available ounce of oxygen like the strenuously exercising muscle-glutton pigs. In fact, the gentle art of walking allows oxygen to be evenly distributed to all of the body's internal organs, which in this particular case is the digestive tract.

Recent studies indicate a three-fold advantage for dieters

in walking before and after meals. As we have previously seen walking before eating quiets down our appetite-control center in the brain and makes us less hungry. Secondly, walking at any time burns calories directly as we walk. And thirdly, new studies in exercise physiology have shown that walking anywhere from one to 1½ hours after eating a small to moderate sized meal will actually burn 10-15% more calories than walking on an empty stomach. This is explained by a term called the *thermic dynamic action of food*. What this means is that the actual digestion of food-stuffs combined with the gentle action of walking results in a slightly higher metabolic rate, thus burning more calories per hour. You can plainly see how walkers stay thin. They just *Walk to Win!*

"I HAVE A WEIGHT PROBLEM—I CAN'T WAIT FOR DESSERT!"

CHAPTER 5

THE EASY 4-DAY DIET— TRY IT!

BE THE BOSS WITH EASY 4-DAY WEIGHT LOSS

DIETSTEP® is not just another diet program!
DIETSTEP® is not just another fitness plan!
DIETSTEP® is not just another pretty face!

DIETSTEP® is the first medically formulated diet and fitness program for all ages, sexes, and body builds. No matter whether you're fat or thin, short or tall, athletic or unconditioned, young or old, muscular or flabby, coordinated or just a klutz—DIETSTEP® is the perfect diet and fitness plan for you.

DIETSTEP® is the only safe, effective, easy, healthful diet and fitness program available anywhere in the world. And what's more, it's free! There are no dues or membership fees, no calories to count, no complicated meal plans to prepare and no back-breaking, death-defying exercises to endure.

Yes, think of all the money you'll save by walking instead of driving everywhere, and by eating sensible, basic, nutritious, inexpensive foods instead of expensive gourmet diet foods that, incidentally, take forever to prepare. There are no designer sweatsuits or monogrammed shoes to buy, no costly health club fees, no diet pills or protein mixes to buy, no fancy meals to prepare, no exotic health foods to buy and no diet clinics to join.

You won't have to look at exercise video cassettes anymore and you won't need any expensive exercise equipment.

You will also save money on doctor's visits for muscle sprains and fractured bones. And you won't need all those tubes of linaments and bottles of aspirin or analgesics for repeated sore muscles. And, best of all, you can stop buying all those silly diet and fitness books written by those so-called experts who don't know their asp from a snake in the ground.

* * * * * * *

Strenuous exercises, jogging and gimmick diet plans are referred to as the **4D plans**:
   4D: They're **DANGEROUS**, causing **DISABILITY, DISEASE** and **DEATH**

* * * * * * *

The **DIETSTEP®** plan is called the **4E and 4F plan**:
   4E: EASY, EFFICIENT, EXERCISE FOR ENERGY and good health

   4F: FAST, FREE, NO FRILLS DIET FOR FITNESS and weight control

* * * * * * *

THE DIETSTEP® DIET—TRY IT!

The **DIETSTEP® DIET** plan is a **high fiber diet** combined with a diet that is **low in cholesterol, saturated fat, salt** and **sugar.** When combined with a regular **walking** program, it is the only diet that has been proven to be effective in both weight control, fitness and health maintenance.

The **high fiber** content of this diet provides a built-in mechanism against gaining weight and developing many diseases. By reducing the **saturated fat and cholesterol and fat** content of the diet we eliminate many high fat calories that add extra weight and can block our arteries with cholesterol.

The **low sugar** content of the diet eliminates nutritionally deficient calories that add senseless pounds and may contribute to the development of heart disease and diabetes. Reducing the **salt** content prevents excess accumulation of fluids and may help to prevent hypertension in susceptible people.

Even the amount of **caffeine** is limited in this diet, since excess amounts of caffeine can stimulate the appetite center—the very thing we are trying to prevent. Excess caffeine can result in nervousness, insomnia, palpitations and headaches, and it may actually cause many breast, pancreas and heart disorders.

These factors are what makes the **DIETSTEP**® program effective in both weight control and disease prevention. Finally you have a diet that is as good for your insides as it is for your outsides. Here is a safe, effective diet and fitness program that can be continued for a lifetime, providing permanent weight control, good health and physical fitness.

THE EASY 4-DAY DIETSTEP® MEAL PLANS ARE SIMPLE TO UNDERSTAND

The following diet was named the **EASY 4-DAY DIETSTEP**® **PLAN** because it is an easy and simple diet to follow. The diet is divided into the following **4-day meal plans:**

MONDAY & THURSDAY	**MEAL PLAN #1**
TUESDAY & FRIDAY	**MEAL PLAN #2**
WEDNESDAY & SATURDAY	**MEAL PLAN #3**
SUNDAY	**MEAL PLAN #4**

Once you've completed the first few weeks of your diet, the **EASY 4-DAY DIETSTEP**® **PLAN** will become an automatic part of your everyday schedule. The diet is extremely easy to follow. There is no need to remember what to eat at home or what to order in a restaurant for any particular meal. You only have to remember the 4 diet meal plans each week.

Won't this type of diet become boring? Definitely not! There is such a variety of foods included in this diet that your taste buds will never tire of this healthful, nutritional, palatable diet program. By varying the nutrients in the diet, there are never any hunger pangs or food cravings.

Remember, the **EASY 4-DAY DIETSTEP**® **PLAN** is the only diet that in addition to controlling weight, will add years to your life by providing essential, healthful nutrients and eliminating harmful components. This is a diet and exercise plan for fitness and health as well as weight loss and weight control.

After you have reached your ideal weight on this easy 4-day diet program, you will never again have to worry about

rebound weight gain. The **EASY 4-DAY DIETSTEP**® plan
enables you to stay thin, trim and fit utilizing only these
4-simple menu plans during your weight-loss program.

By just following these 4 meal plans you will lose **1 pound
every 10 days** or **3 pounds every 30 days.** To lose additional
weight, you can vary the amount of time that you walk each
day. For faster weight-loss, see Table VI which appears on
page 74 of this chapter.

You can lose weight quickly and safely with the **EASY
4-DAY DIETSTEP**® **PLAN.** Just follow the four easy meal
plans and you will be trim and full of pep, when you do the
DIETSTEP®.

"COUNTING CALORIES MAKES ME HUNGRY"

MONDAY & THURSDAY - MEAL PLAN #1

BREAKFAST:

1 whole medium orange or 4 oz. (½ cup) fresh or unsweetened orange juice

1 slice whole or cracked wheat bread
(½ teaspoon whipped/diet margarine or 1 tsp. jelly)

1 cup coffee or tea (artificial sweetener & non-fat milk)

LUNCH:

1 cup/bowl soup (vegetable, tomato, lentil, bean, pea,
celery, minestrone, consomme, chicken noodle/rice,
manhattan clam chowder - no creamed or pureed
soups) and 2-3 whole wheat crackers.

1 tossed salad with lettuce, tomato and cucumber (lemon and/or vinegar or 1 tsp. low-cal dressing)

1 cup decaffeinated (coffee, tea or diet soda)

DINNER:

1 LT/4C salad (lettuce, tomato, celery, carrot, cucumber, cauliflower)

3-4 oz. pasta primavera (fresh veg. and marinara sauce)

or

Vegetable platter (broccoli, asparagus, squash, cauliflower, baked beans, carrots, green beans, spinach,
mushrooms, stewed tomatoes); choose any three (1/2
cup each); or 3 oz. baked eggplant or zucchini parmesan without oil, butter or breading

1 cup decaffeinated (coffee, tea or diet soda)

EVENING SNACK:

2 cups unbuttered, unsalted popcorn
(hot air popcorn popper without oil)

1 glass decaffeinated (diet soda, coffee or tea)

or

¾-1 oz. cooked or cold whole grain (bran type) unsweetened cereal with ½ cup non-fat milk, ½ medium
banana or 2 dozen raisins (½ oz.)

* * * * * * * * * * * *

WALK ½ HOUR DAILY OR 1 HOUR EVERY OTHER DAY

TUESDAY & FRIDAY - MEAL PLAN #2

BREAKFAST:

½   medium grapefruit or 4 oz. (½ cup) fresh or unsweetened grapefruit juice

1   bran, whole wheat or English muffin
(½ teaspoon whipped/diet margarine or 1 tsp. jelly)

1   cup coffee or tea
(artificial sweetener and non-fat milk)

LUNCH:

2-3 oz. (⅓-½ cup) tuna or chicken salad stuffed in pita
bread (1 tsp. mayonnaise), with lettuce, tomato and
⅓ cup coleslaw. Use tuna packed in water without
mayonnaise if possible

1   cup coffee or tea with artificial sweetener and non-fat
milk, or diet soda

DINNER:

1   LT/4C salad (lettuce, tomato, celery, carrot, cucumber, cauliflower)

3-4 oz. baked or broiled fish (flounder, haddock, halibut,
cod, sole, bass, bluefish, perch, trout) with lemon

1   medium baked potato including skin (no butter, margarine or sour cream)

1   cup decaffeinated (coffee, tea or diet soda)

EVENING SNACK:

2   medium unsalted hard pretzels

1   glass decaffeinated (diet soda, coffee or tea)

or

½-¾ cup low-fat vanilla yogurt or low-fat cottage cheese
with 2 tsp. wheat germ or Miller's bran

* * * * * * * * * * * *

WALK ½ HOUR DAILY OR 1 HOUR EVERY OTHER DAY

WEDNESDAY & SATURDAY - MEAL PLAN #3

BREAKFAST:

3-4 medium dried or stewed prunes (or cantaloupe or honeydew melon or any fresh fruit)

1 slice whole or cracked wheat bread (½ teaspoon whipped/diet margarine or 1 tsp. jelly)

1 cup coffee or tea (artificial sweetener and non-fat milk)

LUNCH:

½-¾ cup fresh fruit salad on bed of lettuce with ½ cup low fat cottage cheese and 2 whole wheat crackers

or

small chef salad with turkey and cheese only; use lemon, vinegar or 1 tsp. low-fat dressing

1 cup coffee or tea with artificial sweetener and non-fat milk, or diet soda

DINNER:

1 LT/4C salad (lettuce, tomato, celery, carrot, cucumber, cauliflower)

3-4 oz. broiled or baked chicken breast, skin removed

½ cup brown long whole grain rice; or ½ cup frozen or 1 small ear whole kernel corn (no butter, margarine, or salt)

1 cup decaffeinated (coffee, tea or diet soda)

EVENING SNACK:

2 cups unbuttered, unsalted popcorn (hot air popcorn popper without oil)

1 glass decaffeinated (diet soda, coffee or tea)

or

1 small/medium piece fresh fruit (apple, pear, peach, plum, banana, apricot or nectarine); or ½ cantaloupe or melon with ¼-⅓ cup raspberries, strawberries or blueberries

* * * * * * * * * * * *

WALK ½ HOUR DAILY OR 1 HOUR EVERY OTHER DAY

SUNDAY - MEAL PLAN #4

BRUNCH:

¾-1 oz. cold whole grain cereal (bran-type) with any fresh fruit (½ cup) and ½ cup non-fat milk and artificial sweetener

or

¾-1 oz. cooked whole grain cereal with artificial sweetener, ½ cup non-fat milk, cinnamon and 2 dozen raisins (½ oz.)

or

1-2 scrambled artificial eggs with 1 slice rye or pumpernickel (½ tsp. whipped or diet margarine)

(Any of the above may have 2 cups coffee or tea with artificial sweetener and non-fat milk and 2 oz. (¼ cup) fresh or unsweetened orange or grapefruit juice.)

DINNER:

3-4 oz. steak (lean), and 1 baked potato with skin and 1 cup cooked vegetable of choice - without butter or margarine

or

3-4 oz. veal tenders, baked with stewed tomatoes, onions, peppers and mushrooms, and 1 small baked potato, including skin (no butter, margarine or sour cream)

or

3-4 oz. roast turkey (white meat) with one small sweet potato (no butter or margarine) and ½ cup of any green vegetable

(Any of the above may have 2 cups decaffeinated coffee, tea, diet soda, and 1 LT/4C salad and either 8 oz. light beer or 4 oz. white wine)

EVENING SNACK:

½   cup mixed raisins and dry roasted unsalted peanuts

or

1   baked apple (artificial sweetener) and cinnamon and raisins

or

½-¾ cup low-fat ice cream

* * * * * * * * * * * *

WALK ½ HOUR DAILY OR 1 HOUR EVERY OTHER DAY

DIETSTEP® NOTES:

1. The 1st measurement of food listed in any meal plan is the amount of food for a woman. The amount that follows is the amount of food for a man. (Ex. 3-4 oz. of roast turkey means 3 oz. for a woman and 4 oz. for a man). (Remember measurements are approximate, not exact).
2. Once you've reached your ideal weight, you can then follow the meal plans for only 4 days every week (Mon., Wed., Fri., & Sun.) to maintain your weight. Or you can follow the Alphabet Maintenance Diet which begins on the next page.
3. Check with your doctor before beginning this diet plan or any other diet program, especially if you have a medical condition of any kind. Do not diet if you are pregnant or are a teenager.

HOW MUCH WEIGHT CAN YOU LOSE AND HOW LONG WILL IT TAKE?

By following **THE EASY 4-DAY DIETSTEP®** meal plan exactly as outlined in this chapter, you will lose **1 pound every 10 days** and **3 pounds every 30 days**, as long as you stay on the diet. This may vary a few ounces depending on your starting weight and your body build. Now you're probably saying that you'd like to lose weight more quickly. Not to fear! The additional amount of weight that you lose will depend on the one variable in the diet — the **TIME** that you walk each day.

The following chart (Table VI) indicates the various times that you may decide to walk each day of the week. The last 2 columns show how many additional pounds you will lose every 10 days and each month. Remember, your **diet meal plan always stays the same**. Only the time you **walk** each day can be changed according to how much weight you want to lose. If the weather does not permit walking, then ride your stationary bike according to the calculated times in the following table: (**Table VI**).

The additional weight loss indicated on the following chart is above and beyond the **1 pound** that you'll lose every 10 days or the **3 pounds** that you'll lose every 30 days, while you're following the **4-DAY DIETSTEP® DIET MEAL PLANS**.

TABLE VI

THE EASY 4-DAY DIETSTEP® PLAN

TIME WALKED OR PEDALED EACH DAY		ADDITIONAL AMOUNT OF WEIGHT YOU WILL LOSE EVERY:	
Walk (3mph) (Minutes)	Stationary Bike (15mph) (Minutes)	10 Days (Pounds)	30 Days (Pounds)
15	7½	¼	¾
30	15	½	1½
45	22½	¾	2¼
60	30	1	3
75	37½	1¼	3¾
90	45	1½	4½

Note: The weight loss indicated on Table VI is the additional amount of weight you will lose by just walking or pedaling on the stationary bike. Remember, when you are on the Easy 4-Day Diet, **you'll lose 1 pound for each 10 days** that you follow the **EASY 4-DAY DIETSTEP® DIET PLAN. And you'll lose 3 pounds for every 30 days** that you stay on the **DIETSTEP® DIET PLAN.** Example: Walk 60 minutes every day and you will lose 3 additional pounds walking every 30 days, and 3 pounds by following the **DIETSTEP® DIET PLAN**—for a total of 6 lbs. every 30 days. Sound easy? It is! That's why it's called the Easy 4-Day Dietstep® Plan.—IT REALLY WORKS!

* * * * * * * * * * * *

THE EASY ALPHABET MAINTENANCE DIETSTEP® PLAN

1. After you have reached your ideal weight on the Easy 4-Day Dietstep® Plan, then follow the **EASY ALPHABET MAINTENANCE DIETSTEP® MEAL PLANS.** (Outlined on the next several pages).
2. The **ALPHABET DIETSTEP® PLAN** is an alphabetic device only to make it easy for you to remember what foods to eat every day. Monday uses only *M* - **Foods**, Tuesday - *T* - **Foods**, Wednesday - *W* - **Foods**, and so on.

3. **Walk** 60 minutes every other day or 30 minutes every day, so that your weight will remain constant. If the weather is bad, ride your stationary bike 30 minutes every other day or 15 minutes every day.
4. If you have the urge to cheat, then turn to the **Dietstep®** **Cheater's Snack Plan** in the last chapter and walk off your favorite snack. How about a pizza or an ice-cream cone?
5. Remember to eat high fiber, low cholesterol foods and avoid those foods that are high in sugar, salt and saturated fat. **The EASY ALPHABET MAINTENANCE DIET-STEP® PLAN is high in fiber, and low in saturated fat and cholesterol**, just like the **Easy 4-Day Dietstep® Meal Plan**.
6. If you notice that you start to gain a few unwanted pounds, then start back on the **Easy 4-Day Dietstep® Meal Plans** for a few weeks.

MONDAY - "M" - DAY

BREAKFAST: 1 Muffin (Bran, Oat, Wheat or English) - Jelly or whipped diet margarine
½ Melon (Cantaloupe, Honey Dew, Mango, etc.)
2 cups Coffee/Tea - skim milk and artificial sweetener

LUNCH: Macaroni (Pasta Salad without mayonnaise - Cold) - (4 oz.)
or
Melon Balls (fruit salad) - (2 oz.)
Diet Decaffeinated Beverage/Coffee/Tea

DINNER: Meat (Veal or Lamb)- 4 oz./with clear mushroom gravy
Mashed or Baked Potato - dry (1)
Mixed Tossed Salad/with low-cal diet dressing (1tsp)
Milk (Skimmed) - 8 oz. or decaffeinated Coffee/Tea/Diet Soda

BED-TIME SNACK:
Mango or fruit juice - 6 oz.
Munchies (Pretzel/Popcorn/Peanuts) - (2 oz.)

TUESDAY - "T" - DAY

BREAKFAST: Toast (Wheat) 1 Slice/Jelly or whipped diet margarine
Tea/Coffee 1-2 Cups
Tomato/Orange Juice 4 oz.

LUNCH: Tomato (stuffed with tuna - 2½ oz. packed in water)
Toast - Melba 2-3 pieces
Tea/Coffee - decaffeinated 1-2 Cups/skim milk and artificial sweetener

DINNER: Turkey/or Chicken - baked or broiled - 4 oz.
Taters - Baked or Boiled 1 med. (or 3 small new red)
Tossed Salad - with low cal. diet dressing (1 tsp)
Turnips or other veg. - 1 cup (no butter)

BED-TIME: Two medium hard pretzels *or*
Two cups pop corn - hot air popper/no butter and no salt
Tea - decaf./or decaf. diet soda

WEDNESDAY - "W" - DAY

BREAKFAST: Wheatena/Wheaties/or any cold or hot cereal with skim milk and artificial sweetener
Wheat Toast - 1 slice - jelly or whipped diet margarine
Water/Coffee/Tea - 1-2 cups

LUNCH: Wegetable salad with low cal diet dressing (1 tsp)
Wafers/crackers - 3
Water/Diet Soda - decaffeinated

DINNER: Wegetable Casserole/Baked Eggplant Parmesan - 4 oz.

Watercress Salad with diet low cal dressing
(1 tsp)
Water/Diet Soda - decaffeinated

BEDTIME: Watermelon or Fruit Salad (1 cup) or Fruit
low-fat yogurt - ½ cup *or*
Wheat germ (1 tblsp.) - sprinkled on fruit or
fruit yogurt
Water/Diet soda - decaffeinated

THURSDAY - "T" - DAY

BREAKFAST: Toast (Wheat) - 1 slice - jelly or whipped diet
margarine
Tomato or juice of choice
Tea/Coffee - 1 - 2 cups/skim milk and artificial sweetener

LUNCH: Turkey Sandwich on Toast (Whole wheat)
with Tomato and Lettuce - dry or with ½ tsp.
light mayo
Tea/Coffee - decaffeinated

DINNER: Tuna Casserole - baked with tomatoes, onions, celery and chives- (4 oz)
Turnips or other vegetables - 1 cup
Tossed Salad with low-cal diet dressing
(1 tsp.)
Tea/coffee/Diet soda - decaf.

BEDTIME: Two Medium Hard Pretzels (unsalted) *or*
Two cups popcorn - hot-air popper/unbuttered/unsalted)
Tea - decaf. or decaf. diet soda

FRIDAY - "F" - DAY

BREAKFAST: French Toast made with artificial eggs
Fruit Juice of choice - 6 oz.
Coffee/Tea

LUNCH: Fish/Baked or Broiled - 4 oz (lemon juice or
              wine - no butter)
              Fresh Vegetable - 1 cup - no butter
              Fruit Juice/Coffee/Tea - decaffeinated

DINNER: Fresh tossed salad
              Fowl - Baked Chicken - 4 oz/or Fish - broiled
              - 4 oz.
              Fresh Vegetables or baked potato (no but-
              ter) - 1 cup
              Fruit juice/Coffee/Tea - decaffeinated

BEDTIME: Fruit Salad - 1 cup

SATURDAY/SUNDAY - "S" - DAYS

SELF SELECTION SERVINGS

Select any combination of **high fiber, low cholesterol** foods
that appear in this **Chapter** or in **Chapter** 14 or in the **Appendix.** Since you're selecting the servings yourself, the foods
don't necessarily have to start with an S. Also be careful to
avoid foods that are high in sugar, salt and saturated fat.
Saturdays and Sundays are fun days!

* * * * * * * * * * * *

This easy alphabet diet
Keeps your appetite center quiet
Remember however not to be too quick
With the food items that you pick
You can always mix and match
But be careful of the hidden catch
For example, if you eat too many F's
You'll never get into your pants or dress
So if you carefully choose just a few
The alphabet diet will be kind to you

YOUR EASY DIETSTEP® PLAN
WEIGHT-LOSS RECORD

Week	Time	Mon.	Tues.	Wed.	Thurs.	Fri.	Sat.	Sun.	Wed. AM Weight
1	Walked or Pedaled								
2	Walked or Pedaled								
3	Walked or Pedaled								
4	Walked or Pedaled								
5	Walked or Pedaled								
6	Walked or Pedaled								
7	Walked or Pedaled								
8	Walked or Pedaled								
9	Walked or Pedaled								
10	Walked or Pedaled								
11	Walked or Pedaled								
12	Walked or Pedaled								
13	Walked or Pedaled								
14	Walked or Pedaled								
15	Walked or Pedaled								

"OH NO! SHE'S STARTED ANOTHER DIET AGAIN!"

CHAPTER 6

DIET TIPS
FOR SLIM HIPS

FAT'S FIRST FLING

At a recent American Heart Association meeting, a study showed that men and women store fat in different places: men are more likely to store fat in their abdomens, whereas women store fat more easily in their buttocks and thighs, because nature gives women more fat cells there. What's the significance of these findings?

Extra abdominal fat increases the risk of stroke, high blood pressure, diabetes and high cholesterol levels. The extra fat stored by women in the thighs and buttocks appear to be a harmless place to store fat according to this study; however don't tell any woman that or she'll bop you one. No woman wants to have fat thighs and buttocks.

The good news is that walking seems to take the weight off mens' abdomens and decreases their risk of heart disease and stroke. And women who walk seem to lose weight more easily in those trouble spots—the thighs and buttocks, making these areas firm and trim. So no matter where fat's first fling is, whether in your belly or in your buttocks, *walking women stay trim and walking men stay slim.*

YO-YO DIETS—NO-NO!

The Framingham Heart Study, which has followed more than 5,000 people for almost 40 years, recently indicated a health hazard for chronic dieters. People who lost 10% of their body weight had an almost 20% reduction in the incidence of heart disease. So what's the problem? These same dieters who gained back the 10% of their body weight, *raised their heart disease risk by almost 30%*. So if you weigh 160 lbs. and lost 10% or 16 lbs. you cut your heart disease risk by 20%. But if you gained back that 16 lbs. you increased your risk of heart attack by 30%, an overall net gain of 10% and you still weigh the same 160 lbs. *Sounds scary to me, folks!*

How many times have you heard the old saying that "I've lost enough weight over the years to equal two or three whole persons and I've gained every bit of it back." But what you didn't realize is that the whole person's weight you gained back isn't the "old you." Yo-yo dieting or weight-cycling makes it harder to permanently lose weight and much more dangerous to your health.

Experts in the fields of physiology, bio-chemistry, psychology, nutrition and medicine have come up with the following startling findings about yo-yo dieting:

1. The weight-loss/weight-gain cycle actually increases your desire for fatty foods. Animal research studies at Yale University showed that rats who had lost weight rapidly on low-calorie diets, always chose more fat in their diets when given a choice between fat, protein, and carbohydrates. These rats always put on more weight than when they started and in a much shorter time than it had taken them to lose the weight.

2. Yo-yo dieters increase the percentage of body fat to lean body tissue with repeated bouts of weight gain and weight loss. People who lose weight rapidly on a crash diet, particularly one low in protein, can lose a significant amount of muscle tissue. If the weight is regained again they usually regain more fat and less muscle because it is easier for the body to gain fat than it is to rebuild muscle tissue.

3. Body fat gets redistributed in the abdomen from the thighs and hips after weight-cycling. Yo-yo dieting almost invariably shifts weight to the abdomen from the thighs and buttocks. Medical research has definitely shown that fat deposits above the waist increases the risk of heart disease and diabetes, not to mention an unsightly paunch.

4. When you lose weight by cutting calories, your basal

metabolic rate (BMR) goes down, because it is the body's defense mechanism against starvation. The body can't tell the difference between starvation and low calorie dieting; consequently, your body is trying to conserve energy by burning fewer calories. This is the reason it becomes harder to lose weight after a week or two, even though you are eating exactly the same amount of calories as you did when you first started your diet. This slow-down in the basal metabolic rate (BMR) persists even after the diet is over and accounts for the rapid-rebound, excessive weight gain that always happens to the dieter when he/she goes off their diet. This slow-down in metabolic rate can occur even after a single attempt at dieting. However, the repeated effects of the yo-yo diets can effect the basal metabolic rate (BMR) much more, making additional weight-loss almost impossible and rebound weight gain almost inevitable. The yo-yo dieter is often heard to say—"I'm fatter now than I was before I started this damn diet."

5. An enzyme called lipo-protein lipase (LPL) becomes more active when you cut calories. This enzyme controls the amount of fat that is stored in your body's fat cells. Dieting, therefore, makes the body more efficient at storing fat—which is exactly opposite of what a dieter wants. As you reduce your calorie intake, the enzyme LPL starts to activate the fat-storing process. This is another defense mechanism that the body uses to prevent starvation. Remember, the enzyme LPL doesn't know that you are dieting, it thinks that you are starving to death.

6. Human dieters who lost a substantial amount of weight were compared to people of normal weight. After they lost weight the previously obese people needed surprisingly fewer calories to maintain their weight than the normal-weight people. In one study at New York's Rockefeller University, obese patients who lost weight needed only 2000 calories a day to maintain their weight (125 lbs.) compared to 2300 calories per day to maintain the exact same weight (125 lbs.) by normal-weight people.

7. Chronic male dieters who exhibited repeated cycles of

weight gain and weight loss showed an increased risk of sudden death from heart attacks, according to a Northwestern University report. This study followed 1800 men for a period of 25 years who had engaged in cyclic-dieting.

So what's the answer? We know that losing weight lowers blood pressure, reduces the risk of heart disease, lowers blood cholesterol and triglycerides, increases the HDL ("good" cholesterol) and so on and so forth. The answer is that dieting alone is not the best way to lose and maintain weight. The following is a list of the reasons why *walking is the only safe and effective method* to lose and maintain normal body weight:

1) Exercise, particularly walking, is the real answer to preventing the weight-loss/weight-gain cycle from occurring. Walking makes it less likely to gain the weight back again because you lose more fat and less muscle tissue with exercise. Also, walking prevents the slow-down in basal metabolic rate that always occurs with a yo-yo diet. Actually walking slightly increases the BMR which helps to burn calories at a faster rate. Walking also reduces the production of the enzyme lipoprotein lipase (LPL) which in turn decreases the amount of fat stored in the fat cells.

2) Walking also regulates the brain's appetite controller, the *appestat*. The more you walk, the more you decrease the appestat's hunger mechanism. Inactivity, on the other hand, stimulates the appetite control mechanism to make you hungry.

3) Walking, by increasing the aerobic metabolism of the body, redirects the stomach's blood supply to the exercising muscles, which in turn decreases your appetite.

4) And finally, walking encourages the body to burn fat rather than carbohydrates. This enables the body's blood sugar to stay at a relatively constant normal level. When the brain's blood sugar is normal we are not hungry. Both strenuous exercise and low-calorie dieting burn carbohydrates rather than fats, causing a sharp drop in the blood sugar. When the brain's blood sugar drops as it does in dieting or strenuous exercises, then we feel hungry in order to counteract this low blood sugar.

So again, the answer is *walking!* If you want to have a fit and trim figure — *walk!* If you want thin thighs and firm buttocks — *walk!* If you want a flat tummy and firm breasts — *walk!* If you want superior posture and good looks — *walk!*

To be fit and trim—Walk to Win!
To be nice and slim—Walk to Win!
To be beautiful and thin—Walk to Win!
So let life begin—Walk to Win!

WATCH OUT FOR THAT DIET— YOUR HEART MAY NOT BE IN IT

Researchers at Emery University studied two groups of overweight women. The first group was restricted to 800 - 1000 calories per day. The second group was allowed 1,300 - 1,600 calories daily. One half of the women in each group were allowed to exercise and the other half of each group remained sedentary.

After 3 months, the women who exercised from each group showed less shrinkage of heart muscle than the sedentary half of each group. This underscores other studies which show that people on very low calorie diets can develop dangerous shrinkage of heart muscle (myocardial atrophy) from this type of severe calorie restriction. Regular exercise may prevent this dangerous condition from developing.

Severe calorie restriction is not only dangerous to heart muscle, but it can have a damaging effect on the nervous and immune systems. Regular walking and moderate calorie restriction is the safest and most effective way to lose weight.

DR. WALK'S® DIET TIPS

1. DON'T SKIP MEALS

Skipping meals lowers your blood sugar which brings on cravings for high-carbohydrate, high-calorie foods. In many people, going hungry can bring on "hunger headaches" similar to migraine-type headaches. Eating 3-4, even 5 small meals per day is far superior to eating one or two large meals. If your blood sugar remains constant, then you're less likely to overeat and gain weight.

Have you ever noticed thin, wiry men and women who seem to be eating all the time but never get fat? That's because small frequent meals are lower in calories and the metabolism seems to burn them up at a faster rate, rather than having to deal with a large number of calories all at once. And besides, small frequent meals are usually consumed by active rather than sedentary people. The high-calorie, large-meal eater usually eats and sits and sits and eats. And when he/she is finished eating, they sit some more, because they're too bloated to get up and move around. The small meal eater is up and about before you know it.

2. ELIMINATE THE FAT IN YOUR DIET

Most people do not realize the amount of fat calories that they consume each day. The first order of business is to find the fat in your diet and eliminate it. Everyone knows that there's fat in bacon, lunch meats, eggs, butter, ice cream, milk and cheese. But not everyone realizes that there's considerable fat in donuts, cakes, pies, muffins, margarine, mayonnaise, chicken and tuna salad, coffee creamers and yogurt, cream cheese and cottage cheese - (even the ones marked low-fat).

Your body metabolizes fats and carbohydrates together in a set ratio governed genetically by your individual body metabolism. When you restrict the number of fat calories that you consume, then your body's metabolism automatically controls the amount of carbohydrate calories that you actually eat. By restricting the fat calories eaten you crave less carbohydrates in your diet. The combination of less fat eaten combined with less carbohydrates craved, makes it next to impossible for you to put on excess weight. So when *you eat less fat you're less likely to get fat*. Sounds simple? It is!

3. AVOID EATING FAST AND FAST-FOOD EATING

If you're a fast eater or a fast-food eater—watch out! When you consume food at a rapid pace, you have a greater tendency to consume excess calories by overeating. The reasons for this is that it takes 15-20 minutes for the brain's appetite regulator (the appestat) to receive the signals that your body's stomach is full. If you eat your meal rapidly in 5 or 10 minutes as you often do in fast-food restaurants, then your appestat will never know that you've eaten. Subsequently, you'll still be as hungry as you were before you wolfed down that double bacon-cheese burger. And you'll probably order a milk-shake and a large order of french fries. By the time you get those down the hatch your brain will just be receiving the first signals that you're full from the original double bacon-cheese burger that you ate in the first 5 minutes. Well it's too late by then. The appestat will never know that you added another 450 calories to your fast-food lunch. Only your waist-line, hips and thighs will be the wiser.

4. CHEW FOOD THOROUGHLY AND EAT FOODS THAT NEED CHEWING

This is the direct corollary to Dr. Walk's® tip number 3. Foods that require a good bit of chewing like apples, corn, celery, carrots, salads, cucumber, raw vegetables (cauliflower, broccoli, string beans, radishes, etc) are excellent diet foods since they take time to chew and consequently the brain's appetite regulating mechanism (appestat) is satisfied long before you've had a chance to consume too many calories.

An apple a day not only keeps the doctor away, but it also keeps the fat away from your body. Apples are high-fiber foods which not only take longer to eat than most other comparably sized-foods, but offer many nutritional advantages over low-fiber foods. One reason the appestat is appeased early is the time that it takes you to eat an apple. The other reason is that the high-fiber content of apples and similar high-fiber foods produces more bulk in the stomach, making you feel full faster. Also the high-fiber contents of apples and other fresh vegetables, fruits and grains combine with water in the intestinal tract to form a bulky, lighter stool that prevents constipation, hemorrhoids, diverticulosis and even varicose veins in the legs. This is the result of less straining with bowel movements.

5. EXERCISE WORKS ONLY IF YOU WORK AT IT

One half hour of jogging, calisthenics or aerobics three times a week may make you feel good, but it does very little for cardiovascular fitness and next to nothing as far as weight-loss is concerned. Since most of the calories ($\frac{2}{3}$) burned during the first 20 minutes of exercise are burned as carbohydrates, very little weight is lost by short bursts of strenuous activity. Actually after you've finished with one of these mini torture-type exercises, you're more likely to be famished because of the sudden drop in blood sugar caused by the burning of all those carbohydrates.

On the other hand, if you're walking 30 minutes daily or 60 minutes every other day, you're more likely to lose weight on a regular basis and you won't be hungry after you walk. Reason: after the first 20 minutes of exercise ⅔ of the calories burned came from fat. **And fat is where it's at!** Walkers who walk an hour a day burn 350 calories (at 3 miles/hour) and most of these calories are fat calories. Ten days of walking for 1 hour daily, burns 3500 calories or 1 pound of body weight lost. It works out the same if you walk 30 minutes everyday— then you'll lose a pound every 20 days.

6. DON'T SKIP BREAKFAST

People who never eat breakfast usually make up for it sometime during the day and then some. By the time lunch comes your low blood sugar gives you a ravenous appetite and you're sure to overeat. Or you may get hungry long before lunch time arrives and you'll find yourself stuffing donuts and coffee into your face. Remember, too, that caffeine is an appetite stimulant also and you should be careful not to drink too much coffee or tea. People who skip breakfast seem to make up for it three-fold by snacking mid-morning, midafternoon and late evening. This appears to be due to the fact that the metabolism seems to slow down later in the day in the non-breakfast eaters. The body reacts to a lack of breakfast as if the body is trying to starve itself and so it slows down your metabolism to keep you from starving to death. This results in sluggishness and fatigue which in turn causes the person to "just eat something" in order to feel better. Eating speeds up the metabolism and elevates the blood sugar, and lo-and-behold you feel better. Then the blood sugar rapidly drops again and you feel fatigued again and so you eat again. This is called *functional hypoglycemia* or low blood sugar which results from just skipping meals. Other causes of hypoglycemia are the result of excess alcohol, caffeine, nicotine, sugar and stress.

7. DIETING IS DISCIPLINE!

The most important part of any successful diet is starting it. Once you've made up your mind to begin your diet you're half way there. You must be ready from the very beginning to discipline yourself. Just like any other part of your life, discipline is a must. You know that you have to get up for work each day, so you do it. You know that you have to take the bus to school or work every morning, so you do it. You know that you have to get that report or that project done, so you do it. So what's the problem about dieting? Most people know that they have to do it, but they don't! Reason: you don't have any outside pressure squeezing your insides, like you do when you *know* that you have to get up for work. What you actually have is inside pressure squeezing your outsides out—making you fatter. And the inside pressure which is your own free-will, sometimes isn't strong enough to counteract the fat outside force. So what you need to do is to give your inside pressure or free-will a kick in the pants, so that you can get back into the size pants that fit you last year. **DISCIPLINE! DISCIPLINE! DISCIPLINE!**

8. HEALTHY FOODS LIKE YOU!

Foods that are good for you are also good for your figure. Most of the foods that promote good health are also foods that help you stay slim and trim.

FRUITS — are high in fiber and low in calories. They fill you up without filling you out. Fruits satisfy the appestat by taking longer to consume and they promote good bowel health by providing adequate roughage, which in turn also reduces your appetite. Fruits are not only low-fat, low-calorie foods, but they are especially rich in *potassium*. Potassium is an essential element which appears to have blood pressure lowering properties. In a recent medical study, potassium-rich foods reduced the risk of strokes by more than 30% in individuals who had known hypertension.

Fruits are also good sources of pectin, a fiber found in many fruits and vegetables. This particular type of fiber helps to lower blood cholesterol. Many of these fruits which are high in pectin also contain vitamin C, which helps the pectin lower cholesterol even more than pectin alone. Vitamin C also is important in boosting our immune system and has a cancer-inhibiting factor built into its structure. Some of the fruits that are rich in both pectin and vitamin C are oranges, pears, grapefruit and bananas.

FISH — Studies show that diets rich in fish lower blood

pressure 15-20% in hypertensive men. A study conducted at the Cardiovascular Research Institute in West Germany showed that men with mild hypertension who ate 3 cans of mackerel per week, had a significant reduction in their blood pressures.

Fish oil has been shown to reduce blood fats and consequently slow the formation of deposits of cholesterol in the arteries. In a study at the University of Chicago, monkeys on a diet high in fish oil developed less cholesterol deposits in their arteries than monkeys fed a diet high in saturated fat and coconut oil. The monkeys fed fish oil also had lower total cholesterol and LDL cholesterol levels than the monkeys fed the high saturated fat diet.

Another study conducted at Harvard Medical School appears to indicate that fish-oils also have a cancer-inhibiting factor. In a study of rats with breast cancer fish-oils seem to slow the spread of the disease significantly more than diets high in saturated fat or poly-unsaturated fats and even more than a low-fat diet. It appears that the omega-3 fatty acids present in fish oils is the ingredient responsible for the cholesterol-lowering and cancer-inhibiting effects.

Fish is not only low in saturated fat and calories but it's high in omega-3 fatty acids that help to lower both your cholesterol, and triglyceride levels. Eat fish 2-3 times per week for a healthy heart and a slim body.

CEREAL — GRAINS ESPECIALLY, OATS AND BRAN — provide water-soluble fiber that helps to lower both cholesterol and triglyceride levels. These high fiber cereals also promote good bowel health by reducing constipation and preventing hemorrhoids, diverticulosis, appendicitis and varicose veins.

FOWL — lean white meat of turkey and chicken is low in calories and fat, promoting good health and a slim figure. Make sure you remove the skin, which contains high amounts of saturated fat, before eating fowl.

ONION, GARLIC AND PEPPERS — help to lower levels of blood fats, lower blood pressure and help to make the blood less likely to clot. These foods contain certain natural chemical substances that actually thin your blood.

VEGETABLES — It's important to eat more vegetables of the cabbage-family: particularly broccoli, cauliflower, spinach, brussel sprouts, and squash. These foods are not only high in fiber but they are also high in both vitamins A and C.

Many vegetables also rich in potassium are sweet potatoes, potatoes, squash, spinach, beets, tomatoes and green peppers. Boiling destroys more than 35-40% of the potassium in vegetables, so remember to eat more raw vegetables and steam or microwave vegetables rather than boil them, in order to reduce potassium loss.

Carrots and leafy green vegetables contain *beta-carotene* which is a chemical pre-cursor to vitamin A. Beta-carotene is converted to vitamin A in the body. Vitamin A inhibits compounds called free-radicals in the body which may cause normal cells to turn cancerous. Vitamin A also maintains the integrity of the lining of the lungs and the intestinal tract. Beta-carotene appears to have a protective effect against both lung and colon cancer. A recent study conducted at the New York State University in Buffalo, found that people with lung cancer had significantly lower blood levels of beta-carotene than a similar number of people who were free of the disease. Similar studies have shown that patients with colon cancer also have lower levels of beta-carotene than a comparable number of healthy individuals.

* * * * *

WHY IT'S REALLY TOUGH TO LOSE WEIGHT!

Remember, no one loses weight in a straight line. When you are on a diet you initially lose weight, and then your weight loss levels off. This occurs even though you are eating exactly the same amount as you were when you lost the weight. This leveling off period or **plateau** is the single most hazardous part of any diet program.

The reason is that once this plateau is reached, you begin to become discouraged and you'll say, "I'm still on the same diet but I haven't lost a pound in over a week." Discouragement leads to frustration and next you'll say, "the heck with the diet, I may as well enjoy myself and eat something I really like since I haven't lost weight anyway." At this point 90% of all diets are doomed to failure since the weight-loss pattern now reverses itself and becomes a **weight-gain pattern**.

If you stick out this plateau period, which incidently is

always temporary, you'll be surprised to see that the weight loss begins to pick up speed again. It may take a week or two at the most, but if you are patient, you will again start to lose those unwanted pounds.

No one has ever satisfactorily explained this plateau period; however, physiologists believe that it is probably due to a **temporary re-adjustment of the body's metabolism** in response to the initial weight loss. No matter what the reason is, however, you will always break through the plateau period providing you don't become discouraged or frustrated. Weight loss will again resume its downward progress toward your ideal weight goal.

This plateau period is one of the main reasons that I insist that my patients do not weigh themselves daily; in fact, **weighing yourself every day is hazardous to your diet.** Psychiatrists have found that people who weigh themselves daily never lose weight. The reason for this is two-fold. **First,** when you weigh yourself daily and see that you are losing weight, you become happy and elated, and subconsciously you will eat to celebrate. **Secondly,** if you see that you are not losing weight as fast as you "think" you should, you become depressed and anxious, and sometime during that day you will subconsciously eat because of frustration.

So the rule of thumb is: **the more you weigh yourself, the more you eat!** Believe me, it is true. I've seen my patients go through this frustrating daily weighing process thousands of times. No one on a diet should weigh themselves more than once a week and then you will get a true measure of the effectiveness of your diet. **Wednesday** is the best day to weigh yourself each week. Monday and Friday are the worst days for weighing in, since they precede and follow the weekend and lead to frustration-type eating binges. It took a long time to gain all that weight; you can't take it off overnight. Be patient! Another thing to remember is that bathroom scales can vary 3-5 pounds depending on the temperature of the room. This occurs because the spring inside the scale will expand or contract depending on the room temperature.

And remember, a diet plan without a walking program is like Fred Astair without Ginger Rogers—it doesn't work! Walking is the only sure method of losing weight and keeping it off permanently. Fat people sit and trim people walk! It's as simple as that!

DR. WALK'S® DIET FALLACIES

1. **Calories don't count. False!** This is the first of the many fallacies that people use in the weight-loss business. On the contrary, calories do count in a weight-gain/weight-loss program. In order to gain or lose a pound of fat you must eat or not eat 3,500 more calories than you use up. The type of calories are not important in this particular fallacy, since it is the total number of calories involved in weight loss and weight gain.

2. **A crash diet is an excellent way to begin a weight-loss program. False!** This is probably the worst way to begin a diet program since crash diets, which are usually low in carbohydrates, produce rapid fluid loss. This fluid loss has nothing to do with the amount of liquid that we drink, and it is only reflecting a change in the body's ability to hold fluid. The fallacy is that fat is not coming off in this type of program, and, in fact, protein can be lost during a crash diet, which may be harmful to the kidneys. When these diets are abandoned weight is gained rapidly, usually in the form of fat, and the dieter may wind up with more fat than he/she started with.

3. **Exercise is unimportant in weight reduction and control. False!** Nothing can be further from the truth. Regular physical exercise and activity is the key point in a long-term weight-control maintenance program. Exercise not only burns calories, but has an appetite-regulating effect on the brain's appetite-control mechanism. Exercise also favorably affects the metabolism by lowering blood pressure, blood cholesterol, blood sugar, and in general by contributing to good health.

4. **Certain foods can burn up calories, such as grapefruit. False!** This is entirely erroneous. The digestion of food does consume a small amount of energy from the process of digestion, but there is no food that expends enough energy during digestion to promote weight loss.

5. **It is better to smoke than be fat. False!** The initial weight gained from decreasing or stopping smoking can always be lost by a diet and exercise program; however, the permanent lung, heart and artery damage done by smoking can never by undone.

6. **Toasting bread reduces its calorie count. False!** Toasting

only changes the bread's texture and taste but does not burn away calories.

7. **It does not make any difference whether you eat slowly or quickly as far as appetite or weight gain are concerned. False!** Eating a meal slowly and chewing the food thoroughly gives the body metabolism a chance to regulate and reduce its appetite-regulating center in the brain. This subsequently can reduce the appetite and make you more satisfied with less food. Eating rapidly does not cause overweight; however, since many overweight people tend to eat rapidly and do not give the appetite suppressing mechanism time to work, they eat more.

8. **Since meat is high in protein, it does not cause weight gain. False!** Protein, no matter what the source contains 4 calories per gram. Carbohydrates also contain 4 calories per gram. Fat, however, contains 9 calories per gram, more than twice as many calories as a gram of protein or carbohydrate. Since any excessive calories above the body's basic metabolic requirements results in an increased storage of fat, eating meat not only can cause weight gain but can cause a greater proportion of fat to be deposited in the body, because of its high fat content. Therefore, meat not only gives 4 calories per gram for its protein content, but it also gives 9 calories per gram for its fat content. Therefore, the greater the percentage of fat in the meat, the higher the caloric value.

9. **Since protein is the most important nutritional requirement of the body, high protein diets are the most beneficial and the healthiest. False!** Protein is a very important part of the body and is necessary in the diet for providing the amino acids (building blocks) for cellular activity, tissue repair and general maintenance of the body. However, protein is not the only essential requirement of our bodies. Carbohydrates, fats, vitamins, minerals, essential fatty acids and proteins are all necessary to provide energy and the basic ingredients to work the body's physiological and biochemical machinery properly. Any diet that is weighed in favor of one item or another, for example, the high protein diet, is not a healthful or nutritious type of diet.

10. **As long as you take a vitamin supplement every day, it doesn't matter what foods you eat or drink. False!** Vita-

min supplements will not provide all the daily requirements of protein, carbohydrates, minerals, amino acids
and essential fatty acids that the body needs. This is a
widespread misconception about nutrition and dieting.
Many complications have been noted by people on very
low calorie diets combined with protein-vitamin supplements, because of the inability of the body metabolism,
particularly the kidneys and liver, to adjust to this type of
diet.

11. **If I skip breakfast and lunch and just eat a large supper,
I will lose weight. False!** No matter when the calories are
consumed in a given 24 hour period the total end result is
the same. The basic formula is: calories consumed vs.
calories expended; whether you eat 400 calories 3 times a
day or 1,200 calories at one meal, the body does not know
the difference. In addition, skipping meals is not a healthful way to embark on a diet program, since the appetite
becomes overstimulated late in the day and you not only
eat a large dinner but continuous snacks throughout the
evening.

12. **If I eat or snack at bedtime, the food will not be digested
properly and I will gain weight. False!** Again, the same
principle exists as to the total calories consumed in any
24 hour period vs. the total calories expended. This is the
basic formula needed for either weight gain, weight loss,
or weight maintenance. Eating at bedtime will not put
any more weight on than eating any other time of day of
night. Some people however, may develop indigestion
when they eat immediately before bedtime.

20 MORE TIPS FOR SLIM HIPS

1. **Eat more slowly** with each meal. This involves taking
smaller, less frequent bites and chewing each mouthful
for a longer period of time. Pause between each section of
the meal.

2. If you are still hungry when you are finished your first
portion, **wait at least fifteen minutes** to see whether or
not you really want another portion. In most cases your
appestat (the brain appetite control mechanism) will be
more than satisfied at the end of that period of time and
you will not need a second helping.

3. Also restrict your meals to one, or perhaps two, locations in your home for eating. If you have no regular place to eat, then you will find that you are eating in every room; however, when food is restricted to **one main dining area**, there will be less tendency to snack during the day.

4. Make sure you **leave the table** as soon as you are finished eating and spend **less time in the kitchen** or areas that have a tendency to remind one of eating.

5. Make sure that you do not place **serving dishes** on the table during a meal for there will be more of a tendency to take second and third helpings. Be sure that you **do not leave food out** where you can repeatedly see it during the day.

6. Never go to the market on an empty stomach; you will buy snack foods (carbohydrate cravings). Also make it a point not to eat while watching **television** or **reading** since you will eat more while not concentrating on your meal.

7. Remember not to start a weight reduction program just prior to the **holiday season** or before **vacation time** since these are the most unsuccessful times to begin this type of project.

8. **Fried foods** should be avoided, since, even though you drain excess fat away, the fried foods still retain a large percentage of fat which adds to the calories. **Boiling, broiling, baking** or **steaming** are the best techniques for preparing foods.

9. **Fat on poultry and meat:** Always trim away visible fat from meat and fowl before cooking and remove visible fat at the table when eating. The skin of the chicken contains 25% of the fat content of the chicken and will add tremendously to the calories. Canned fishes, such as tuna and salmon, should be packed in water or the oils drained away.

10. **Hot foods** such as soups, and foods that require a lot of **chewing** will leave you with a greater feeling of satisfaction because they take a longer time to swallow and absorb.

11. Eat **salad greens** and **vegetables** before the main course since these will take the edge off your hunger for higher calorie meat, poultry and fish portions. The best salad dressing is none. Salad dressings are high in fats and calories. Use calorie-free herbs, spices, lemon, vinegar, or occasionally a small amount (1 tsp.) low-fat, low-calorie

dressing. **Restaurant tip:** dip your fork in a side cup of salad dressing every 3-4 mouthfuls of salad and you'll enjoy the taste without the extra calories.

12. **Teflon coated pans** and the new **edible spray-on coatings** which are made of vegetable oil will help reduce the amount of caloric fat that you consume. Although **margarine** is lower in saturated fats than butter, it is still 100% fat and has almost as many calories as butter.

13. **Alcohol:** Alcohol is one of the most serious hazards in any diet program, whether it is dining out or at home. The additional calories which are consumed in the American diet from alcohol have a tendency to cause and maintain overweight problems. Alcohol has more calories (7 calories per gram) than most foods on a weight basis. Try to substitute club soda with a twist of lemon or mineral water for drinks. When you do have a drink, drink a small amount of white wine or a light beer.

14. You may have any of the following **low** or **no calorie** items: sugar-free decaffeinated soda, fresh lemon or lime juice (not reconstituted), artificial sweetener, seasonings and spices (except salt), decaffeinated coffee and tea, vinegar, herbs, club soda, bouillon and mineral or tap water.

15. **Baking** and **broiling** are permitted when done on a rack. You may **broil** or **steam** vegetables, meat, fish or poultry. Do not stew, fry or saute. Cook with seasonings, not salt or salt products.

16. Get in the habit of always asking for **milk** (preferably non-fat) when ordering coffee. Creamers (dairy & non-dairy) are high in saturated fat and calories.

17. Limit **caffeine** to two cups coffee, tea or diet soda daily, since excess caffeine may make you nervous and can also increase your appetite. Make it a habit to order decaffeinated for your "2nd cup."

18. Decrease the amount of **salt** since it has a tendency to retain fluid and may mask actual body weight reduction. Salt also may cause or aggravate hypertension in susceptible people.

19. Do not diet if you are a **child, teenager** or **pregnant.** During the growth process or when nourishing a fetus, nutrients must not be restricted.

20. Always check with your **physician** before starting any diet program, especially if you have a medical problem.

"YES, DEAR, I STARTED MY DIET AND EXERCISE PROGRAM TODAY. I PICKED UP A CASE OF LIGHT-BEER!"

III. TRIM-STEP®: BODY-SHAPING PROGRAM

"Walking is considered the perfect weight-control and body-shaping exercise. Not only does it burn up 350 calories an hour, it also suppresses the appetite. Walking also raises the level of endorphins, those feel-good chemicals in our bodies. Walking tones muscle and trims fat, while it lowers both your blood pressure and your blood cholesterol."

Fred A. Stutman, M.D.
"Barbara Bush Gets In Capital Shape — By Walking"
Star Magazine, Mar. 14, 1989

"THIS LOOKED EASY ON TV. NOW HOW DO YOU LET GO?"

CHAPTER 7

A FIGURE SUPREME— A BODY THAT'S LEAN

STRIDE AND PACE — IT'S NOT A RACE!

A lot has been written about what type of stride is best for a walking program. " Stretch your stride." "Don't stretch your stride too much." "Land on your back heel." "Land on the middle of your foot." "Push off with your toes." "Push off with the ball of your back foot." "Pull your body forward with your front foot." "Push your body forward with your back foot." "Lean forward when you walk." And so forth and so on. If you try to follow any or all of these rules you'll probably never get started on your walking program. Or if you do get started, you'll either fall flat on your face or knock yourself unconscious as you crash into a tree while you're watching your feet.

Stride, schmide! Walk comfortably! Don't concentrate on your feet at all, just walk naturally. Your stride will develop automatically as you begin your walking program. Stride is as individual a trait as the way you brush your teeth. Everyone does it differently and no one way is the right way. The way that's comfortable for you is the correct way. Don't let anyone tell you otherwise.

You've also read that your stride has to be synchronized with your arm swing. I've seen people who start walking as though they're trying to do cross-country skiing without the skis. When you walk your arms will swing naturally in a motion that's comfortable for you. It's not necessary to concentrate on how your arms are moving. You're out there to take a nice refreshing walk, not to give flag-signals to a passing ship. Arm motion, like stride motion, is developed naturally. It should be comfortable for you and not exaggerated. Swinging your arms up and down is not a necessary part of a fitness walking program. Bending arms at the elbow and pumping them vigorously like the race-walkers do is ridiculous to say the least. You should not have to concentrate on swinging your arms when you're walking. Arm swing will come naturally as you walk and will vary with the speed that you're walking and the length of the stride that you take. Leave your arms to themselves. They'll know what to do when you're taking a brisk walk. Arm swing, like stride, is an individual characteristic of each walker. There is no right or wrong way to swing your arms.

And lastly, remember—*pace is not a race*. The amount of nonsense that has been written about stride and arm swing doesn't compare to the amount of absurd rhetoric that has been written about pace. "Walk fast." "Walk briskly." "Don't walk too fast." "Don't walk too slowly." "Walk this way." "Walk that way." "Walk which way?" "Get your pulse rate up." "Change your pace." "Increase your pace." "Walk 5 miles per hour." "Walk 6 miles per hour" "Don't ever stop until you drop." The advice we're given by the so-called fitness experts goes on ad-infinitum.

I'll state it straight out for the umpteenth time. **A rapid pace is not necessary for an effective health and fitness program!** No one alive or dead for that matter has ever proven that a rapid walking pace which produces an even more rapid heart rate is good for physical fitness. Yes, you've read about it over and over again in all of the health magazines and fitness books that have been written over the past decade.

Some time in the distant past (maybe 10-15 years ago), some nut, somewhere out there, stated that in order to attain maximum physical fitness you had to exercise fast and hard. Fast enough to get your pulse rate up to the *mythical target heart rate,* which would insure the poor recipient of this misinformation—life, liberty, and the pursuit of fitness. They forgot to mention—disease, disability, and death. Someone started this myth. No one living will admit it. No heirs of any dead, so-called fitness experts have come forward to admit that their dear-departed was the first to start this myth. I certainly don't know who started it. However, since this myth was started, everyone who has written about the fitness and health benefits of exercise has taken this untruth as the gospel. Well, just like the TV evangelists who have been preying on an unsuspecting public, these so-called health experts have been handing you a load of cow manure.

On the contrary, most of the new medical evidence based on physiological and biochemical studies of exercise, reveal that moderate, not extreme, physical activity is the most beneficial for maximum health and fitness benefits. All that is essential for cardiovascular fitness in the maximum oxygen uptake capacity of the body. This is accomplished with relative ease by a moderate walking pace of approximately 3 miles/hour. At this rate, studies show that the body is working at peak efficiency to extract, distribute and deliver all of the oxygen and nutrients required by every living cell in your body. Once these cells receive their precious cargo of oxygen and nutrients, they operate their own individual metabolic machinery at maximum efficiency.

So what's all this talk about "faster is better?" Even at 4,5 or 6 miles per hour, your body can only extract, distribute and deliver so much oxygen to the cells. These cells can't extract any more oxygen from the blood stream than they are already doing when you're walking 3 miles per hour. They are actually extracting the maximum amount of oxygen that they can hold, at a walking pace of 3 miles/hour. Remember, *stride and pace are not a race. A moderate walking pace is full of grace.*

WALKING FAST WON'T LAST

So what happens to the rest of the oxygen when you start to exercise more rapidly? The extra oxygen that the body breathes in when you're walking or exercising too fast is just the extra oxygen that is needed by the fast moving muscles that are exercising. This extra oxygen is therefore only going to your arms, legs, back and chest wall muscles. Nothing else is benefiting but these muscles. No other living cell inside your body is getting even an extra iota of oxygen.

And as we have previously seen when you start to exercise more rapidly, your living internal cells actually start to get less oxygen than they originally got when you were just walking 3 miles per hour.

So don't let the so-called fitness experts fool you. *Walking fast won't last!* Walking briskly at approximately 3 miles per hour is best. How do you know if you're walking 3 miles per hour? That's easy. Just measure off some distances beforehand with your car's odometer or your kid's bike odometer. Or go over to the local school's running track which is usually a ¼ mile, or just measure city blocks (approximately 10-12 blocks equal one mile). Now if you know how far a mile is, then just time your walk. You should walk 1½ miles in 30 minutes if you're walking at a pace of 3 miles/hour, or 1 mile in 20 minutes, or ½ mile in 10 minutes.

Once you've determined your walking speed, then make your adjustments accordingly. If you're walking slower than 3 miles per hour, try to gradually build-up to that pace. However, if you find that walking 3 miles per hour is too fast for you then slow down to where it's comfortable. Three miles per hour is not a magic number, it's only an approximate guideline! You'll get the same fitness benefits at a slightly slower rate if you're too tired walking at a 3 mile/hr rate. On the other hand if you're walking under 2 miles/hour then you're actually window-shopping walking and that's not adequate for cardiovascular fitness. As long as you're walking faster than 2 miles/hr and slower than 4 miles/hr, you will derive the maximum health and fitness benefits of walking.

If you find that your walking speed is somewhat faster than 3 miles per hour, that's fine, provided you're not pushing yourself to the point of fatigue or shortness of breath. Remember it's not necessary to walk fast for cardiovascular fitness. However, if you find that walking between 3 and 4 miles per hour is comfortable for you — go right ahead. Any speed above 4 miles per hour approaches race-walking speed, and is counter-productive to cardiovascular fitness, not to mention the high rate of injuries.

You should be able to gradually build-up to ½ **hour a day or one hour every other day** for your regular maintenance walking program. This amount of walking at approximately 3 miles per hour is all that is necessary to operate the cellular machinery of your body at peak efficiency. On the days that you're not walking, your body is still operating on the improved maximum oxygen uptake that it received on the previous day. As long as you don't let more than two days elapse between walking, then you're sure to reap the fitness benefit of walking.

Take a steady even stride
Not too difficult , not too wide
Swing your arms, and away you go.
Not too fast and not too slow
Remember to keep your 3 mile pace
Walking should be fun, and not a race.
So if you start out walking fast
Slow down or you'll never last.

LET'S DO THE TRIMSTEP®

When you walk, don't slouch. Walk tall! One way to walk is with your head up, shoulders back, stomach in, and your chest out. Remember, however, there is no correct way to walk except the way that is comfortable to you. Learning to walk tall comes with practice but after awhile this stance will become a natural part or your Trimstep® walking style.

Your **stride** is one of the most important aspects of your walk. There is no correct stride length. Stretch as much as you can without straining when you are walking. Thrust your legs forward briskly, swing your arms vigorously and feel your energy surge forth as you walk with the Trimstep® stride.

Keep your **pace** steady, never push and don't try to accelerate your speed when walking. If you do get tired after a short period of time, stop and rest and then re-start again at a steady and even pace. Don't rush, just walk at a comfortable Trimstep® pace.

Your **rhythm** of walking is a condition that will come naturally as you continue your walking program. Keep your body relaxed and your stride steady and even, and your rhythm will develop naturally. Uneven walking surfaces that you encounter will control your rhythm, especially going down or up hill. Don't fight it, just walk naturally and you'll be doing the **Trimstep®**.

A FIGURE SUPREME AND A BODY THAT'S LEAN

The **Trimstep® walking plan** will shape your body beautifully. You'll never have to worry about having a pot belly, flabby thighs, sagging breasts, rounded shoulders, a curved spine, jelly upper arms, drooping chins or a protuberant posterior. By just walking a half hour a day or 1 hour every other day with a brisk step (3 - 3½ miles per hour) and lots of pep your body will begin to take on a new firmer shape.

Stretch your stride, swing your arms, throw back your chest, lift up your head, suck in your gut and you'll Trimstep® like you've never walked before. Put energy into each Trimstep® you take and your body will burn lean from this energy steam. As you burn away the pounds your body will take on its new trim shape.

The Trimstep® body shaping plan depends on one factor only—*walking briskly for one-half hour daily or 1 hour every other day*. There are no calories to count, no diets to follow, no starvation tactics to endure and no diet aids to depend on. Your body will automatically slim down gradually every day that you take your brisk walk. Your figure will become trim as you lose those unsightly flabby pounds. And as you walk briskly for one hour every other day or one-half hour daily, your muscles will tighten, firming up your figure that was hidden under all that flab.

Walking briskly every day for at least one-half hour daily or 1 hour every other day is all the exercise you'll need to firm and shape your body beautifully. There are no strenuous calisthenics, back-breaking exercises or painful mangle machines to endure. To shape your figure all you have to do is walk at a brisk pace of 3 - 3½ miles per hour with a healthy stride and a brisk arm motion. This is the only step you need for the Trimstep® Plan to a figure supreme and a body that's lean.

You will start to develop a sprightly step as you do the Trimstep®. Your stride will become smooth and effortless as you thrust your legs forward. You will begin to develop a lively spring and bounce with every step that you take. You'll see later in this chapter how to walk with the **Trimstep® Heel-Toe-Method**. This walking method helps to stimulate the circulation throughout the entire body.

As you do the Trimstep® your chest will expand, providing more room for your heart and lungs to work efficiently. Your stomach muscles will tighten and suck in that unsightly gut, supporting your internal organs properly, in the fashion that they were accustomed to being supported when your abdominal muscles were in their prime.

Your posture will improve as your shoulders find their way back to their upright position. Your head will once again assume the erect position that it had when you were a young man or woman. Your back and spine will straighten like the shoot of a young branch. Your buttocks and thigh muscles will tighten and firm up, and your upper arms will lose their flabby appearance.

Your figure will slowly go through a metamorphosis and you will appear younger, feel better and be healthier than you ever were before. You will actually slow down the aging process to the point at which you will look and feel 10-15 years younger. Your weight will decrease to its teenage level as you travel the Trimstep® program. *You will burn steam, as your energy beam keeps you lean, with a figure supreme.*

Walk off weight, walk off worry, walk off stress and tension as you walk away the years and the ravages of aging. The Trimstep® program will give you a perfect "10" body as you feel and look younger and younger and younger.

I guarantee you a better figure, a leaner body and a younger you, when you do the Trimstep®. Don't give in to the ravages of the aging process which cause spineless jelly figures of men and women. Don't let inactivity sap your bones of their calcium, your muscles of their strength and your body of its life. Don't let your body start to sag before its time. Use your only defense available against the aging process—**walking every day the Trimstep® way—towards a figure supreme and a body that's lean.**

LOOK GOOD WITH OR WITHOUT YOUR CLOTHES ON

America has terrible posture and according to recent studies adults have worse posture today than their parents had. Adolescents nowadays slouch more, and young athletes overdo exercises that cause hollow backs to develop from muscle imbalance. Foot and leg problems which are often the result of sports injuries also tend to cause poor posture.

Poor Posture eventually causes many chronic low and mid-back problems in addition to leg and shoulder deformities and pain. To correct poor posture you must improve muscle tone. A **walking program** is the best exercise to develop good posture and to prevent structural abnormalities. According to orthopedic surgeons you should walk briskly while straightening the upper back and tightening the lower abdominal muscles. Remember, you must concentrate on always maintaining good posture. Walking will develop the proper muscular tone needed to look and feel good with or without your clothes on.

Keep your shoulders back, your head up and your stomach in. Walk briskly taking big strides and swing your arms vigorously. Don't be afraid to step on by those slouching, creeping, crawling, so-called window-shopping walkers who inhabit the sidewalks. Let's show those lazy laggards just what a lean, mean walking machine is.

A WALK EACH DAY KEEPS BACK PAIN AWAY

According to many orthopedic surgeons, walking puts considerably less stress on the lower spine than if you were just sitting without a back-rest. Walking strengthens the muscles in the pelvis and lower back, which helps many people with back problems. In fact, most people with back problems feel much better while they're walking than when they're sitting.

It has been suggested that over 100 million dollars are spent each year on workmen's compensation costs for back problems which are directly related to prolonged sitting. Back pain was the primary reason given for the time lost from work on over 50% of workmen's compensation claims. And the most startling finding in this study was that office workers who sat all day had an even higher incidence of back problems than workmen who did heavy lifting and other physically demanding jobs.

Anatomically, sitting puts considerably more strain and stress on the spine than does standing or walking. When you stand, the weight of the body is supported by the back, hips and legs; therefore, the pressure exerted on the back is evenly distributed throughout the entire length of the spinal column. When you walk, there is even less pressure exerted on the spine, because the forward thrust of your body reduces the force of gravity on your back. However, when you sit for prolonged periods of time the weight of your body is unevenly distributed to the lower back and hips.

Prolonged sitting puts 45% more pressure on the inter-vertebral discs (cushions between the spinal vertebrae) than does either standing or walking. This usually leads to spasm of the lower back muscles resulting in chronic back pain. Over a long period of time, prolonged sitting can eventually lead to a slipped or herniated disc. These discs contain a gelatin-like material which under extreme pressure can actually be squeezed out like toothpaste, resulting in what is called a slipped disc. A recent study conducted at Yale University found that people who sat at work more than 6 hours daily had a 60% greater risk of developing a slipped disc than workers who walked or stood most of the day.

Other similar studies have also found a significantly higher incidence of back problems in people whose jobs re-quired prolonged driving each day. Statistics show that people who spend more than two-thirds of their day driving have a 75% higher risk of developing a slipped disc than people who stand or walk most of the day. The cause of this high incidence resulted from both the weight of the sitting body on the low back and the pneumatic drill-like effect of road vibration on the spine. These two effects can eventually lead to degener-ation of the intervertebral discs.

The only way to prevent back problems from occurring is to get out of your chair and walk. If you're desk-bound at your job, make sure you go out for a walk at lunchtime, rather than sitting for another hour. Make it a point to get up from your desk frequently to get a drink, go to the bathroom or just to walk around the office. And for those who drive a lot each day, make frequent pit-stops, just to get out and stretch your legs. Remember, *a walk each day keeps back pain away*.

KEEP YOUR BODY LEAN AND YOUR ARTERIES CLEAN

In order to walk comfortably and efficiently without tir-ing, you should balance your body weight over the feet or just slightly ahead of them. Keep your body relaxed, and your knees bent slightly, utilizing a steady, even pace, and a brisk walking stride. To obtain the most benefit out of your walking program, it is helpful to walk with the **Trimstep® heel-and-toe method**, pointing your feet straight ahead. By utilizing this method, your leg muscles are used more efficiently, and this results in an overall increased blood supply to the peripheral circulation (in particular the legs and feet). This walking method is especially beneficial in the treatment of poor circulation to the legs (Fig. 1).

The leading leg is brought forward in front of the body, thus enabling the heel of the lead foot to touch the ground just before the ball of the foot and the toes. Your weight is then shifted forward so that when your heel is raised your toes will push off for the next step. Your arms and shoulders should be relaxed, and they will swing automatically with each stride you take. Before long you will develop a natural rhythm, pace and stride as you walk. Remember to walk with the **Trimstep® heel-and-toe method** (Fig 1). This uses the calf muscles productively to pump the blood up through the leg veins, back to the heart and lungs, and then out through the arteries to all of your body's cells, tissues and organs. This walking method keeps your *body lean* and your *arteries clean*.

"ISN'T THAT CUTE? THEY WANT YOU TO TAKE THEM OUT FOR A WALK."

FIGURE 1

DON'T BE A HEEL, SAID THE TOE

To get the most out of your walking program, walk with the Trimstep® heel-and-toe method. Proper walking uses calf muscles more productively and improves blood flow to these muscles. The diagram below explains heel-and-toe walking.

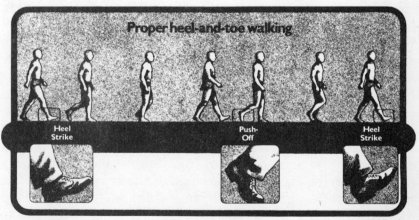

Proper heel-and-toe walking

Heel Strike	Push-Off	Heel Strike

Heel Strike:
Heel of leading
foot touches the floor before
the ball of the foot and toes.

Push-Off.
Knee is bent so heel is raised:
weight is shifted forward. (This is essential
and you should feel the action in the calf
muscles.) Toes push off to next step.

Heel Strike:
Leg is accelerated
forward to get in front of
body. Foot is positioned for
next heel strike.

With permission of Rorer Pharmaceuticals, Fort Washington, PA

YOU REALLY ARE A HEEL, SAID THE SOLE

Researchers at the Center for Locomotion Studies of Penn State University found out that the heel of the foot supports most of the weight when walking. Using a computer to measure weight distribution, the heel supported 60% of the weight and the forefoot supported 28% of the body's weight. The midfoot only carried 8% of the load and the toes a measly 4%.

What's the significance of their studies? First of all, when you buy a walking shoe, make sure that the heel and the forefoot padding are thick and solid. If the shoe doesn't have adequate support in these two areas, you're not only throwing your money away but you're throwing your foot a curve ball. Most injuries in walking occur to both the heel and the forefoot bones and ligaments from inadequate support. Once these areas are injured it may take months for them to heal properly. The incidence of the so-called "March Fracture" that occurred so often in soldiers was a result of inadequate padding in the forefoot areas of their marching boots.

The other important finding from this study relates to the efficiency of your walking stride. Since the heel is already supporting most of your weight, be careful not to slam your heel down with each step. This is a characteristic of the so-called "race-walkers" who are not content enough to be walkers, yet are too scared to be runners. So what results is a ridiculous type of exercise that looks and sounds like a duck waddling and a wart-hog grunting. Race walkers invariably sustain injuries, including fractures of the small bones of the heel and forefoot, just like their big brothers—the runners.

An effective push-off with the toes with each step leads to an improved efficiency of walking because of an even distribution of your total body weight. No matter how fat or how thin you are, your weight distribution results in the same pressure points on your feet. The heel still supports 60% of your body's weight, the fore-foot 28% and the remaining 12% distributed between the mid-foot and toes.

So remember, an even steady stride will make the most of your walking program. Let the force of gravity propel you forward with an effortless, almost weightless stride. Walking properly keeps your feet in good shape so that they can keep the rest of you in tip-top physical shape, *a foot in time, saves nine—lives that is!*

GIVE YOUR FEET A TREAT

Proper foot care is essential to any exercise program since the feet are vulnerable to injury and disease. The foot is a very complex structure consisting of 26 bones, 56 ligaments and 38 muscles. The feet not only carry the entire weight of the body, but they are essential in holding the body in an upright position and maintaining the body's balance during walking. Since your feet are the parts of the body that are located furthest from your heart, their circulation generally tends to be decreased, especially as you get older.

Constant pounding on hard surfaces causes the feet to absorb considerable shock and consequently subjects them to injury. The feet are also prone to the growth of fungi and bacteria because of the moist warm climate created by shoes and socks. These factors all point to the necessity of proper foot care in your Trimstep® walking program.

FOOT FACTS FOR FEET

1. Avoid the use of **tight-fitting garments**, including stockings, socks and garters, which can reduce the circulation to the lower extremities.
2. Avoid **prolonged sitting**, especially with your legs crossed, as this can also reduce the blood supply to your legs.
3. If you develop a cramping pain in your legs and feet while you're walking, which is relieved by rest and resumes again upon walking, see your doctor at once. You may have **poor circulation** in your legs. This can be caused by a narrowing of the arteries, preventing blood from reaching your legs and feet.
4. Dress sensibly since extremes in **temperature** can impair the circulation in the legs.
5. **Nicotine** constricts (narrows) the blood vessels and can result in impaired circulation. Smoking also causes a build-up of carbon monoxide in your blood and a decrease in the amount of oxygen carried to your legs.
6. **Exercise your feet** daily without shoes by walking barefoot on a carpet and flex your toes up and down any time you take off your shoes.

7. Keep feet **clean and dry**, especially between toes. Wash with deodorant soap and dry carefully. Use foot powder when necessary.
8. **Clean, soft, loose-fitting stockings and socks** prevent odor forming bacteria and sweat from building up. They also help to prevent the formation of blisters and calluses.
9. **Cut nails** straight across, never down in the grooves on the sides of your toes.
10. **Dry scaly feet**—use a skin moisturizer lotion at bedtime. Check with your doctor if the condition persists.
11. **Tired, aching feet**—treat to a warm water soak after walking, dry thoroughly.
12. **Foot problems**: corns, bunions, calluses, blisters, ingrown toenails, sores, ulcers, cracks, pain or swelling should be reported to your doctor.
13. **Walk, don't run**, and your feet will still be able to have fun.

TRIMSTEP® INTO THE
BEST SHOE FOR YOU

1. Wear a *properly fitted*, low-heeled shoe for maximum comfort and safety. Remember, make sure the shoe fits, no matter what the style. Shoes should be at least ½-¾ of an inch longer than your longest toe.
2. The *toe-section* should be wide and high enough so as not to cause compression of the toes.
3. The *shank* (section between heel and ball of foot) should be wide enough to fit the bottom of your foot comfortably.
4. The *uppers* (part of the shoe above the sole) should be soft and flexible enough to bend with your foot, such as soft leather, fabrics and suedes. Avoid synthetic materials (man made) such as vinyl and patent leather since they are not porous or flexible.
5. The *sole and heel* of the shoe should preferably be made of a thick resilient material (foam rubber or crepe). These are the most practical for every day use, since they are the most durable. Well-cushioned soles are extremely comfortable and give resiliency to your step, thus absorbing some of the shock encountered when walking on a hard surface. They also lessen your chance of slipping.

6. *Sneakers or running shoes* should only be worn if they have a wide, high, flexible toe box. This allows enough space to prevent crowding of the toes, which can result in toe and nail injuries. Most of them however, do not provide good support or adequate cushioning. Many of them also cause blisters and foot infections because of inadequate ventilation.

7. *High heels* cause the whole foot to slide forward, making the formation of corns, bunions, calluses and occasionally hammertoes more likely. Also continual use of high heels can actually shorten the Achilles tendon making it more susceptible to injury. They also prevent the foot from acting as a natural shock absorber and this leads to ligament strain in the foot and leg and recurrent backaches.

8. Avoid the use of *boots* with extremely high heels, since they interfere with your balance. These boots may also cut off the circulation and cause inflammation of the calf leg veins (phlebitis).

9. Avoid high *platform shoes and clogs*. These shoes often lead to ankle and foot injuries, and may cause painful bleeding under the toenails.

10. *Hiking shoes or boots* are cumbersome and are usually not necessary unless you plan to hike over rough terrain.

11. *Flat shoes* may actually strain a woman's calf muscles since most women usually have tight calf muscles to begin with.

12. *Shoes with 1 to 2 inch heels* are the best type for walking since they help to relax the leg muscles by removing tension on the tendons and ligaments.

13. *Shoes usually smell,* not your feet. Foot odor is caused by bacteria on the shoe leather which absorbs sweat from your feet. Give shoes time to air out. If however, you find that it's your feet and not your shoes that smell, check with your doctor. You may have a bacterial or fungal foot infection.

"THIS IS CERTAINLY MORE FUN THAN JUMPING WITH JANE, DANCING WITH DEBBIE OR ROMPING WITH RICHARD."

CHAPTER 8

WALKING WOMEN WIN!

SHE WALKS IN BEAUTY

"She walks in beauty, like the night
Of cloudless climes and starry skies
And all that's best of dark and bright
Meet in her aspect and her eyes"

Lord Byron

WALKING WOMEN SEXIER

A new study released at a meeting of the Society for the Scientific Study of Sex, revealed that moderate exercise increases women's sexual drive. Over 8,000 women who exercised regularly were interviewed for this research study. The following are a summary of the findings of this study:

- 98% of women interviewed stated that exercise boosts self-confidence.
- 89% of women reported an improvement in sexual self-confidence.
- 40% stated that their capacity for sexual arousal had been enhanced.
- 31% reported an increase in making love more often.

The following reasons were postulated for these extraordinary findings. First was that exercise increases the brain chemicals *endorphins,* which are the body's natural chemicals which make you feel good. Walking also acts as a natural anti-depressant and makes you feel better about yourself. Walking also not only makes you feel good but it actually makes you look prettier and healthier by increasing the blood supply to the skin and scalp. Walking regularly also seems to regulate the natural release of female hormones from the ovaries. Whatever the reasons are — **Walking Women Are Sexier!**

WOMEN ARE DOING THE TRIMSTEP®

A recent Gallup Poll sponsored by *American Health Magazine* showed that approximately 58 percent of women exercise regularly. Walking was the type of exercise that 3 out of 5 women engaged in most often. Almost 50 percent of those questioned said that they were walking for their health, 30 percent exercised to stay in shape, and approximately 20 percent stated that it was to lose or control weight.

This survey showed that women are walking again and feeling better. The responses given for choosing walking as their favorite exercise were, "easy, safe and comfortable, not too strenuous, beneficial and an exercise that you can continue for a lifetime."

Let's get out there and start walking again as if our lives depended on it. They probably do! Put life into each step and walking will repay you tenfold by putting extra years into your life. When you use your Trimstep® walking machine, you'll have a figure supreme and a body that's lean.

HER LEGS WERE MADE FOR WALKING

Women are structurally built for walking, but not for running. Since the runner pounds the ground with a force equal to three to four times her body weight, she is more likely to sustain injuries than the walker. Walking is one of the most natural functions of the human body. Due to the structure of a woman's musculo-skeletal system and the shape and flexibility of her spine, her body is perfectly constructed for walking.

As she walks the muscular and skeletal systems perform synchronously together. Her curved flexible spine has a spring-like function, made up of many vertebrae, each separated from the other by a tiny cushion (intervertebral-disc) which is designed to absorb shock. These discs also give the spine its resilience and flexibility. When she walks she uses the hinge-like joints in her feet, ankles and knees while the ball and socket joints in her hips move effortlessly with a fluid-like motion.

The muscles that are attached to the long bones of the legs and the pelvis are specifically designed for walking. The leg, hip and back muscles are used for support and the mechanics of propelling the body forward. The long bones of the legs form a framework of levers which are moved by these muscles, and subsequently help to propel the body forward. The abdominal muscles support the weight of the abdominal organs when she walks and her chest wall and diaphragm muscles assist in respiration.

As her legs thrust forward, she is in effect catching the forward motion of the upper part of her body. This natural motion in walking creates a perfect balance between gravity's force and the forward thrust of your body. The act of walking is therefore an almost effortless bio-dynamic mechanism, structurally more efficient than any woman-made machine.

PERFECT POSTURE — PHOOEY!

Check your posture before you start walking. Stand tall. Tuck your tummy in and straighten your spine. Throw your chest out and pull back your shoulders. Now that you're standing tall and straight like a soldier, take a deep breath and let it all out. Feel better? Good! Now let yourself relax and go back to your normally slouched over posture. Nobody is his right mind is going to walk like a marionette, unless you're a Nazi doing the goose-step. I love to read the magazines and books that describe what your posture should be like when you walk. If anyone walked like that, they would fall over on their faces after just a few steps. You can even ignore to some extent, what I've said about posture and walking in the last chapter.

It's important to try to maintain good posture when you're walking, but its equally important not to let it interfere with your walking program. Walking should be fun. *Walking isn't marching.* If you find that you can straighten up a little when you're walking, well and good. If you find that it hampers your walking stride, then forget it. Who said you had to look like a straight stick. Don't you remember how your mother and your teacher always used to say, "Stand up straight" or

"Sit straight in your chair." Well tell them to go "fly a kite." If you want to walk slouched over a little and you feel more comfortable that way—go ahead! It's time we took control of our lives and our posture for that matter. Walking lets us have the freedom to be individuals. Walkers don't have to follow any set of exercise rules. Walking is supposed to be fun. Let's keep it that way.

If you feel like walking in the most comfortable position for you—be my guest. If you want to occasionally throw out your chest and pull back your shoulders—go right ahead. If you want to tuck your tummy in now and then—do it. But don't feel that you have to do anything out of the ordinary, if it interferes with your comfort and stride while you're walking. Let's leave the perfect posture to the soldiers and the gymnasts who get medals for it. Walking is supposed to be fun, not torture. Rules were made to be broken, so forget what I said in the last chapter and just go out there and walk every day, any way that feels comfortable to you. *Perfect posture—phooey!*

BE A LEAN, MEAN WALKING MACHINE

Walking produces a remarkable number of changes that occur inside of your body. Your *blood volume* and the *red blood cells* increase in number. Your h*eart* pumps blood more efficiently. Your *lungs* expand, taking in and distributing more oxygen. Your *muscles* tighten and contract giving you a firmer figure. Your *energy* level increases, and you feel strong and fit. The results of these changes will make your figure lean and mean and your posture supreme.

Your overall appearance will improve following your daily work, since walking will improve your *circulation* and enable you to feel and look great. Your skin, complexion and hair texture will also improve with walking because of the increased blood circulation to the skin and hair follicles. Your complexion will literally glow after your walk and your skin will stay healthy and fresh looking all day long.

After you have been walking for awhile you will notice that your muscles will become firm and many of the fatty deposits on your thighs and buttocks will start to decrease in size. Your *stomach* will become flatter and the muscles of your *calves, thighs* and *buttocks* will become firmer. These changes result from improved muscle tone and also from the strengthening of muscles and ligaments which are attached to the spine.

You don't have to kill yourself to stay fit, trim and healthy. Walking actually provides better long-term figure control and fitness benefits than jogging or other strenuous exercises, without the hazards and dangers. Always remember that exercise does not have to be painful or uncomfortable to be effective. The **Trimstep**® walking plan provides the easy steps needed for a trim, beautiful body. Be *lean!* Be *mean! Be a walking machine!*

BONES OF YOUNG WOMEN MAY BE THINNING

Women who over-exercise to the point where their menstrual cycles are disrupted, may develop irreversible loss of bone mass. This is due to the loss of calcium from the bones because of the lack of the female hormone estrogen. The results can be devastating, even in young women, since this calcium loss leads to fragile bones with subsequent loss of bone strength. In essence, a 25-year-old female who exercises strenuously enough to disrupt her menstrual cycle significantly, could conceivably have the bones of a 50-year-old woman.

It was previously thought that these bone changes could be reversed by reducing the amount and severity of the exercise. Unfortunately, this is not always the case. Even after women regain their regular menstrual periods by reducing exercise, their bones in some cases may not fully recover. These bone changes appear to be similar to the condition known as osteoporosis that occurs in post-menopausal women.

Walking on the other hand produces no sudden changes in estrogen production and therefore no changes in the menstrual cycle. Consequently, there is no bone-loss and no loss of bone strength. In fact, a regular moderate walking program actually causes an increase in bone-mass. According to a new study from the Washington University School of Medicine, moderate exercise, like walking, increased bone mineral content of the lumbar spine by 5.2% to 6.1% in 76% of post-menopausal women. This increase in bone mass remained constant throughout the walking program; however, the bone mass returned to 1.1% above baseline levels after the training period was discontinued.

The results of this study underscores the principle behind a life-long moderate type of walking program. Exercise must be consistent and moderate in order to have long lasting beneficial effects. Sporadic, seasonal or short-term, high-intensity exercises showed no correlation with increasing bone mineral content. The stimulus needed for increasing and maintaining bone mass is moderate weight-bearing exercises like walking.

WALKING WOMEN UNITE!

Osteoporosis is a serious debilitating disease, affecting over 20 million Americans, mostly women over the age of 45. This condition is actually a degeneration of bone throughout the body resulting in a loss of bone density. The bones actually become thinned out as a result of a loss of the mineral calcium from the bone structure. Osteoporosis is especially marked after menopause because of a reduction in the secretion of estrogen by the aging ovaries.

Osteoporosis leads to approximately 1½ million fractures each year. Fractures of the hips are particularly common in older women. Approximately one out of five older women who sustains a hip fracture dies of secondary complications. This results in almost 35,000 deaths every year, making osteoporosis a leading cause of death among senior citizens. Another 25% of these women who break their hips become permanently crippled. Other serious complications of osteoporosis are fractures of the spinal column. These fractures can cause a collapse of the spinal vertebrae resulting in a shortening of actual height, a severe curvature of the spine ("dowager's hump"), or a paralysis of the spinal cord.

There are many therapies that are currently undergoing investigation for the treatment of osteoporosis. The most common form of treatment is the use of calcium supplements to replace the calcium lost from bone. Other recommended treatments include the use of estrogen, sodium fluoride, vitamin D supplements and calcitrol (a form of vitamin D that helps the absorption of calcium). Enough about treatment. What do you think is the most important way to prevent osteoporosis? You guessed it again! **Walking!**

In a recent study reported in *The Journal of Orthopedic Research,* women who remained physically active after menopause or after age 50 had stronger, denser bones. Compared with inactive women ages 50-75, the active women had considerably greater arm and spine bone density measurements, almost in the same range as women 10-15 years younger. This study supports earlier research that shows that **osteoporosis** (thinning of the bones) can be slowed or halted by a regular walking program combined with a high calcium diet, and that the incidence of bone fractures is 10 times less frequent in **walking women**.

Walking outdoors when the sun is shining also helps to strengthen bones, because sunshine helps the body produce vitamin D, a nutrient needed for calcium absorption. And if these walking women ever do have the misfortune to break a bone—their bones **unite** (heal) faster!

LADIES WHO LUNCH—LEARN TO PUNCH!

According to Dr. William Castelli, director of the Framingham, MA Heart Study, high levels of triglycerides (a type of blood fat) increase the risk of heart attacks and strokes. It seems that the body converts triglycerides into low-density lipo-proteins (LDL's), the so-called "bad" type of cholesterol. The LDL cholesterol is the type that clogs up your arteries and can make you prone to developing either a heart attack or a stroke.

Women seem to be more at risk than men for developing heart attacks and strokes from high triglyceride levels. Men, on the other hand, seem to be more at risk for strokes and heart attacks when their cholesterol levels, rather than their triglyceride levels, are high. Triglyceride levels usually go up when excess refined sugars are consumed, like cakes, candies, pies, ice cream, etc. Women who usually eat more sweets than men seem to develop higher triglyceride levels, since the body's metabolism converts excess sugar into triglyceride. If you have to limit your sweets don't cry, because *triglycerides may make you die*.

Now for the good news. Walking lowers both triglycerides and LDL cholesterol. So when you sit down for coffee and cake, remember to get up and walk those triglycerides off, before they walk their way into your heart for a long unhealthy stay. *Punch-out triglycerides with a brisk walk, before they K-O you with a "real fat" punch.*

WALKING WOMEN WIN BATTLE OF VANDALIZED VEINS

Once your blood has circulated throughout the arteries, supplying oxygen and nutrients to all of your body's cells, it must return to the heart and lungs for a fresh supply of oxygen. The blood must pass from the arteries into the veins before it can be returned to the heart and lungs. Except for the blood returning to the heart from the upper third of the body, the return of all the rest of the blood to the heart from the lower two-thirds of the body must go upwards against the force of gravity.

This flow of blood through the veins back to the heart is assisted by the contraction of your *leg muscles* when you walk. The leg muscles actually squeeze the blood up the veins against gravity. This upward flow of blood is also aided by the small *one-way valves* located inside the walls of the veins. These valves actually prevent the blood from falling back down the veins.

Prolonged sitting actually causes a pooling of blood in the leg veins because of the force of gravity. This results in a build-up of pressure inside the walls of the veins which subsequently impairs the return flow of blood back to the heart. I'm sure you've experienced *numbness* and *tingling* in your legs when you've been sitting in one position for a long time. Once you get up and walk around, your leg muscles begin to squeeze the pooled blood back up the leg veins, and the symptom of numbness quickly goes away.

Many women unfortunately have genetically weak veins. These individuals are prone to develop varicose veins. Prolonged sitting, as we have seen, builds up the venous pressure in the leg veins which is caused by the pooling of blood. Anyone who has weak veins to start with now faces a more serious problem than just numbness and tingling in the legs.

The excessive pressure that builds up in the veins actually balloons out these weak veins. This, in turn, stretches out the walls of the veins, and the small valves located inside the walls of the veins lose their resiliency.

After a period of time these weakened veins permanently dilate (enlarge), and their valves no longer are able to prevent the flow of blood from dropping back down the veins. This results in what is commonly called *varicose* or *incompetent* veins, which are unable to return all of the blood back to the heart. Sometimes fluid leaks out of these veins into the tissues of the legs causing edema (swelling of the feet and legs). Walking and support stockings are the only ways to control this condition. Surgery sometimes is necessary if these veins become worse.

Prolonged sitting can result in another more serious, often life-threatening, condition of the veins. The blood that pools in the leg veins of those people who sit in one position for long periods of time may begin to clot. The stagnated blood starts to irritate and inflame the inside walls of the veins that it is pressing against. This inflammation of the leg veins is called *phlebitis*. This condition requires prompt medical treatment and can be a potentially life-threatening condition. If a blood clot actually forms in these veins it could conceivably become dislodged and travel to the heart or lungs with fatal consequences. Although this condition occurs more frequently in people with varicose veins, it can occur in anyone who sits in one position for a long period of time (example: long flights or auto trips).

After you have been sitting for a long time, especially when traveling, your circulation slows down. This is why your feet often swell after a long trip. The upward flow of blood from the leg veins can also be impaired by constrictive clothing or by crossing your legs, which causes further swelling in your feet and ankles. Always make it a point to walk around on a plane or train. Make frequent stops when riding in a car to stretch your legs. Walking will start your leg's muscle-pump working, so that it squeezes the blood up your leg veins and back into your heart for re-circulation. Don't let your leg *veins' vital valves* become *vandalized victims* of the *sedentary sitter*. Walking women can win the battle of these vandalized veins.

WITH CHILD—TAKE IT MILD!

The so-called fitness experts have been telling pregnant women for the past 10 years that exercise is beneficial for them. Magazines, videotapes and books have been giving the same messages loud and clear—"it's okay to exercise when you're pregnant, you'll have a healthier baby."

Well, guess what? This advice is all wrong. Recent animal studies show that strenuous exercise during pregnancy may be potentially harmful to the fetus. This apparently happens because of two reasons. First, strenuous exercise may redirect the blood flow away from the uterus and placenta toward the mother's exercising muscles and skin. Any decrease in the blood's supply of oxygen to the developing fetus can be hazardous—causing birth defects, miscarriages, premature births and even fetal deaths.

Secondly, strenuous exercise causes an elevation of the body temperature in the pregnant woman. This rise in temperature is transmitted through the bloodstream to the fetus. This elevated temperature may cause damage to the fetus' developing nervous system resulting in neurologic birth defects. Recent studies in humans have verified these experimental animal studies.

Pregnancy itself makes greater demands on the cardiovascular and muscular system, so it stands to reason that physical exertion should be limited. Strenuous calisthenics, especially leg exercises, strain the ligaments supporting the uterus. And pregnancy causes a woman's center of gravity to shift, making a fall or injury more likely while exercising.

Always check with your own physician before embarking upon any exercise program, even walking. Most physicians, I'm sure, would agree that walking is the safest, most beneficial form of exercise for at least the 1st half of your pregnancy. The fitness industry isn't concerned about your health. They are interested in one thing only—to make money selling equipment, apparel, books, video-cassettes, magazines and the rest of their snake-oil remedies. First have a baby that's healthy and serene. Then start walking to make your figure trim and lean.

WALKING WOMEN WIN AGAIN!

Women who began exercising and playing sports as young girls appear to develop body changes that reduce their risk of breast and uterine cancers. In a recent study at Harvard School of Public Health these findings were presented based on the fact that exercise in young girls delays the onset of menstruation by several years. The early onset of menstruation is a known risk factor for developing breast cancer.

Women who continue their exercise program into later life have less body fat and more lean muscle mass. These women also tend to eat a low-fat diet throughout their adult years. It is a known fact that excess fat makes excess estrogen, which increases the risk of breast cancer. In this study of over 5,000 women, it was also found that the lean women produced a less potent form of estrogen, which was not as likely to cause breast and uterine cancer as the more potent form of estrogen produced by heavier women.

These findings presented at the 1988 meeting of the American Association for the Advancement of Science, showed that sedentary women had a 2½ times greater risk for cancer of the uterus and twice the risk of developing breast cancer. It was also shown that inactive women had 3½ times the risk for developing diabetes. Adult-onset diabetes is more likely to develop in obese, inactive women than in leaner active women, regardless of any hereditary factors.

Active young women also have fewer and more irregular menstrual periods. Less periods in young girls and women usually reduces the risk of uterine cancer because of a decrease in the production of female hormones. This reduction in hormones also decreases a girl's fertility level. I doubt if exercise, however, can be counted on as an effective method of preventing pregnancy. But it just might be an answer to why there aren't more teenage pregnancies than there are already. In any event the fertility level usually returns to normal once exercise is decreased somewhat and the periods became more regular.

Women who remain active during their adult years were found to have a lower risk of developing heart disease also.

Walking regularly contributes to the production of this less potent form of estrogen. When this type of estrogen is combined with the hormone progesterone which is naturally produced by the ovaries, active women have lower levels of total cholesterol and higher levels of HDL (the "good" cholesterol).

Walking Women Win Again! Long May You Reign!

A WOMAN WINS FOR HER & HIM

Two patients of mine, a husband and wife, wanted to lose weight and start "some sort of an exercise program." Actually it was the wife who wanted to lose weight and look good. She was forcing her husband to participate along with her because as she exclaimed, "he's getting too fat and is starting to get out of breath when he goes up steps." John weighed a little over 220 lbs and Lois weighed-in at about 165 lbs. Both had been my patients for years and each had tried a variety of diets and exercise plans with little or no result. John was now 51 years old and Lois was 48. Lois said she finally made the decision to come in after she and her husband went to a neighbor's pool party. She said even though her husband seemed unconcerned about his "big belly," she had had it with her fat thighs and hips.

Lois, who came in one day for a routine physical exam, stated, "I know you're always recommending walking for your patients and have written a good deal about walking, but does it really work?"

"Yes," I said, "it works, but you have to work at it." She wanted to know what I meant by "work at it." "Lois," I said, "walking is like any project or activity that you begin. You must first have a good attitude about what you're planning to do. Then you must start properly and follow through carefully, but most of all you must be consistent. And above all else, you have to be committed to the program for the rest of your life."

Well, Lois looked skeptical at first, stating that she hadn't realized that this was to be a life-time project. I explained that walking, like anything important in your life, has to become a part of your everyday living. Walking must become a way of life for anyone who's interested in fitness, good health and weight-control. Unlike most diet and exercise programs, walking is not a short-term program.

Lois looked somewhat bewildered. "If all I want to do is to lose 15-20 lbs, why must I make such a long-term commitment?"

"Well," I said, "if you want those pounds to stay off and you want to maintain good health, then you can't just stop when you've lost those unwanted pounds." I attempted to explain to her that once she started walking, she would want to continue walking long after her 20 pound weight-loss. "Walking will become a part of your everyday activities," I exclaimed, "and believe me you won't want to stop your walking program."

I don't think she was totally convinced but she agreed to start a walking program with her husband. I explained to her that she and John should start slowly and build-up their exercise tolerance gradually. I outlined a simple walking program for her and her husband that is outlined as follows:

15 minutes every-other day for the 1st week
30 minutes every-other day for the 2nd week
45 minutes every-other day for the 3rd week
60 minutes every-other day for the 4th and following weeks.

I explained that if they found that they couldn't walk an hour every other day, then a ½ hour walk daily will provide exactly the same health, fitness and weight-control benefits as the 1 hour walk every-other day.

Lois asked me if that didn't seem to be an awfully slow way to start an exercise program. I explained to her that since she and her husband hadn't exercised for the last 15-20 years, this was the safest and most effective way to start her walking program. She again reluctantly agreed to start slowly. But she said, *"walking seems like it's too easy a method to lose weight and trim me down.* Don't you need to do something more strenuous to burn calories?" I assured her that walking was the safest and most effective way to lose weight with the least chance of injuring herself or quitting the program.

"How fast should I walk?" Lois suddenly asked. "I hadn't thought about that at all." "I've read," Lois stated matter of factly, "that you're supposed to walk very fast, swinging your arms rapidly."

"Believe me," I stated, "you don't have to walk that fast in order to attain maximum physical fitness and weight control. In fact it's not necessary to walk very fast at all." "Brisk walking," I explained, "is walking anywhere from 3 to 4 miles per hour. Anything under 2 miles per hour is too slow and anything over 4 miles per hour is walking too fast. Studies show that walking at any speed is beneficial, so never give up a walking program because you think you can't walk fast enough for fitness."

"Do I have to time my pulse?" Lois asked.

"Most certainly not," I stated vehemently. "That's one of the fitness hoaxes that have been perpetrated on the American public, by the so-called fitness experts and exercise enthusiasts. A rapid pulse rate is defintely not an essential ingredient in an exercise and fitness program. And besides, a rapid pulse rate may do more harm than good," I stated categorically. "As your pulse rate and heart beat become more rapid, your blood pressure starts to rise. As your blood pressure goes up, so does the stress and strain on your arteries. If the blood vessels themselves become stressed enough, they develop tiny cracks in their lining walls. These cracks become ideal seeding-beds for deposits of cholesterol and calcium to accumulate on. If these deposits become extensive, they may obstruct the flow of blood through the arteries, subsequently producing a stroke or heart attack."

"Walking at a moderate speed of approximately 3 miles per hour is more than adequate to get your pulse rate up to 85-100 beats per minute," I explained. "This is more than sufficient to allow your lungs to extract oxygen from the atmosphere, transfer it to your arteries, and finally to distribute this oxygen to all of your body's cells, tissues and organs. Anything faster than that is completely wasted, since the lungs can only pick up so much oxygen from the atmosphere and distribute it via the arteries to your cells. Any pulse-rate higher than 100 beats per minute can't extract any more oxygen and distribute it any faster than a pulse rate of 85-100."

"In fact," I exclaimed, "a rapid pulse rate in addition to being harmful, as I had previously stated, is actually wasteful. All of this extra oxygen that is brought into the body with strenuous exercise is supplied only to the exercising muscles themselves, to provide them with enough oxygen to keep up the strenuous exercise. Once they've run out of oxygen to use, they go into "oxygen debt" and must stop exercising shortly in order to pay back any extra oxygen that they borrowed from the rest of the body."

"And remember," I insisted, "that when you're exercising too fast, you're only doing your body harm. Not only does a rapid pulse raise your blood pressure and damage your arteries, but the rapid pulse rate also robs oxygen from your internal organs, tissues and cells. It does this because the exercising muscles use up all of the available oxygen and actually cause some of the blood and oxygen to be shunted away from your internal organs to these exercising muscles."

Suffice it to say, Lois seemed satisfied and we agreed to check her weight, blood pressure and general physical condition every two weeks. Before starting her program, however, I insisted that she and her husband come in for complete physical exams, blood work, a urinalysis and a resting EKG. I told her that if either she or her husband had any abnormalities on the resting EKG or developed any chest pain or discomfort or shortness of breath when they were walking, then I would insist on a stress EKG.

Well, both Lois and John passed their complete physical exams except for the fact that Lois's blood sugar and triglycerides were slightly elevated and John's total cholesterol, LDL cholesterol, triglycerides and uric acid were all moderately elevated. Although John had no family history of gout, I explained that the uric acid is frequently found to be elevated with obesity. Lois's blood pressure was 140/90 and John's was 160/94. I stressed a low-salt diet and I told John that if the diet and the walking program didn't bring down his blood pressure, he would need medication. I recommended that both John and Lois begin a modified low-fat, low-cholesterol, low-sugar, low-salt diet. I told them that combined with their walking program, the diet would help them to take off their unwanted pounds and lower their blood pressures.

Well, as expected, 12 weeks later, John had lost 24 lbs. (an average weight-loss of 2 lbs. per week), and Lois had lost 18 lbs. (an average weightloss of 1½ lbs per week). Lois's blood sugar and triglycerides were now within the normal range. Her HDL cholesterol, which was essentially low-normal on the initial examination, was now in the high-range of normal which is a excellent indicator of good health, since the higher the HDL ("good" cholesterol) is, the less likely you are to have a stroke or a heart attack. Lois's blood pressure was now 130/80, a 10 point drop in both the systolic and diastolic pressures.

John's total cholesterol had come down from 285 to 240 and his LDL ("bad" cholesterol) had come down approximately 20%. This was an excellent result for the first 12 weeks and I told him that I'd expect another significant drop over the next 12 weeks. His triglycerides and uric acid both came down into the high-range of normal. The most remarkable finding on John's 12-week examination was that his blood pressure had dropped from 160/94 to 144/86. I told him that with further weight reduction and dietary restriction he would probably not need medication if his blood pressure went down a few more points and remained within the normal range.

Approximately 3 months later, Lois and John come in for follow-up check-ups. Lois was now 135 pounds, and John was now 184 lbs. Each had lost an additional 12 lbs. All of their blood chemistries were now well within the normal range and both of their blood pressures were now within normal limits.

I asked Lois what she now thought of that easy exercise called walking. She stated that she was literally amazed that anything as simple as walking could have so many benefits. "True" she said, "we were following your diet, to some extent, but we often cheated, especially on the weekends. I can truly say," she said, "that walking has not only made me look better, but I actually feel 100% better. I can do things that I couldn't do for years. John and I go bowling once a week and we get up and go out for a ½ hour walk every night, a few hours after dinner. Sometimes on the weekends, we drive out to the country and take a walk in the woods. We go to the movies and dances more often, and we just feel like doing more each day than we thought about doing over the past 20 years. Now John's stomach doesn't look like he's pregnant anymore and I can wear slacks or shorts without feeling self-conscious."

"You were so right, Dr. Stutman. I wouldn't stop this walking program for all the tea in China. We'll modify our diets a bit because neither of us is interested in losing too much more weight, but we'll never stop walking. Walking has given me a new perspective on life and it has given me the push I needed to enjoy life to the fullest. As hard as John works each day, he looks forward to our evening walks and he said just the other day, that there's really not anything on TV that's that good in the early evening."

TURN THOSE EYES—WITH A FLAT TUMMY, SLIM HIPS & THIGHS!

Tell most people that walking produces a flat tummy, slim hips and thighs and they'll tell you that you're crazy. "You need to do strenuous calisthenics and exercises to reduce fat deposits in those areas." Don't be too sure! Walking can give you a flat, firm tummy and slim hips and thighs without any additional exercises—and that's a medical fact!

First of all, when you walk briskly with an even stride you are contracting and relaxing muscles in your chest, back and abdomen. With each forward motion of your legs, these muscles contract to keep your body erect. Your abdominal muscles tighten automatically, exactly as they would if you were doing strenuous sit-ups, with one exception—you're not straining your back muscles. As you swing your upper arms, the upper chest wall muscles that are tied in with the upper abdominal wall muscles aid in tightening these abdominal muscles. This combination of upper body and lower abdominal muscle contractions are what produces a firm, flat tummy.

With repeated bouts of walking come repeated bouts of muscle tightening, until a point is reached when your abdominal muscles are firm and taut all of the time, whether you're walking or not. This firm, flat tummy will continue to last as long as you walk regularly. Also as you walk, the forward and backward motion of each hip stretches the hip muscles. This hip motion tugs at your lower abdominal muscles, further flattening your tummy.

Now what about those lumpy, bumpy hips and thighs. First of all, don't let anyone give you the baloney about *"cellulite deposits."* There's no such thing as cellulite! It's a term coined by diet promoters to encourage people to purchase diet-gimmicks to rid themselves of the mythical cellulite. Microscopic studies of fat show that fat cells are connected by strands of connective tissue. When these connective tissue strands stretch, they lose their elasticity and subsequently the fat gives a lumpy appearance. Regular fat cells and the so-called cellulite fat deposits are indistinguishable under the microscope. *Fat is fat!* And cellulite is **phoney-baloney!**

Let's get back to *thin and trim thighs*. When you walk briskly your pelvis shifts forward and your buttock muscles contract as you stride forward. Your lead leg pulls you forward as your back leg pushes you forward. Both of these motions contract and relax your leg muscles both in front and in back of your thighs. This alternate flexing and relaxing of the thigh muscles tones and trims your thigh better than any machine can do and with considerably less likelihood of injury. Repeated regular bouts of brisk walking also burns away fat deposits in your thighs. Since walking is a moderate aerobic exercise, it burns fat rather than muscle tissue. The result: *trim and thin thighs*. When this fat burning process is combined with the contractions of your thigh muscles you will also lose those unsightly bumpy and lumpy (the mythical cellulite) fat deposits. Sound too easy? It certainly is! I guarantee it! If I'm wrong, you can call me Ray or you can call me Jay, but you desen't call me Dr. Walk®.

O.K. let's get on to those *wide-spread hips* and *flabby buttocks*. Now I know you'll tell me that you inherited those from your mother or your grandmother and there's nothing you can do about it. Well, I'll tell you that you didn't inherit those characteristics from anyone. First of all, your mother and your grandmother probably never did much walking at all, and that's why they had wide bottoms and fat hips. Too much sitting is bad for the derrière and the hips. Inactivity in these areas leads to the accumulation of fatty deposits and the loss of connective tissue elasticity. These factors combine to give what's known as the spread-hip, wide-bottom look. Not a look designed for today's modern womens' fashions. You don't have to accept it as inevitable. You don't have to contend with flabby buttocks and fat thighs even if you've already got them.

Walking will prevent flabby thighs and a wide bottom. Walking will get rid of fat thighs and a flabby bottom. Don't let anyone tell you that they're permanent. As you walk briskly your upper legs and hips stretch forward and backwards with each stride that you take. Your hips and buttocks also move from side to side by rotating, as your legs swing forward. This motion tightens your hip and buttock muscles, which starts the slimming process almost immediately. The forward motion of your legs combined with the tightening of the lower abdominal muscles also produces a tightening effect of your lower back and buttocks muscles. This combination of alternate muscle groups contracting and relaxing produces firm, tight buttock muscles. This firming effect actually lifts the buttocks so that they lose their saggy appearance. Your thighs also become thin and trim with walking and remain that way as long as you continue a regular walking program.

> Don't despair you don't have to be like mummy
> Walking regularly will give you a nice flat tummy
> It's not necessary to throw any fits
> Walking alone will produce trim, slim hips
> Don't put up with a fat bottom, my dear
> Walk every day to firm and tighten that rear
> If your bottom sags, don't you mind
> Walking will firm up that drooping behind

"MMM, DOESN'T THAT LOOK JUST YUMMY?"

"WOW, THAT WALKER IS TRIM—AND NO TUMMY!"

"THEY SHOULD BUILD THESE FITNESS CENTERS CLOSER TO THE HOSPITALS!"

CHAPTER 9

I SAID BODY-SHAPING— NOT BODY BREAKING!

"NO PAIN, NO GAIN" — THAT'S INSANE!

Millions of Americans who have joined fitness clubs in the past 10 years have been brain-washed by their so-called fitness instructors into believing the *"no pain, no gain"* fallacy. They have been intimidated into exercising "until it hurts," or when at the point of total exhaustion their instructors say—"do 5 more good ones." And if you want to look fit and trim like the 21 year old fitness instructor, you'd better "use it or lose it."

Well guess what? You've been handed another load of fertilizer. In a recent survey of over 1500 aerobic class participants, over 53% sustained injuries. These injuries included pulled muscles, sprained ligaments, stress fractures, dislocated joints, torn cartilages and slipped discs. Several cases of stress-induced heart attacks and strokes were included among the list of injuries.

Most of these so-called fitness centers are run by instructors who've had no training at all in exercise physiology. Less than 10% of fitness instructors have degrees in exercise physiology or have been accredited by the *American College of Sports Medicine*. Many fitness clubs display a sign reading "our fitness instructors are certified." This probably means that the instructor attended a 2-day class to receive an exercise fitness certificate.

Most of these crazy calisthenic clubs don't even bother to take a medical history from their members. As long as you pay your dues up front, they could care less what happens to you! The fanatical fitness instructor freaks who run these side shows, think that everyone regardless of age, weight, sex or body build should be able to keep up with their continuous aerobic acrobatics. And when the first casualty occurs, and someone cries—"Who knows CPR?"—Who do you think is the first one out the door? You guessed it—our muscle bound fitness instructor!

> **Save your money and save your time**
> **Fitness clubs are a pain in the behind**
> **If all you want is fitness and pep**
> **Then take a walk with a vigorous step**
> **These health clubs say "no pain, no gain"**
> **That's not only false, but that's insane**

MASS MASOCHISM

Americans follow, for all intents and purposes, the pain-pleasure principle. In order for an activity, exercise, or diet to be good for you, it must hurt first, and if it is too easy, it certainly can't be beneficial. In other words, we follow the punishment-reward principle. If you follow a strict diet, that will lead to a thin, trim body. Or if we engage in strenuous, back-breaking exercises, then, of course, we will become fit and trim.

The diets that we follow usually are aimed at fast results, so we look for the fast gimmick or fad diet in order to lose weight rapidly. Other extremes can be seen in the health food and vitamin industry. If a certain amount of a vitamin or mineral is listed as the correct dosage for good health, we then assume that larger amounts must be better.

And finally we come to the exercise-fitness mania which has become a major industry overnight in America. We have gone from a sedentary existence to marathon-type exercises and have overlooked the simpler, more moderate forms of exercise. If it's flashy and aerobic, it must be good. Not since the days of the Roman gladiators has a population engaged in such dangerous sports. Injuries and deaths by the thousands have resulted from these *awful aerobic acrobatics*. Mass masochism has overtaken America—*"if it hurts bad, it must be good"!*

BODY-BREAKING—NOT BODY-SHAPING

One out of every two people who engage in aerobic exercises are injured. In a study of over 1,500 aerobic students, more than 800 of them reported injuries ranging from simple shin splints to fractured bones and slipped discs. Contrary to popular belief, the more frequently you exercised, the chances of injury increased significantly.

These injuries were thought to be caused by over-exercise, improper shoes, and hard, non-resilient floor surfaces. However, injuries occurred even in many individuals who took proper precautions. The fact of the matter is that there is no medical benefit to jumping up and down whether the floor is hard or soft, or whether you are wearing the correct shoes. Aside from stretching your muscles, which incidentally is completely worthless as an exercise, you are doing nothing to improve your level of fitness.

Calisthenics and aerobic dancing are social functions, not fitness builders. Yes, to some extent you are increasing the maximum oxygen consumption, but only for short spurts which produces no lasting cardiovascular benefits. Remember, no one has ever proved that getting your heart rate up to astronomical numbers for short periods of time improves your level of cardiovascular fitness. On the contrary, most recent medical studies indicate that this rapid pulse rate theory may actually be potentially hazardous to you health.

Calisthenics cripple by breaking bones, pulling muscles, stretching ligaments, and ripping tendons. **Aerobic dancing damages** feet, ankles, knees, hips and spines by pneumatic-drill type bouncing. **Weight machines mangle** by straining ligaments, ripping muscles, tearing tendons and bulging biceps. Many of these musculo-skeletal injuries cause temporary damage; others result in permanent disability. As far as I'm concerned aerobics are awful and calisthenics are crazy.

Well you're saying, what's so bad about a few pulled muscles or torn tendons? Wait! I haven't finished yet with the more serious complications of these crippling calisthenics. *Irregular heartbeats* are common among both men and women who engage in aerobic classes. They are caused by the extreme stress of the exercise and an unconditioned cardiovascular system. In most cases they are not harmful. However, in many cases they are potentially dangerous, leading to more serious heartbeat irregularities, heart attacks, and even sudden death.

Many people who start aerobic classes and think they are in good health may have *underlying congenital or acquired heart abnormalities* that they are completely unaware of. They may have had a heart murmur as a child and were told that it would probably go away when they got older. Many relatively minor heart conditions in childhood have remained undiagnosed because of the lack of accurate diagnostic tests 20-30 years ago, and because these people have never had any symptoms of heart disease. They feel fine, have no chest pain or palpitations and are leading perfectly normal lives—until they start these crippling calisthenics. Then they may develop chest pain, shortness of breath, marked fatigue or palpitations. Often it is attributed to "just being out of shape" and these aerobic robots continue on their casualty-course toward disability and death. How many aerobic classes give *free EKG's and echocardiograms* to new members!

How about our typical overweight middle-aged male with underlying, *undiagnosed coronary heart disease or hypertension*. He has no symptoms, joins the awful acrobatic aerobics class, starts his crazy calisthenics and drops dead. He probably had some chest pain and shortness of breath when he started his jumping jacks aerobics class. But he just ignored it and thought he too was "just out of shape" like the rest of his overweight classmates. And he certainly wasn't going to stop in the middle of his exercise class while the rest of the aerobic robots, including the 21-year-old athletic instructor, were effortlessly jumping and stumping. So he just exercised on through his pain and strain and kept on "looking good" as they wheeled him out on the stretcher. How many fitness clubs offer *free stress EKG's and coronary arteriograms* along with their membership fees?

Leave the calisthenics for the crazies, the weight machines for the maniacs, and the aerobics classes for the acrobatic asses. *Walk, Don't Jump and you won't be a chump!*

AEROBIC ACCIDENTS

Aerobic dancing may be good for the waistline but it's bad for the back and legs. In a recent study reported in *The*

Physician and Sportsmedicine Journal, injuries occurred in over half of the women who participated in aerobic dance classes. In a related study almost 75 percent of participants suffered some form of injury.

The most common injuries were:

1. **Shin splints** (injuries to the ligaments over the shin bone with resultant pain when walking)
2. **Ankle injuries** (ligament tears and pulled calf muscles)
3. **Sprain of the Achilles' tendon** in back of ankle
4. **Stress fractures** of the small bones of the feet
5. **Lower back injuries** ranging from pulled back muscles and torn ligaments to slipped discs

Most women who engaged in aerobic dancing were not sufficiently conditioned to take the excessive strain put on their ligaments, muscles and joints. Once these joints and ligaments are injured, the re-injury rate almost doubles because of inadequate healing time given for recovery in most cases.

Why do a *dangerous dance* when you can take a *wonderful walk* with all the same health and fitness benefits, and without the hazards and dangers. **Walk, don't limp!**

MANGLE-MACHINES & OTHER THINGS

There are many types of indoor exercise mangle machines that can be found at your expensive health club. Most of these are extremely dangerous and difficult to use. Muscle injuries, ligament tears, tendon ruptures, back and neck muscle spasms are but a few of the many treats in store for you when you *tangle with the mangle machines*.

1. **MULTI-PURPOSE GYM MUSCLE MACHINES:** These include the so-called new ball-bearing weight-stack-lifting machines and various springs, cables, pulleys, and elastic stretching devices. This type of exercise stresses the stimulation and strengthening of the large muscles of the body. These machines do very little for the heart and lung capacity and do not increase the consumption of oxygen; therefore, they are not useful in fitness conditioning, nor in burning

calories to help you to lose weight. Many of these muscle gym machines can be dangerous and have been known to cause elevation of blood pressure in susceptible persons. Fitness centers lead you to believe that because these weight-stack machines are on ball-bearings, they are safe to use. That's sheer nonsense. Weight lifting with weight-machines has the same dangers as free weights.

2. **ANKLE AND WRIST WEIGHTS:** Whoever thought of exercising or doing calisthenics with weights on your ankles and wrists should have weights tied to his hands and feet and be dropped in the ocean. There is enough strain on the heart during exercise without making it more hazardous to your health. Remember, exercise doesn't have to be painful for it to be beneficial.

3. **SIT BACK AND DO NOTHING MACHINES** (Belt Vibrators, Roller Machines, and Whirlpool Baths): These so-called exercise devices contribute absolutely nothing towards the development of cardiovascular fitness. They are not aerobic exercise or any other exercise for that matter, and are potentially dangerous. Roller machines can cause small blood vessels to break under the skin, causing hemorrhages. Belt vibrators have been implicated in jarring internal abdominal organs with occasional damage to these vital structures.

4. **BARBELLS, DUMBBELLS, AND OTHER HEAVY FREE WEIGHTS:** All are dangerous and can cause back, arm, leg, and hip injuries. Some people have developed hernias from weight lifting. Heavy weights may aggravate or cause high blood pressure in some people. Barbells are for dumbbells.

5. **MINI-TRAMP:** These miniature trampolines are often called rebounders. They are three or four feet wide and are approximately 4-8 inches off the ground. There are many injuries reported with these rebounders. They include falls from loss of balance, ankle and knee sprains from twisting, head and neck injuries from bouncing too high and hitting an overhang, and back and hip injuries from twisting.

6. **ROWING MACHINES:** This particular mangle ma-

chine is really designed to develop upper body strength, not cardiovascular fitness. These machines also can be dangerous to people with high blood pressure. They can also cause a variety of back problems ranging from pulled muscles to slipped discs.

7. **TREADMILL:** The treadmill is actually a conveyor belt supported by a steel frame. They come in both motorized and non-motorized varieties and both are extremely dangerous to use. They put excessive strain on the back and leg muscles, causing a variety of injuries ranging from simple muscle and ligament sprains to more severe back injuries.

8. **INDOOR SKI TRACK MACHINES:** The newest and perhaps most dangerous entry into the home exercise market is the indoor ski track machine. These contraptions supposedly simulate cross country skiing in your living room. You hook your feet into two wooden ski-like contraptions which slide back and forth as you move your legs forward and backward. Then you grab on to two pulleys with each arm and attempt to pull them simultaneously as you slide back and forth on the wooden slats. The only problem is that you have to pull the pulley with the arm opposite to the leg that is moving forward? Sound easy? Forget it. Even if you've skied before, unless you are a contortionist, this complicated apparatus is for the birds. Reports of fractured leg bones, torn arm muscles and broken hips are but a few of the reported injuries related to the use of these new mangle machines.

9. **BODY WRAPS AND STEAM BATHS:** Body wrapping has become one of the new fad weight-loss and muscle toning gimmicks that has been perpetrated on the American public. By wrapping a person in plastic strips or wraps, the body retains heat and moisture, and excessive perspiration leads to excessive fluid loss, not actual weight loss. Because of the pressure exerted by these wrappings, it appears that you have lost inches where you were wrapped. This, however, is only an illusion created by the indentation caused by the tight wraps. According to the FDA, these wraps have no effect whatsoever on fat deposits nor will they dissolve fat in any part of the body. The

weight initially lost because of excessive perspiration comes back almost immediately after adequate fluids are consumed. These wraps also have the added danger of causing dehydration and mineral loss with resultant cardiac rhythm abnormalities. These same hazards apply to steam and sauna baths. If used excessively, they not only can cause dehydration and heart rate abnormalities but they can also raise blood pressure to dangerous levels.

10. **ELECTRICAL MUSCLE STIMULATORS:** Pseudo-diet and fitness promoters claim that these devices tone muscles and promote weight-loss by stimulating the muscle fibers with low-levels of electrical shock. Actually these muscle stimulators are prescription medical devices used for alleviating pain in some chronic back conditions, which incidentally are prescribed only by a medical doctor. These devices, used in the wrong hands, can cause electrical burns or shock and are particularly hazardous to people with heart conditions, nervous disorders such as epilepsy, cancer patients and pregnant women.

11. **STEROIDS:** Steroids increase muscle mass to the same extent that they increase the risk of heart disease. A new study according to The National Heart, Lung and Blood Institute found that steroid users had dangerously low levels of the good cholesterol-HDL and higher than normal levels of LDL-the so-called bad cholesterol. These findings put all steroid users in the extremely high risk group for developing heart disease.

Besides heart disease, steroid users are at significant risk for developing liver disease including liver cancer, hypertension, failure of the immune system and a variety of mental disorders, ranging from chronic anxiety to severe psychoses. Women body-builders, in particular, who take these steroids are also at risk for developing menstrual abnormalities, ovarian damage, infertility, unsightly facial hair, loss of breast tissue and deepening of the voice. Many of these changes may become permanent even if women attempt to counteract them with female hormones.

The following is an updated list of the hazards and dangers of taking steroids (anabolic) for weight-training and muscle building:

1. Facial hair growth and baldness in women.
2. Severe pustular acne in men and women.
3. High blood pressure and clogged arteries in men and women.
4. Liver cancer in men and women.
5. Prostrate cancer in men.
6. Breast growth in men; breast cancer and decreased breast size in women.
7. Atrophied testicles and sterility in men; menstrual irregularities and ovarian damage in women.
8. Increased hostility, aggression and emotional disorders.
9. Abnormal growth of muscle tissue.
10. "Reverse anorexia"—eating compulsions.

Anabolic steroids are synthetic variants of the strongest male hormone, testosterone. They are mainly taken in tablet form but may also be injected. They may be acquired legally by prescription only; however, there is a growing black market in Mexico, Canada, Europe and the USA.

12. **PERSONAL FITNESS TRAINERS:** These are the newest entries into the physical fitness arena. For $150 an hour you can sweat and strain under the watchful eye of your very own fitness guru. These so-called trainers come to your office or home and supervise your work-out program. Most of these self-acclaimed fitness experts are not qualified for anything more than to make a fast buck. No license is required to set up shop and the most training that the majority of these so-called trainers have is a 2-day seminar at the local gym.

13. **VIDEO-TAPES:** The video-tape industry has claimed millions of captive Americans in their homes to *Dance with Debbie* or *Jump with Jane* or *Romp with Richard*. The problem with these tapes is that they're all variations on the same theme. They're *aerobics for the masses, by famous acrobatic asses.* They do nothing for physical fitness and car-

diovascular conditioning. In fact, they are actually hazardous to your health. Many participants have sustained a variety of ligament, muscle and bone injuries while using these videos. By increasing the heart rate to very rapid rates, they can also cause hypertension and heart rhythm abnormalities. In fact, these strenuous aerobics have even been implicated in causing strokes and heart attacks in people with underlying heart disease and hypertension. *Walkers don't need videos. They just goes!*

14. **LOW-IMPACT AEROBICS:** Even the so-called, *low-impact aerobics* are hazardous to life and particularly limb. Over 65% of aerobics participants sustain some form of ankle, knee or hip injury during this senseless jumping up and down and swaying to and fro. Most of these injuries are temporary; however, many result in permanent ligament and joint injuries, particularly if the participants return to their exercises before the damaged parts have time to heal. There have also been reported cases of arthritis, fractures, back injuries and herniated (slipped) discs from these acrobatic aerobics. *Low-impact aerobics are high-impact pseudo-heroics!*

HAVE YOU EVER SEEN A JOGGER SMILE?

Walking remains the safest, most effective form of exercise known to man. With all of the hazards of jogging and competitive sports you may wonder why anyone would participate in so violent an exercise as jogging. Well, the answer is simple—we live in a masochistic society and we have been conditioned to believe that an exercise or activity has to be painful in order for it to be beneficial. For instance, how many of you have attempted to diet with vigorous starvation diets to obtain a thin figure, engaged in backbreaking exercises to have a well-conditioned trim body, or suffered a painful sunburn to obtain a beautiful tan? *Have you ever seen a jogger smile?* They can't; it hurts too much.

Medical research has proven that exercise does not have to be painful in order to have beneficial results. Walking produces the same—let me repeat—the same health, fitness and weight control benefits as jogging and other strenuous exercises without the hazards. The cardiovascular benefits are exactly the same without the strain.

These are not only my own observations, but are the conclusions of thousands of medical investigators in this country and abroad. The medical journals are filled with studies about the health benefits of walking, and they are also filled with an equal number of reports listing the hazards of jogging and other strenuous exercises. So, don't be dumb; let's have some fun—*Walk, Don't Run!*

Remember, you can achieve better health and fitness without stress and strain and inconvenience—and let me point out to you that a walking program is the only exercise that you can safely carry out for the rest of your life. Walking, then, is the road to a healthier, happier, and longer life.

ONCE, TWICE, THREE TIMES YOU'RE OUT!

It is now widely known that strenuous exercise can cause sudden death. Cardiac deaths which occur while jogging have been reported with increasing frequency in the past 10 years. Now, if you're lucky enough to survive the hazards of jogging, you may get your chance to die again—*immediately after jogging*.

Post-exercise sudden deaths have now begun to occur frequently, especially after marathon races. Recent studies indicate that during the cooldown phase the joggers' blood pressures dropped dramatically. In order to compensate for this drop in blood pressure, the body pours out large quantities of the hormones norepinephrine and epinephrine. Norepinephrine blood levels can increase to 10 times the normal amount which increases the heart rate and constricts the blood vessels. Epinephrine levels may increase to 3-4 times the normal level, markedly increasing the blood pressure.

This flood of hormones into the bloodstream is actually a reflex effort on the part of the body to restore the blood pressure to normal, following exercise. However, these dangerously high hormone levels may put a fatal strain on the heart, especially in people with underlying coronary artery disease. Researchers suggest that a gradual cool-down phase like **"walking"** following jogging may help to prevent the possibility of post-exercise sudden death.

Did I hear them say walking? Am I nuts? Are they crazy? How many times do you need to be hit on the head to find out that jogging is dangerous? *Once! Twice! Three times, you're out!* Now you not only get the chance to die while you're jogging, but if you manage to survive, you can try again immediately after jogging. And get their nerve! They're trying to salvage their "dead joggers" with my walking program. I won't have it. Either they walk first and finish walking like any intelligent two-legged mammal, or they can finish on all fours—dead or alive!

JOGGER'S HIGH CAN MAKE YOU DIE

The brain chemicals (endorphins) which are released in very high amounts during running have an almost morphine-like effect, allowing these runners to tolerate the pain of stress fractures, muscle injuries, torn ligaments and even angina (heart pain). Heart attacks and sudden deaths in runners may be related to the runner's inability to feel pain while running because of the analgesic effect of these endorphins. Ordinarily a heart attack victim has the warning signs of chest pain or shortness of breath and will usually seek medical treatment promptly. The jogger who has reached the so-called "jogger's high" or "jogger's euphoria" may not be able to feel this pain until it is too late. *Walk to Win, with low-dose endorphins.*

JOGGING JEOPARDIES

The following list includes many of the injuries and disabilities that accompany not only jogging but other strenuous exercises as well. These disorders are being reported with increasing frequency in medical journals, hospitals and doctors' offices nationwide. I have personally treated patients who have developed many of these injuries and disabilities. Unfortunately, many of these conditions can lead to chronic disorders lasting a life-time. Be safe not sorry. Don't let injuries do you in—**Walk to Win!**

Musculo-Skeletal System:	Muscle cramps and sprains, ligament and tendon injuries, cartilage tears and bone dislocations. Stress fractures (bones of feet, long bones of leg, pelvis, hip, and spinal vertebrae). Also arthritis flare-ups and back injuries.
Nervous System:	Compressed nerves in the neck, arms, legs and low back resulting in pain, numbness and weakness. Slipped discs resulting in nerve damage.
Metabolic System:	Chemical imbalances in the blood (ex. calcium and potassium loss), and blood sugar abnormalities (hypoglycemia). Heat exhaustion and heat stroke.
Immune System:	Itching and redness of skin, hives swelling, and anaphylaxis (shock, swelling, irregular heart beat—sometimes leading to death).
Obstetrics and Gynecology:	Menstrual irregularities, miscarriages, birth defects, prolapse (dropping) of the uterus and ovarian damage.
Genito-Urinary System:	Blood and protein in the urine, bladder bruised, kidney damage and prolapse of bladder. Penile and testicular frostbite.
Cardiovascular System:	Palpitations, chest pain, heartbeat abnormalities, heart attacks and sudden death. Hypertension and strokes from ruptured arteries in the brain (aneurysms).
Respiratory System:	Shortness of breath, fatigue, wheezing, exercise induced asthma, partial lung collapse (pneumothorax) and respiratory failure.
Gastrointestinal System:	Abdominal cramps, nausea, vomiting, Stress ulcers of stomach and bloody diarrhea (caused by decreased blood supply to the colon).

The Eye:	Inflammation, irritation, conjunctivitis, vitreous hemorrhages and retinal detachments.
Environmental:	Frostbite, dehydration, heat exhaustion, heat-stroke, hypothermia, dog bites, auto accidents, lung damage from polluted air and high levels of ozone.
Psychiatric:	Anxiety, depression and obsessive-compulsive behavior (running mania).
Endocrine (Hormone) System:	Decreased sex drive, impotence, infertility, menstrual abnormalities, adrenal and thyroid gland disorders. Also ovarian and testicular damage from poor blood supply.
Orthopedic:	Metatarsalgia (inflammation) of toes; osteoarthritis of ankles, knees and hips; tendonitis feet and ankles, runner's knee (bursitis/arthritis); swelling of muscles over shinbone (anterior tibial compartment syndrome). Stress fractured small bones (feet, ankles and legs); hip dislocations; vertebral fractures and slipped discs; groin injuries.
Hematology:	Sports anemia (pounding feet break down red blood cells); blood in urine (bladder bruises or kidney damage).

THE WEAKENED, WEEK-END WARRIOR!

In a recent symposium at Rutgers Medical School, Dr. Aapo Lehonen, a lecturer in medicine at Finland's University of Turku, stated that moderate exercise has been proven to increase the "good" cholesterol (HDL) in the blood. **HDL cholesterol** has been noted to have a protective mechanism against the development of heart disease. Moderate aerobic exercise, according to Dr. Lehonen, seems to have the greatest effect on raising the HDL cholesterol, and, therefore, the most beneficial effect on the blood fats.

Aerobic exercise is defined as the type of exercise in

which the oxygen demand of the large muscles of the body does not exceed the oxygen supply. This type of aerobic exercise usually occurs in constant, sustained exercise such as walking, but not in strenuous high-intensity exercises where the oxygen demand exceeds the oxygen supply.

Jogging and other strenuous exercises result in anaerobic metabolism, in which the oxygen demand is greater than the oxygen supply, resulting in a condition known as oxygen debt. Since the body has to spend all of its time trying to pay off this oxygen debt, it has no time or energy to sustain a high level of HDL cholesterol. Consequently, the protective effect on the heart is lost during these brief bursts of high-intensity activity.

The 9-5 desk worker who dashes on to the tennis or racquetball courts each weekend is wasting his time and maybe his life. The weary business executive who gets up at dawn to jog or run every Saturday and Sunday morning should have stayed in bed, for all the good his exercise is doing him. These *week-end warriors* are *actually weakened,* not strengthened.

THE LEGS ARE THE FIRST TO GO

Osteoarthritis is a condition which eventually affects the majority of people over 60. The knees are often the first joints to be affected. Several recent studies show that people who walk regularly have less pain, greater flexibility and less joint inflammation than sedentary people. **Walking** and the **stationary bike** are the most suitable exercises for this condition since they put less pressure on the knees and ankles than strenuous exercises or calisthenics.

Jogging, calisthenics and aerobics are by far the worst forms of exercise for this condition. This type of exercise puts undue pressure on the ligaments and cartilages of the ankle, knee and hip joints. This continued trauma results in chronic inflammation of the joints, leading eventually to osteoarthritis. The joints become inflamed, swollen, painful, and lose their mobility. Strenuous exercises only tend to aggravate the arthritis.

The incidence of **osteoarthritis** in runners is approximately 15.5 percent as compared to 0.1 percent for the general population. Although osteoarthritis is one of the conditions that affects many people over the age of 60, its incidence is relatively low in younger population groups. The mean age of runners affected with osteoarthritis is 47.8 years—approximately 13 years earlier than the general population. The incidence is related directly to the total number of years and the distance these runners ran each week. More miles and more years combined to produce more arthritis as a result of the continued trauma to the legs, hips and back.

Walking, on the other hand, does not cause arthritis and it can actually benefit people who have already developed certain forms of arthritis. Recent studies indicate that the moderate stimulation of arthritic joints by walking induced cartilage cells in the joints to grow, which helped to heal the damaged joint. In a study of 280 people over the age of 65 with moderate arthritis, a walking program helped these patients regain mobility in the ankle, knee, and hip joints.

NOW YOU MUST SURELY SEE, ALL BUT WALKING IS INJURY FREE

If you have a fever, muscle aches, a bad cold, an intestinal upset or any illness whatsoever—don't exercise. The body's defense mechanism is telling you to lay off any exercise program. And especially if you sustain an injury of any kind (which is highly unlikely in walking), then by all means discontinue exercising until you're feeling better. If any symptoms or signs of illness and/or injury persist or re-occur contact your physician immediately.

People who engage in strenuous exercises like jogging, aerobics, weight lifting and contact sports are by far the worst offenders. Once they injure themselves, they rarely give their bodies enough time to heal properly. Usually it starts as a simple tendon injury or a pulled muscle; however, without adequate rest and medical treatment, it may progress into a long standing tendonitis (tendon inflammation), muscle injury or tear, or a stress fracture (small hair-line fractures of any bone) or even more serious types of joint or bone injuries.

The compulsive exerciser who has been injured, often returns to his exercise long before proper healing has taken place. He's either "icing his back" or "soaking his foot" or "taping his ankle" or "splinting his finger." All of these home first-aid remedies that these exercise enthusiasts read about in the so-called sports-medicine books are usually not medically authorized treatments.

Another common mistake that these exercise-nuts make is to continue to take anti-inflammatory drugs without medical supervision. The over-the-counter drugs such as ibuprofen, taken for long periods of time can reduce the swelling and inflammation of an injured joint or muscle to a minor extent only. The patient begins to feel better even though the damaged part hasn't healed properly and he then begins exercising again, long before adequate healing has taken place. The result: the injured joint, ligament, muscle, or bone becomes further damaged, often leading to irreparable injury to the damaged body part. These injuries are termed *overuse injuries*. The longer it takes the patient to get medical help, the longer it takes to heal the injured part.

> *If you're sick or you're ill*
> *Take doctor's rest and his pill*
> *Or when you're injured or hurt*
> *Keep your feet up off the dirt*
> *Never be afraid to stop and rest*
> *Later you'll be able to do your best*
> *Always let your doctor do the talking*
> *So that you can resume your walking*
> *Strenuous exercise may damage your knee*
> *Try walking — it's almost injury-free*

"IF YOU WANT TO LAST AS LONG AS ME—TRY WALKING, IT'S INJURY-FREE!"

"TAKE YOUR CREW BACK TO THE HOSPITAL, YOUNG FELLOW. I'VE OUTWALKED MY LAST THREE DOCTORS!"

IV. WINSTEP™: LIFE-EXTENSION PROGRAM

"Walking every day is one of the only defenses that we have to win the war against the degenerative diseases of aging. Walking controls weight, lowers blood pressure, reduces stress and tension, retards cancer, prevents heart disease and strokes, and slows the aging process. If you want to live an additional 15, 20, even 25 years, then you'd better start walking as if your life depended on it—It does!"

Fred A. Stutman, M.D.
"The Today Show": NBC, July 1980

"IT WAS PROBABLY THE FALL THAT KILLED HIM. HOWEVER HE RARELY WALKED AND DID HAVE A VERY HIGH CHOLESTEROL."

CHAPTER 10

FIGHT FATS & HEART ATTACKS

BABY, BABY—STICK YOUR HEAD IN GRAVY—"I TOLD YOU SO!"

Finally the medical reports are starting to say what I've told you all along about exercise for the past 10 years in numerous medical articles and books. In the most recent study on exercise and heart disease the findings were that *"just a small amount of exercise prevents the development of heart disease in the majority of people."* Haven't I been telling you over and over again, that exercise doesn't have to be stressful, painful, or exhausting to be beneficial? Didn't I tell you that walking at a moderate rate of 3 miles per hour was adequate to develop cardiovascular fitness and good health? Wasn't it Dr. Stutman who fought it out tooth and nail with all of those jogging and aerobics enthusiasts who said that exercise had to be strenuous for it to be beneficial?

And wasn't that Dr. Stutman who said over and over again that getting your heart rate up to the mythical target-heart rate zone was both ridiculous and dangerous? Remember that I said that no one living or dead had ever proved that a rapid heart rate was essential for cardiovascular fitness, and that in fact it was extremely hazardous to keep the heart beating rapidly for a long period of time. And wasn't it yours truly who said that strenuous exercise was not only hazardous but that it was counter-productive to cardiovascular fitness and good health? Strenuous short bursts of exercise contribute nothing towards the prevention of heart disease and strokes, and in fact strenuous exercise may actually cause a heart attack or a cerebral hemorrhage to occur. Have I finally made my point? (Not so much to you loyal readers, who have known all along how beneficial a moderate walking program is, but for all those skeptics and so-called fitness experts who have been trying to tell Dr. Stutman and his merry-band of fellow walkers that his moderate walking program wasn't enough, I have this to say to all of you: **Baby, Baby, Stick Your Head in Gravy!—I Told You So!**)

Let's however, get back to this medical report. I think I got carried away a little. In a study of over 17,000 people by the Institute for Aerobics Research in Dallas, it was concluded that moderate exercise is an independent factor in the prevention of deaths by cardiovascular diseases. The following findings were presented at the 1988 American Heart Association's conference in Santa Fe, N.M.:

- Despite blood pressure, cholesterol or age, moderate exercise has an independent effect in preventing heart disease and strokes.
- Men in the lower 20% of physical fitness had a three times higher rate for heart disease than men falling between the 20-40% range of fitness development.
- Women in the bottom 20% zone of fitness had a 70% higher incidence of heart disease than those women in the 20-40% range of fitness development.
- The major conclusion was that **"just a little bit more exercise"** is all that is needed to lower your risk of cardiovascular diseases. And I think it is a bit ironic that the report ended with my long standing quotation—*"You don't need to run a marathon in order to reduce your risk of heart disease."*

NO HEART DISEASE, IF YOU PLEASE

Researchers at the Disease Control Center in Atlanta revealed a startling finding after reviewing 43 previous studies on heart disease. The one statistically significant, predisposing factor in the development of heart disease which appeared in every single study, was a *"lack of exercise"*.

Their research revealed that people who exercised the least had almost twice the risk of developing heart disease as those who exercised regularly. This particular study brought together the findings of the 43 previous studies which had all measured physical activity in many different ways. Walking was as effective as any other type of exercise in preventing heart disease without the added risk of injury and disability which occured in more strenuous exercises.

This analysis suggests that the lack of exercise on its own may be as strong a risk factor for developing heart disease as high blood pressure, smoking and high cholesterol. The Disease Control Center also stated that about 59% of adults in the USA get little or no exercise at all. This in effect would translate into a major heart disease risk factor for all of these sedentary Americans. *Don't sit around and get obese. Otherwise you're at risk for heart disease!*

I DON'T LIKE THOSE ODDS!

In a recent study in *The New England Journal of Medicine*, it was reported that vigorous, strenuous exercise helps to protect people from sudden heart attacks even though the odds of having a heart attack are higher during the work-out than at other times. Well, "excuse me"! Those odds are lousy. It sounds like the ones who survive the work-out are the only ones that live longer. You have a better chance playing Russian roulette.

The study found that men who exercise regularly have a lower than normal risk of having a heart attack only at times when they are not vigorously exercising. However, during their work-out they are more likely than usual to suffer a cardiac arrest. This study was trying to show that strenuous exercise is more help than harm. It sure doesn't sound like that to me!

I'll stick to walking, where the risk of having a heart attack with or without cardiac arrest is much lower than before walking, while walking and after walking! Even if there's the slightest doubt, **Walk, Don't Workout.** The best defense against heart disease is in—**Walk to Win!**

BEAT THE ODDS AGAINST HEART DISEASE

Coronary heart disease is responsible for over one-half million deaths each year in the United States. It causes more deaths each year than all forms of cancer combined. There are over 5½ million Americans who have been diagnosed as having coronary artery disease. It is estimated that there are at least 2½ million other Americans with undiagnosed coronary heart disease, many of them under the age of 50.

Coronary artery disease is caused by the build-up of fat deposits in the arteries (atherosclerosis). This disease begins slowly, early in life, and usually doesn't produce symptoms until middle age. Unfortunately, this condition often goes undetected until the person has his/her first heart attack, which may in fact be fatal. Although we have made great strides in the treatment of heart attacks, the emphasis must rest on preventing this slowly progressive disease (atherosclerosis) from occurring. It is estimated that more than 60 billion dollars are spent each year in the treatment of coronary heart disease and less than a million dollars yearly are spent on the prevention of this disease.

In order to prevent or slow the progress of atherosclerosis we must be aware of the *10 risk factors* which contribute to the development of this disease. One risk factor that we can't control is **heredity**; however, those people who have a strong family history of heart disease should pay particular attention to the risk factors that we can modify. The 9 risk factors which we can control ourselves or with medical treatment include: **cigarette smoking, excess alcohol consumption, excess caffeine, obesity, high blood pressure, high blood cholesterol, diabetes, stress** and **inactivity.**

One risk factor increases your risk of a heart attack by 25%. If you have two of these risk factors, it increases your likelihood of getting a heart attack by 35%. Three will increase your chances by 45% and four will increase your risk by 55-60%. If you are unfortunate enough to have five or more of these risk factors, you'd better take out a few more life insurance policies—fast!

How would you like to be able to eliminate or reduce almost all of these risk factors in one fell swoop? There is no need to worry about these risk factors if you start walking like your life depended on it. Believe me, it does! *Walking* can actually help you remove or reduce these risk factors to a minimum with a little additional help from your willpower.

How is this possible? The body that exercises doesn't want or need to *smoke* or drink *alcohol* or *caffeine*. The person who walks stays at his or her *ideal weight*. Walking lowers your *blood pressure* and your *blood cholesterol*. If you're a *diabetic* or have diabetic tendencies, walking helps to improve and regulate sugar metabolism. Walking is a sure fire method to ward off the evils of *stress* and *tension*. And, finally, walking every day completely eliminates the coronary risk factor of *inactivity*. When you *Walk to Win* you are beating the odds against all 9 risk factors of heart disease.

CHILDHOOD CHOLESTEROL CAUTION

In a recent study reported in *The New England Journal of Medicine*, it was conclusively found that heart disease can actually begin in childhood. The study was based on the autopsies of 35 youngsters ages 11-23, who died of causes other than heart disease.

The findings indicated that the higher the level of cholesterol in the blood, the more fatty deposits that were found in the arteries. In six cases the blood cholesterol level and the amount of fat found in the arteries was comparable to that found in adults with heart disease. Three of those studied also had been known to have high blood pressure, and their arteries showed even more cholesterol deposits than those who had had normal blood pressure.

In this study, the type of cholesterol that blocked up the arteries was the LDL form of cholesterol, otherwise known as the bad-cholesterol. As we'll see later in this chapter, this type of cholesterol can be lowered by eating a low cholesterol and low saturated fat diet. Recent medical research has shown that *walking* will also lower this form of bad-cholesterol (LDL), as well as raise the good-cholesterol (HDL). This HDL-cholesterol can help to carry away the fatty deposits that have already started to form in the arteries.

The only way to prevent heart disease from occurring in adults is to prevent it from starting in childhood. Children should be encouraged to stay away from fatty foods, particularly fatty meats, whole milk and dairy products. The only way you can accomplish this is to set the example early in life for the whole family's eating habits. Encourage fresh fruits and vegetables, fish and fowl, whole grained cereals and breads, fat free milk and dairy products, and whole grained baked goods and pastas.

Never hesitate to ask your doctor to check your child's blood cholesterol, especially if there is a family history of heart disease. The prevention of high blood cholesterol must begin in childhood if we are to make any progress in the fight against heart disease. And finally make sure your children walk or play actively every day. Let's not give the LDL (bad) cholesterol a chance to block up your child's arteries. A walk every day will help to keep cholesterol away.

WIN THE WAR AGAINST CHOLESTEROL

Many studies have demonstrated a significant correlation between dietary cholesterol and coronary heart disease. A recent Japanese study demonstrated that Japanese men had lower blood cholesterol and lower coronary heart disease than Japanese-American men living in San Francisco. This was due entirely to the high fat diet consumed by the Japanese-American men.

An international study using 18 different population groups living in eleven countries showed a direct correlation between fat and cholesterol intake and coronary heart disease. The lower the blood cholesterol, the lower the incidence of heart disease.

In a national cooperative pooling project research group, middle-aged men were studied in several different groups (Albany Gas Co., Chicago Gas & Electric companies, Framingham and Tecumeseh studies). All of these various studies pooled together showed a significant relationship between serum cholesterol and the ten-year risk of developing heart disease. In each study the conclusion was the same: the lower your blood cholesterol, the lower your incidence of developing heart disease.

The relationship between high cholesterol in your blood and coronary heart disease has been demonstrated by so many studies that the proof is now irrefutable. If your serum cholesterol is below 200 mg. and stays there, you are virtually immune to coronary artery disease.

The role of elevated serum triglycerides in causing coronary heart disease in some studies is controversial; however, most studies have definitely found some relationship. Many other diseases are associated with high serum triglycerides.

They include diabetes, obesity, thyroid disorders and certain kidney diseases. Since elevated triglycerides often accompany elevated LDL-cholesterol levels, they are indirectly related to the development of early coronary artery disease.

TAKE A TRIP ON THE GOOD SHIP

Since cholesterol will not dissolve in your bloodstream, it must attach itself to a protein. These proteins act as a ship transporting its passenger (cholesterol) through your bloodstream. And now we will take a little journey across the ocean as we go "down to the sea in ships." First we'll travel on the sinister pirate ship called the LDL and then we'll take a little cruise across the sea of blood in the good ship Lolly-Pop.

The **BAD-CHOLESTEROL PIRATE-SHIP** (LDL-low density lipo-protein combination) deposits cholesterol in your arteries when you eat too much cholesterol or saturated fat. If you limit the amount of **saturated fat** and **cholesterol-rich foods** that you eat, the bad pirate-ship will have less cholesterol to carry around and it won't be able to block up your arteries with its cargo of fat. You can sink the bad-cholesterol pirate-ship before it torpedoes your heart. If you stuff your face with fatty foods, you'll surely walk the pirate's gangplank to an early watery grave.

New medical evidence has found that there's another way to sink this pirate ship. A daily walk around the ship's deck will prevent these pirate plunderers from dumping cholesterol into arteries. Regular walkers have less LDL cholesterol and less triglycerides than those passengers who just sit on the deck sunning themselves.

The **GOOD-CHOLESTEROL-SHIP LOLLY-POP** (HDL-high density lipoprotein combination) flies a different flag. It rams the pirate ship and collects the excess amounts of cholesterol in the blood and takes it to the liver where it is eliminated from the body in little barrels of bile juices. Recent medical studies indicate that the sailors on this good-ship lolly-pop (**HDL**) may also be able to remove the cholesterol that has already formed in your arteries and dump it out at sea.

How do we get aboard this good-ship lolly-pop (**HDL CHOLESTEROL**)? Heredity plays an important part in the production of **HDL** cholesterol. Some of us have more HDL cholesterol than others because of a good set of genes. Diet unfortunately has almost no effect in **HDL** production—so a low fat, low cholesterol diet won't budge your HDL cholesterol; however, it will certainly lower the bad LDL cholesterol.

There is however, one thing that you can do to increase the production of **HDL**. You guessed it! Our old tried and true friend—WALKING—will raise your **HDL** levels. If you walk ½ hour daily or 1 hour every other day, you will keep your **HDL** permanently elevated. High intensity exercises like jogging for brief periods of time raise the **HDL** level temporarily and then it falls after the exercise is completed.

A nice long walk every day is the only way to keep the good-cholesterol-ship lolly-pop afloat. By carrying its cargo of fat out of your body, your heart will live to sail another day.

The good HDL cholesterol is very hard to find
But with a daily walk it won't be far behind
The bad LDL cholesterol is not a nice guy
If you eat fatty foods it will make you die
So make sure that you eat a low cholesterol diet
And you'll lead a happy life that's nice and quiet
A walk everyday keeps your HDL elevated
And that's certainly an occasion to celebrate it
When you walk your LDL also goes down and in
So that you'll lead a long life when you *Walk to Win!*

HIGH-FIBER, LOW-FAT—IS WHERE IT'S AT!

Dietary cholesterol is an important factor in the development of coronary heart disease. **Saturated fat** may have as strong an effect on raising blood cholesterol levels as does dietary cholesterol itself. Consequently, the saturated fat in marbelized beef may be as dangerous as the cholesterol in eggs. One must keep in mind, however, that both the **dietary cholesterol** and the **dietary saturated fats** are both very important factors which elevate blood cholesterol and contribute to the development of **atherosclerosis** and **obesity.**

Elevated levels of blood fats have been incriminated as risk factors in the development of **cardiovascular disease**. In particular, blood cholesterol has been implicated in the formation of **cholesterol plaques** which narrow the coronary arteries to a point where the blood supply is unable to pass through, and the individual develops a heart attack. **High fiber** and **low saturated fat/cholesterol** diets are one of the mechanisms involved in the prevention or treatment of elevated blood fats and the subsequent development of obesity and atherosclerosis.

To reduce the blood cholesterol levels we have to increase the amount of fruits and vegetables in our diet and decrease the amount of fatty foods. By increasing fruits, vegetables, fish, skimmed milk, low fat dairy products, poultry and beans in our diet we will most certainly reduce the blood cholesterol. Foods that are high in saturated fat and cholesterol that should be avoided are meats, whole milk products and eggs in particular. The best treatment for high blood cholesterol is a diet which is low in **calories, saturated fat** and **cholesterol.** This diet is currently accepted by the **American Heart Association.** *High fiber, Low-Fat—Is Where It's At!*

KEEP YOUR ARTERIES CLEAN WITH A WALKING MACHINE

A 52-year-old male executive came to see me recently because of pain in his calf muscles when he walked. He was not able to walk more than a block before severe pain in one or both calves caused him to stop walking. After a few minutes of rest, the pain subsided and he could resume walking again. However, after walking another block or two at the most, the pain resumed and he was forced to sit down again. This patient had a history of moderate hypertension and he had smoked 1½ packs of cigarettes every day since he was 20 years old. The diagnosis was relatively simple. The patient exhibited all of the classical symptoms of *"intermittent claudication."* Vascular studies of the lower extremities confirmed this clinical diagnosis.

Intermittent claudication is defined as pain or cramps in the legs, usually the calf muscles, brought about by exercise (usually walking) and relieved fairly promptly by rest. This condition results from an occlusion (obstruction) in the large and medium-sized arteries leading to the legs. This obstruction comes from the build-up of deposits of cholesterol (atherosclerosis) inside of these blood vessels. As this obstruction becomes more severe, the blood supply to the exercising leg muscles cannot be met. Since these muscles cannot get enough oxygen, they cry out with pain (intermittent claudication) due to the lack of oxygen-rich blood. When the exercise (walking) is stopped, the muscles require less oxygen, so that as soon as the limited blood supply reaches these muscles with some oxygen, the pain stops.

The very first step in the treatment of this condition is to stop smoking. Carbon monoxide from smoking promotes atherosclerosis in both the coronary arteries and in the peripheral arteries (those leading away from the heart—example: legs). Carbon monoxide molecules actually jump into the seats on the red blood cells that were reserved for the oxygen molecules. Without its passenger, oxygen, the red blood cells carry this deadly enemy (carbon monoxide) throughout the body. These carbon monoxide molecules get off at various stops along the arteries to do their dirty work. The arteries waiting for oxygen get a big surprise. They get molecules of carbon monoxide instead. This carbon monoxide irritates the artery's inner lining (intima) and subsequently makes it an ideal seeding bed for deposits of cholesterol.

Nicotine from the cigarettes also contributes to piling up more cholesterol in the arteries. It accomplishes this by raising the blood pressure, narrowing down the artery's opening (lumen) and by promoting clot formation in the arteries. When you stop smoking you can prevent atherosclerosis from progressing and in some cases you can actually reverse the process.

The simplest and often most effective treatment for this condition is—yes, you guessed it—*walking!* Now wait a minute, you're thinking, "he just told me that walking is what caused the pain in intermittent claudication." That's absolutely correct. However, most medical authorities feel that a gradual walking program is the best form of conservative therapy for this condition. Patients who have stopped smoking and engaged in a modified walking program have been able to double or triple the distance that they can walk without pain. This occurs because walking dilates or opens arteries, making more room available for blood to reach the muscles. Walking also makes more oxygen available to be carried in its regular seat on the red blood cell. This extra oxygen prevents cholesterol from being deposited in the arteries and it supplies more nourishment to these oxygen-starved muscles. And walking helps to keep the arteries elastic, so that they can stretch and recoil, thus helping to propel the blood along its way.

Finally, walking improves the flow of blood to these muscles by opening up a reserve group of blood vessels, that normally just sit in the wings like understudies in a play. These reserve blood vessels are referred to as the *collateral circulation*. Walking actually calls forth these small little-used reserve blood vessels, much the same as the trumpeter calls forth the cavalry. These small vessels located in the legs open up with regular walking and send the blood around (bypass) the blocked arteries. A regular walking program can help to keep these collateral vessels open permanently.

Walking also can actually eat away at the cholesterol deposits that have accumulated in the blocked arteries. It accomplishes this by supplying oxygen-rich blood to these blocked arteries and by raising the "good" (HDL cholesterol) which carries shovelfuls of these cholesterol deposits out of the body. Walking also lowers the "bad" (LDL cholesterol) in the blood, making less cholesterol available to block up the arteries.

If, however, this disease has progressed too far, then medical treatment may be required. Several new drugs that help to open the arteries and decrease the blood's thickness (viscosity) are now available. If these medications are not effective, then surgery may be necessary. One form of surgery is called *angioplasty,* wherein the artery is dilated with a balloon catheter. The cholesterol plaque is actually squashed against the wall of the artery, making a larger opening available for the passage of blood. The other form of surgery is called *arterial bypass surgery*. In this type of surgery, a vein graft is usually attached to the artery above and below the blockage, so that blood actually bypasses the blocked artery. Often times an attempt is also made to remove the blockage inside the artery *(endarterectomy)*. These procedures, especially the bypass surgery, are risky and are only done in those cases where no other treatment is successful.

There is a similar type of condition in which cholesterol deposits accumulate in the arteries of the neck (carotid arteries). This form of atherosclerosis obstructs the flow of blood through these arteries and results in a decrease in the supply of oxygen-rich blood to the cells of the brain. This decreased blood supply can lead to a condition referred to as *transient ischemic attacks* (TIA's). These are actually temporary small strokes with no permanent damage. These attacks can cause visual loss, speech impairment, weakness or partial paralysis of an arm or leg, memory loss, headaches and other neurological symptoms. These symptoms usually last a few seconds to several minutes and then the patient is normal again. Some cases have been known to last several hours. If this process of atherosclerosis progresses to a point where the carotid arteries are almost completely blocked, then vascular surgery may be necessary to prevent a full-blown stroke from occurring.

The best treatment for both of these conditions is to prevent them from occurring. Always check with your physician if you develop any symptoms that you think might be caused by these disorders. The risk factors for developing these diseases are the same as the risk factors for developing heart disease. Cigarette smoking, high serum cholesterol, inactivity, stress, excess caffeine and alcohol, obesity, diabetes and hypertension can all be modified or improved by walking. Remember, walking keeps your arteries clean and your health supreme. Keep claudication pain and transient ischemia away, with a walk each day.

WALKING AROUND KEEPS BLOOD SUGAR DOWN

Walking enables Type I diabetics (insulin dependent), to reduce their insulin requirements by approximately 35%, and Type II diabetics (non-insulin dependent) to reduce their oral medication dosages by approximately 75% and in some cases to eliminate medication entirely. This occurs because walking not only burns calories including sugar, but walking increases the cells' sensitivity to insulin. Type I diabetics therefore need less injections of insulin and Type II diabetics become more sensitive to the production of their own body's insulin and require less oral medication.

Once the insulin or oral medication doses are reduced, the diabetic's cardiovascular risk factors improve. The diabetic normally has increased risk factors for heart attacks and strokes. Walking appears to reduce these risk factors by controlling blood sugar, decreasing serum cholesterol, making the blood less likely to clot, reducing total body weight and by opening the tiny capillaries that feed blood to the extremities, organs, tissues, cells and to the heart muscle itself.

An exercise program for the diabetic requires careful medical supervision. All patients should get complete physical exams before starting any exercise program. For most diabetics that means complete blood testing, urinalysis, chest X-ray, EKG, and in some cases a stress EKG. The patient's physician will actually determine what type of tests are necessary. Medication dosages (insulin or pills) should never be changed without a physician's approval.

In general, strenuous exercise should be avoided because exercise, like insulin, accelerates sugar absorption which could result in sudden hypoglycemia (low blood sugar) which could result in fainting spells or other serious complications. This is particularly true if the diabetic attempts to exercise too soon after a meal. At least 1½-2 hours should elapse before the diabetic begins exercising.

The beauty of a walking program is that it is a moderate aerobic-type of exercise without any of the hazards of strenuous exercise. This is especially important in the diabetic, since he/she is particularly vulnerable to the side effects of strenuous exercise. Walking avoids the sudden drops in blood sugar that so often accompany strenuous exercise. Walking eliminates the high-impact ratio on the extremities' nerve-endings and blood vessels which are particularly subject in the diabetic to injury from high-impact sports. Walking gently burns calories thus lowering blood sugar moderately. This enables the diabetic to eventually lower his/her dosage of insulin or oral medication, after the body gradually adjusts to the wonderful world of walking. *Walking keeps your feet on the ground and your blood sugar down.*

PEOPLE WHO ONLY SAT, FOUND IT FATAL TO GET FAT

In the majority of cases obesity results from too little exercise and too much food. Life insurance studies have shown that excess weight causes cardiovascular disease with increased mortality. These same studies also reveal that life expectancy improves following weight reduction.

Obese people have a significantly higher incidence of hypertension than non-obese persons. The excess body weight demands a higher cardiac output (pumping out blood) to meet the increased metabolism of the fat person's body. This in turn causes the left ventricle chamber of the heart to gradually enlarge because of this extra workload. The combined effect of obesity, hypertension and heart enlargement may eventually lead to heart failure and death. Weight reduction can lower both the systolic and diastolic blood pressures if it is accomplished before the complications of heart enlargement and heart failure occur.

Obesity also causes an alteration of the body chemistry and metabolism. The blood sugar goes up dramatically with obesity often leading to the development of diabetes. The uric acid in the blood becomes elevated, often leading to kidney stones and attacks of gout. Fat people have higher levels of triglycerides (sugar fats) and the "bad" LDL-cholesterol. They also have lower blood levels of the "good" HDL-cholesterol. These altered blood fats will eventually lead to severe coronary artery disease. These abnormal blood chemistries can be reversed to normal levels, if weight reduction occurs before permanent complications result.

And if all these risks of being fat weren't bad enough, here's another piece of fat to chew on. **Obesity just by itself has been listed as an independent risk factor for coronary heart disease.** Newer data from the 26-year follow-up statistics in the *Framingham Heart Study* (Hubert, 1983) demonstrated that obesity just by itself was enough to cause a significant increase in the risk of coronary heart disease and premature death in both men and women.

Had enough fat to chew on? You certainly know by now all of the risks of being fat, unless of course you don't care about living too long. And by now you should also know that there are only two ways to lose weight effectively. One is to shut your mouth and the other is to move your feet. And since most of us can only shut our mouths long enough to reach the next meal, then we had better get out there and walk every day like our lives depended on it. Walking is the only permanent weight reducer known to man or woman that can be continued for a lifetime.

The results are now finally in
It certainly pays to be thin
So if you want your lifetime to last
Then you'd better start walking fast
Remember that those who only sat
Found it was fatal to get fat
Because when they got obese
They all developed heart disease
But those who always walked
They lived long enough to talk
Remember, life is wonderful and sweet
If you want to prolong it, move your feet

"I TOLD YOU THAT IF YOU DIDN'T GET UP AND WALK, YOU'D TURN INTO A VEGETABLE!"

"THEY WERE RIGHT WHEN THEY TOLD YOU THAT STRENUOUS EXERCISE WOULD ADD YEARS TO YOUR LIFE. YOU LOOK AND SOUND 10 YEARS OLDER ALREADY!"

CHAPTER 11

O.K. FOLKS—K.O. STRESS & STROKES

ON YOUR MARK, GET SET—FORGET IT!

Walking is the exercise of the eighties, and has now surpassed more strenuous exercises like jogging and high-impact aerobics as the exercise of choice for the majority of Americans. Because walking is low-impact and injury-free, it can be done anywhere, anytime and by almost anyone. Walking is recommended for any age group including children and senior citizens. It is an exercise for the thin, the fat, the non-athlete and the professional athlete. In summary, walking provides all of the *fitness* and *weight control* benefits of more strenuous exercises without the injuries and disabilities associated with these high-impact, stressful sports and exercises.

Walking, unlike other types of strenuous exercises, has a built-in safety factor that these competitive, strenuous exercises lack. This safety factor is its *non-competitive* nature. Walking allows you to exercise at your own pace without fear of competition or of following any rigid type of schedule. You walk where you want to, when you want to and with whom you want to. Walking can be done alone or with others. The choice is always yours.

Strenuous exercises including race-walking are all competitive-type sports and lead to stress rather than relaxation. We certainly have enough stress in our everyday lives at home and at work. We don't need additional stress and tension when we're trying to unwind. Competition always is stressful. It raises the body's stress hormones—epinephrine and nor-epinephrine, both of which speed up our heart rates and excite the body's nerve endings to produce anxiety and tension. Isn't stress what we are trying to get away from? Isn't tension what we are trying to avoid? If you have to voluntarily add additional stress to your leisure activities, then you may as well stay at the office a little later or worry about your personal problems for an extra hour or two.

What we want from an exercise is a little peace and quiet. What we need from an exercise is a break from the stress-tension cycle. What we really need is a little relief from the day's monotonous routine. What we need in our lives is a refreshing, pleasant way to enjoy ourselves for a short time— a little slice of order and relaxation amidst the chaos of our lives. What we really need is a *walk*.

If you have to get down on your knees at the starting line like a runner and wait for the starter's gun to go off, then you'd better re-evaluate your exercise priorities. Is this any way to run an exercise and fitness program? Is this the way you want to spend your leisure hours? Is this what you want for your time-off period? Is this the way you want to relax? Doesn't this sound a little like what you're doing all day—**on your mark, get set—GO!** That starter's work gun is always above our heads. "Is that report ready yet?" "Did you see that sales rep yet?" "Why were you late for that conference?" "Did you get in touch with that buyer yet?" When you walk away from the office, *really walk away*. Don't let your leisure hours simulate your office hours by engaging in competitive, strenuous exercises.

And how about at home. Do you remember way back when it all started? "Did you brush your teeth yet?" "Did you do your homework?" "Did you put out the trash yet?" "Did you forget to stop at the store again?" And so forth and so on. Do you remember what you did as a youngster when you had the chance? Right—you went out to play to get away from all those questions. And when you got married and things got tough at home—right, you went out for another walk! And when the boss started up with you about a customer—right again, you went out for a walk to cool-off. No one told you to go out for a walk, your body and your brain knew that they needed it, so out you went.

And now the exercise and fitness nuts are asking you— "Did you run 3 miles today?" "How fast did you jog today?" "How about a third set of racket ball?" "Is that all the weight you can press?" "How come you can't keep up with that young aerobics instructor?" "Did you get the new outfit yet for your fitness class?" "How come you get out of breath so easily?" "You're not in very good shape, are you?"

Tell them all to stop that talk—and then go out for a **walk**!

STRESS CAUSES SUDDEN DEATH

Emotional stress can precipitate heart attacks in patients with a history of coronary artery disease. Type A behavior (high-strung, aggressive personalities) has also been associated with an increased incidence of coronary heart disease, completely independent of other coronary risk factors (The Western Collaborative Group Study: *AM J. Cardiology*, Vol. 37, 1976). And patients who already had coronary heart disease with Type A behavior were shown to have more severe artery involvement than did patients with heart disease who had Type B behavior (non-aggressive, more relaxed type personalities).

In another related study (The Recurrent Coronary Prevention Project: *AM. Heart J.*, Vol. 108, 1984) counseling of Type A heart patients resulted in a reduction of Type A behavior in 44% of those counseled. These patients whose high strung emotional behavior was modified, had 20% less recurrent heart attacks than the Type A heart patients who did not receive counseling.

It is well documented that emotional stress can not only contribute to the development of heart disease but that it can also aggravate existing coronary artery disease. Stress can aggravate angina pectoris (heart pain from poor circulation in the coronary arteries) in patients who have coronary artery disease. When stressed, these people may develop severe chest pain that can usually be relieved by putting a nitroglycerin tablet under their tongues.

Stress can also precipitate heart attacks (myocardial infarctions), heartbeat irregularities (arrhythmias) and sudden cardiac arrest, in patients with pre-existing coronary artery disease. A recent study reported in *The New England Journal of Medicine* (Vol. 311, 1984) showed an increased risk of cardiac deaths among the men with high levels of stress, who had previously survived a heart attack. And emotional stress combined with excess salt in the diet may actually cause some people to develop a permanent form of high blood pressure.

All of these studies prove that emotional stress can cause coronary heart disease as well as aggravate it in patients who already have heart disease. And all of these studies also show that by reducing stress, coronary heart disease and hypertension can often be prevented in normal patients and controlled in patients who already have heart or blood pressure problems. Type A behavior can be modified with stress management techniques. These techniques include personal counseling, avoiding stressful situations, and our true-blue, loyal friend—*walking*. Walking has been proven over and over again to significantly reduce stress and tension, alleviate anger and hostility, decrease fatigue and malaise, and control anxiety and depression. *Walk away from stress today and your heart will be O.K.*

THE DEVIL MADE ME DO IT!

Why do we always feel as if we need to take a trip or change our environment when we're fatigued or stressed? Why do we say, "let's go to the beach" or "let's take a trip to the mountains?" Why is it that after a hard week at the office, you feel like "just getting away from it all." In other words, why don't we just stay put or stand still? What makes us want to get up and go? What inner force is responsible for this feeling that we must seek solace in the great outdoors, someplace far away from our present confining environment?

Science has tried to come up with answers to these questions and has made some startling discoveries. Our bodies give off electromagnetic waves like animals, fish and birds. This electromagnetism is what makes birds migrate every year. It is what enables fish to swim upstream to spawn. It is what makes bears know when to hibernate and then when to awaken again. Electro-magnetic waves, in fact, govern many of the physiological, bio-chemical and psychological functions of all living things.

Men, like animals, are also governed by electromagnetic forces that cannot be seen, heard, felt or touched. They can't be studied with a microscope or a stethoscope. They can't be seen in the retina of the eye with an ophthalmoscope. Nor can they be studied in any way known to medical science. Yes, we can evaluate brain waves on an electroencephalogram. We can study the brain's structure and architecture with a brain scan. We can even study the brain and spinal cord with a new type of X-Ray unit called an MRI (magnetic-resonance imaging). This machine does not really study the electromagnetic impulses of the body, even though the word magnetic is included in the test name. These electromagnetic waves, at the present time, are not measurable by any known machine or instrument.

All we know is that when a certain amount of tension builds up in our bodies we have to release it. "We've got to get out of the house." "We've got to get away from the office." "We just have to get away for the weekend." "We must get out and take a walk." Our bodies are screaming at us to release the tension. These so-called electromagnetic impulses are telling our nervous systems to shut-down the terminals. These waves are starting to short-out our bodies like a faulty fuse. The *synapses* (connecting points) in our brains are becoming inundated with messages of stress and tension. The *neurons* (nerves in the brain and spinal cord) become overloaded like telephone wires with too many calls coming in at the same time. Whether we call this **burn-out,** or **over-load syndrome** or just **high-anxiety**, the message is clear. Our bodies are telling us something. The message is loud and clear, like an SOS from a sinking ship. *"Unplug yourself from the electric current!" "Turn your terminals off!" "Shut down your nuclear reactor before you have a melt-down!"*

You must get away from it all! Whether it's a trip to the country, a drive to the mountains, a vacation at the shore, or just a walk in the woods; your body and mind need a release-valve to let off this built-up steam. We are receiving electromagnetic signals from somewhere inside of us, telling us to flee from stress and tension. Our minds are also receiving these beckoning impulses, through the atmosphere from these distant places, not unlike radio and television waves. And we must act on them or we will be destroyed. You can only stand so much stress and tension before the psychological damage turns into physiological and biochemical damage.

Don't wait for a stroke or heart attack to occur before you start to follow the voice on the airway of your electromagnetic waves. Don't wait until you've had a major ulcer attack, to listen to the message sent on the electrical impulses of your brain. You must get away now! You must heed your body's inner voice. You must go to where you will feel healthier, happier and refreshed. This is nature's way of protecting you from self-destruction and self-annihilation. You can prevent your body from exploding into the atmosphere by getting away from stress and tension as often as possible.

You will actually re-generate yourself each and every time you get away from your daily stresses. If it's not possible to go to the shore, mountains, or country, at least *get out and walk everyday—anywhere and everywhere*. Walking provides the same release of psychological and physiological tension as a trip to the beach. Walking answers the call of the electro-magnetic waves which are telling you to "chill-out." And when you do eventually get away to some favorite spot, make sure you take a walk there also! By combining a *change of location* with a *refreshing walk* you will doubly be able to respond to your body's electromagnetic impulses for release of stress and tension.

You will notice how much better you feel almost immediately after your trip or your walk. Refreshed, relaxed and relieved, you'll be better able to return to the stresses of everyday living with a new perspective on life. You will actually have built-up a type of immunity to the tensions that formerly tore you apart. This immunity, like the immunity to certain diseases, needs to be re-enforced. This re-enforcement will take the form of *more trips and more and more walks*.

Your body will always feel the magnetic pull to certain places where it knows that you feel good. Listen to it! It knows this better than you do, even with your so-called logical mind. The mental processes always fight the electro-magnetic pull with excuses. "I have no time for a vacation." "That report is due next week." "I just can't get away now." "Maybe next month I can get a few days off." "As soon as I finish this project, I'm taking a vacation." Well, your body may not wait until next month or even next week for that matter. It may short out right now, today, even this minute. So you better get away today. You better take that walk right now. And if you feel slightly reluctant to tell yourself or anyone else that you're listening to your body's inner electromagnetic impulses, then just tell yourself or that friend that—**"The Devil Made Me Do It!"**

FEET ON THE GROUND, KEEPS BLOOD PRESSURE DOWN

According to the American Heart Association, more than one out of every four people in the United States has high blood pressure. Among people age 65 years and older, approximately two out of three people suffer from hypertension. There are approximately 57.7 million Americans who have high blood pressure according to the Heart Association Council for High Blood Pressure Research. Many of these people are at considerable risk for developing strokes, heart attacks, heart failure and kidney disease, unless they receive medical treatment. Unfortunately, most people with high blood pressure have no symptoms and may have hypertension for many years before it is diagnosed. Remember, always get your blood pressure checked regularly.

Many cases of mild hypertension can be controlled without the use of medication. These methods include weight reduction, salt restriction, cessation of smoking, alcohol restriction, decreasing saturated fats and cholesterol in the diet, stress reduction and exercise. It should be pointed out that the majority of studies on the benefits of exercise for lowering blood pressure, have used walking as the best moderate intensity exercise for this purpose. Jogging and other strenuous exercises can actually raise blood pressure during the actual exercise.

An Oslo research study of approximately 18,000 men aged 40-49 years recorded lower blood pressures in those men who engaged in regular leisure activity, particularly walking and gardening. Interestingly, no blood pressure differences were noted among different intensities of physical exercise which again emphasizes the point that faster is not necessarily better.

Two major studies reported in a recent issue of the *Journal of the American Medical Association* proved without a doubt that regular exercise, particularly walking, can decrease the risk of developing heart disease and high blood pressure by more than 50 percent.

The first report from the Research Institute in Dallas studied over 6,000 men and women who had no previous history of high blood pressure. Over a period of 4 years, people who did not exercise regularly ran a 52 percent higher risk of developing hypertension. The second study from Harvard University followed 17,000 men over a period of 16 years (from 1962 to 1978). Those men who exercised regularly experienced only one-half the death rate from heart disease and hypertension. This study showed lower blood pressures and lower death rates in those alumni who just walked regularly. The following chart illustrates the reduction in death risk (%) associated with distance walked per week *(Fig. 2)*.

Figure 2

Cardiovascular Benefits of Walking

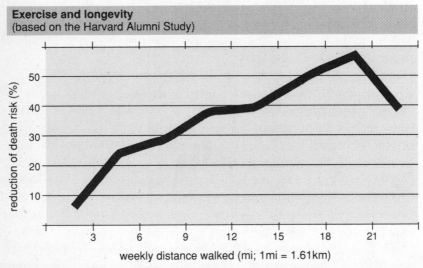

Figure 2. *Reduction in death risk (%) associated with distance walked per week.* (Adapted from Paffenbarger RS et al *N Engl J Med 314:605, 1986;* with the permission of The New England Journal of Medicine)

In a related study reported in the journal *Atherosclerosis* (Dec., 1983), high risk men ages 43 to 60 were tested with a low-fat diet only, and were compared to a similar group which combined the low-fat diet with a walking program. The group that also walked had a significant reduction in weight, cholesterol, triglycerides, total body fat and blood pressure compared with only moderate reductions in the group that only dieted.

In no fewer than seven other separate studies in hypertensive men and women, a walking program produced lowered blood pressure in over 80% of these patients. The periods of exercise training varied in these different studies from three months to three years. It was interesting to note also, that if any patient dropped out of the program, his/her blood pressure gradually went up to its former hypertensive level after six-eight weeks. This confirmed the theory that in order for exercise to be beneficial, particularly for high blood pressure, it must be carried on for a lifetime. And what better exercise than walking can be done for the rest of your life?

The medical evidence is overwhelming that regular exercise, particularly walking, lowers the blood pressure in people with hypertension. There is also increasing evidence that a regular program of walking can help to prevent hypertension from developing in those individuals who have a hereditary predisposition or tendency to develop high blood pressure. There have also been many recent studies on children, showing that the inactive child is more likely to become the obese hypertensive adult than the child who exercises regularly.

There are several physiological mechanisms responsible for the blood pressure lowering effect of exercise. They include improved cardiac output of blood, decreased peripheral vascular resistance to the flow of blood, slower pulse rate, dilation of small arteries, thinning of the blood and a reduced release of catecholamines and angiotensin (the hormones that cause high blood pressure). The fact remains, however, that no matter what the physiological reasons are, walking lowers your blood pressure. All you have to remember is that if you **keep your feet on the ground, you'll keep your blood pressure down!**

STOP SALT—STOP STROKES!

One of the most serious medical problems facing Americans today is **hypertension**. There are approximately 35 million people in the United States suffering from high blood pressure—or 1 out of 8 adults. Because many people are unaware of the existence of hypertension, they do not seek medical treatment for this condition. Since it rarely gives symptoms in the early stages, it is commonly called the **silent disease.** Hypertension, however, can cause serious complications such as heart attack, stroke or kidney disease.

Hypertension can be controlled not only with medicine but with a decrease in **salt** intake. With the reduction of salt to approximately 5 grams daily, we are able to reduce the blood pressure in many susceptible individuals. How do you know if you're one of the susceptible people? You don't! Some recent studies indicate that anywhere from 18-25% of people have a genetic predisposition to developing high blood pressure if they use excess salt. The only safe thing then that we can do is to have our blood pressure checked regularly, and stay away from salt.

The excessive use of salt in the average American diet is the result of an **acquired taste** for salting foods rather than an actual need for salt in our bodies. The first question my patients usually ask is, "won't food taste bland without salt?" Our taste buds gradually adjust to a decreased amount of salt in the diet, and after a short period of time excessively salted food has an unpleasant taste. Food actually tastes better without salt.

Salt, or sodium chloride, is an essential chemical compound necessary for life. However, it is a **potentially deadly substance** if we get too much of it in our diets. The fact is that it is almost impossible to develop a dietary deficiency of sodium since most of our diets contain more than 5 grams of salt daily, and that's in fresh unsalted food only. In the average American diet with processed foods, canned foods and salted food snacks, we consume approximately **10-15 grams** of salt a day. Actually we only need ½ **gram** of salt a day to prevent a sodium deficiency in our bodies.

How does this much salt get into our diets? First of all, salt is used world-wide as a **preservative** in many foods. It is also an essential ingredient in the **canning process**. The salt content of **processed foods** adds 5 additional grams of salt daily to our diets. There is salt, of course, in potato chips, pretzels, pickles, tomato sauce, TV dinners, crackers, tuna fish, sardines and even peanut butter. However, did you also know that there is considerable salt in cheese, butter, margarine, bread, tomato juice, ketchup, beer, soda and most breakfast cereals? Add to that the 2 grams of salt we pour every day on our meat, soups, salads, eggs and vegetables and we're getting 12-15 times more salt than we actually need to sustain life.

This excess salt intake can actually cause a **rise in blood**

pressure by disturbing the kidneys' ability to eliminate this salt in the urine. The excess accumulation of sodium in the blood causes the body to retain more fluid and this **increases the volume of blood**. The heart subsequently has to work harder to circulate this additional volume of blood and high blood pressure can result from this disturbance. This is a temporary condition, if the high salt intake is decreased. However, with a continued excess salt intake, the rise in blood pressure is substantial and may become permanent. **Strokes** and **heart attacks** are the complications which can result from prolonged untreated high blood pressure.

Reduce the amount of salt used in your cooking or baking. Do not add salt to any food at the table. Use herbs, spices and condiments instead of salt. Decrease the consumption of processed foods, canned soups and vegetables, prepared meats and cheeses, bouillon cubes, salted crackers, cereals with high salt content, worcestershire and soy sauce, and seasoned salts. Increase the amount of fresh or frozen vegetables and use unsalted margarine. Be careful of over-the-counter cold and headache remedies which may have sodium as part of their content. Avoid pretzels, potato chips, peanuts, pickles, crackers and most packaged snack foods.

Increase foods with high potassium content since these seem to have a beneficial or protective effect on hypertension. Some foods rich in potassium are oranges and orange juice, grapefruit and grapefruit juice, bananas, raw tomatoes, potatoes, squash, cabbage, broccoli, chicken, turkey and lean beef.

Remember to follow your physician's advice and recommendations in the treatment and control of high blood pressure. You may be able to control your blood pressure without the use of medication but only under a physician's supervision. Have your blood pressure checked regularly. Also check with your doctor before using any of the "salt substitutes." Check the food content guide at the end of this book to determine the salt content of various foods. See **Appendix.**

STOP STROKES BEFORE THEY STOP YOU

Strokes are the third leading cause of deaths in the United States each year. The most frequent contributing factor is high blood pressure. Approximately 65% of all strokes occur in people who never knew they had high blood pressure or in people who had hypertension but did not take their medication regularly.

High blood pressure speeds up the process of atherosclerosis ("hardening of the arteries"). Untreated hypertension damages the lining walls of the arteries and allows fatty deposits to collect in the arteries. This in turn sets the stage for blood clots to form in the blood vessels of the brain, which can cause a stroke. High blood pressure also can weaken the walls of the blood vessels so that a balloon or aneurysm forms. The combination of high blood pressure and extreme physical exertion (example: jogging, weight-lifting, etc.) may cause this aneurysm to rupture, which results in a hemorrhage into the brain producing another form of stroke.

Fortunately, stroke-related deaths have declined by almost 45% in the United States in the past 10 years. This is due primarily to the widespread, successful treatment of high blood pressure. People are beginning to realize that they have to continue taking their high blood pressure medicine indefinitely, in order to prevent strokes from occurring.

Stopping smoking also is important in preventing strokes from occurring. The carbon monoxide from smoking damages the blood vessel walls, and speeds up the process of atherosclerosis. The early treatment of diabetes and obesity also helps to slow down this process of hardening of the arteries, which leads to hypertension and stroke. And we have already seen how the avoidance of salt and stress helps to lower blood pressure and in turn reduces your risk of stroke.

According to most medical authorities, a moderate program of regular exercise is extremely important in controlling high blood pressure and in preventing strokes. You heard it— **moderate exercise!** Walking is the exercise most often prescribed by physicians to control hypertension. Walking lowers the blood pressure and can help to prevent strokes. The following steps show you in detail how the *Win-Step*™ actually lowers your blood pressure, prevents heart disease and strokes, and prolongs your life.

THE WIN-STEP™ WINS THE WAR AGAINST DISEASE, DISABILITY AND DEATH

1. **Walking lowers the blood pressure by:**
   a. **dilating (opening) the arteries,** allowing more blood to flow through them
   b. improving **elasticity** of blood vessels—giving less resistance to the flow of blood
   c. lowering chemicals in blood that can raise blood pressure—**catecholamines** and **angiotensin**
   d. improving **return of blood** to the heart, so that the heart can work more efficiently at a slower rate
   e. increasing the amount of **oxygen** delivered to all tissues and cells
   f. decreasing the rate of **sodium reabsorption** in the kidneys

2. **Walking protects the heart by:**
   a. decreasing the risk of **blood clot** formation
   b. improving the return of blood to the heart from the **leg veins**
   c. increasing the flow of blood through the **coronary arteries**
   d. increasing **HDL (good) cholesterol** which protects the heart and arteries against fatty deposits (plaque)
   e. improving the efficiency of the heart's **cardiac output** (total volume of blood pumped out by the heart each minute)
   f. helping to keep the **collateral circulation** open and available for emergencies

3. **Walking improves lung efficiency and breathing capacity by:**
   a. conditioning the **muscles of respiration** (chest wall and diaphragm)
   b. opening more **usable lung space** (alveoli)
   c. improving efficiency of **extracting oxygen** from the air

4. **Walking improves the general circulation by:**
   a. increasing the **total volume of blood,** and the amount of red **blood cells,** allowing more oxygen to be carried in the bloodstream

    b. **dilating the arteries** thus improving blood flow

    c. increasing **flexibility of arteries** thus lowering blood pressure

    d. compression of **leg and abdominal veins** by the pumping action of the muscles used in **walking**, aiding the return of blood to the heart

    e. using small blood vessels in the legs for re-routing blood (**collateral circulation**) around blocked arteries in emergencies

5. **Walking prevents the build-up of fatty deposits (plaque) in arteries by:**

    a. decreasing the serum **triglycerides** (sugar fats)

    b. decreasing **LDL (bad) cholesterol** in the blood

    c. increasing **HDL (good) cholesterol** in the blood

    d. preventing the blood from getting too thick, thus lessening the chance that **blood clots** will form

6. **Walking promotes weight loss and weight control by:**

    a. directly **burning calories**

    b. regulating the brain center (**appestat**) to control appetite

    c. re-directing **blood flow** away from digestive tract toward the exercising muscles thus decreasing appetite

    d. using **blood fats** instead of sugar as a source of energy

7. **Walking controls stress by:**

    a. increasing relaxation hormones in the brain (**Beta-endorphins**) and decreasing stress hormones (**epinephrine and norepinephrine**)

    b. increasing the **oxygen** supply and decreasing the amount of **carbon dioxide** to the brain

    c. efficient utilization of **blood sugar** in the body regulated by an improved production of **insulin**

    d. literally **walking away** from stress

8. **Walking promotes a longer healthier life by:**

    a. strengthening the **heart muscle** and regulating the **cardiac output** (a slower more efficient heart rate)

    b. lowering **blood pressure** thus preventing strokes, heart attacks and kidney disorders

    c. improving **lungs' efficiency** in extracting oxygen from air

    d. improving the efficiency of the delivery of **oxygen** to all the body's organs, tissues and cells

e. strengthening **muscle fibers** throughout the body thus improving reaction time and maintaining muscle tone
f. maintaining **bone strength and structure** by preserving the mineral content of the bone, thus preventing osteoporosis (bone thinning) and certain forms of arthritis

SITTING OFTEN PUTS YOU IN AN EARLY COFFIN

Physical inactivity is actually a double risk factor for developing coronary heart disease. First of all, inactivity is associated with obesity, hypertension, and elevated blood fats, uric acid and blood sugar. All of these factors in themselves are risk factors for developing heart disease. Secondly, epidemiological studies have demonstrated that physical inactivity by itself is a major risk factor in the development of heart disease.

These studies have also proven that physical activity, both occupational and recreational, significantly reduces the chances of developing heart disease. Those people who walk regularly also have a much better chance of surviving a heart attack should they be unfortunate enough to sustain one. Walking actually protects you from developing coronary heart disease.

Walking also helps to reduce the other coronary risk factors. Several recent studies have shown that walking may not only prevent heart disease from occurring, but it may actually reverse the changes in the coronary arteries that have already occurred in people with heart disease.

Walking accomplishes these miraculous changes by lowering the bad LDL-cholesterol and triglyceride levels in the blood. It also raises the good HDL-cholesterol which has a protective effect on the heart. Walking also decreases the blood vessel's vascular resistance thus lowering your blood pressure. It also decreases both the resting and exercise heart rates. Walking promotes weight loss and prevents the blood sugar and uric acid from getting too high, otherwise, diabetes and gout could possibly develop. Walking also helps to prevent clot formation by decreasing clot-forming agents in the blood. And, finally, walking decreases neuromuscular tension which combats anxiety and depression.

Now if you need another reason
Why you should walk each season
You should know that sitting often
Will put you in an early coffin
So, follow the Walk to Win sign
And you'll live a real long time

"I SEE YOU FOLKS BROKE OUT OF THE RETIREMENT HOME AGAIN!"

CHAPTER 12

LOOK YOUNGER— LIVE LONGER

THE SECRETS OF THE WALKATHONIANS

In a little known study of a small province in lower Slobovia, walkers appear to live forever. No one has ever reported a death in this community in over 350 years. The elders known as the *Walkathonians* have never allowed any outsiders to view their walking rituals. But legend has it that these *Walkathonians* have been walking regularly for over 350 years and have never developed any disease or disability whatsoever. The only reported deaths have been from falls off the sides of steep mountains and these people have been buried quickly and quietly in unmarked graves to prevent word of their deaths from reaching the outside world.

It is said that *Walkathonians* feel that their longevity record will be tarnished if any deaths whatsoever are reported. The elder Walkathonian Council has been keeping their written record free of deaths, so that they may qualify for medical notation in either the famous Framingham Heart Study or the Guiness Book of World Records. Reliable sources stated that they will also be publishing their medical longevity report in next month's Journal of the American Medical Association. Once the word is officially released, people worldwide will be clamoring for the *Walkothonians'* secrets of eternal life. As one famous *Walkathonian* told me in a private confidential interview—**"WE JUST WALKS!"**

WALK AS IF YOUR LIFE DEPENDED ON IT—IT DOES!

The facts are irrefutable: you live longer and have an improved quality of life if you're a walker. Recent medical studies indicate that walkers live at least 10-15 years longer than non-walkers, and in many cases up to 25-30 years longer.

In a recent study conducted on over 17,000 Harvard school graduates, it was determined that those people who exercised regularly lived significantly longer than those who remained sedentary. Those individuals who exercised consistently had a significantly lower incidence of heart attacks and strokes than those in the sedentary group. And the exercise that most of these graduates reported was—*walking*. Those that walked the most had the lowest incidence of early death. The individuals who walked 9-10 miles per week (that's only about ½ hour daily or an hour every other day) had a 20% lower risk of heart attacks than those who walked 2-3 miles per week, and a 30% lower risk than those who didn't walk at all.

Walking adds years to your life and life to your years. *Walk as if your life depended on it*—It Does!

EAT LESS—LIVE LONGER!

Reducing your daily calorie intake by just 20-25% daily can extend your life by 10-15 years, according to a recent study released by the National Center for Toxicological Research. Based on animal studies, their findings regarding decreased calorie consumption, were as follows:

- Extends life and delays the aging process by enhancing DNA's ability to repair cell damage that results in disease and aging.
- Slows or prevents cancer by making the metabolism more efficient in eliminating carcinogens from the body.
- Slows the metabolic rate and lowers the body temperature, which in turn slows the aging process.

These findings are based on studies which appear to delay the aging process by reducing both the total daily caloric intake and the intake of total fats in the diet. It is essential to provide adequate vitamins, minerals and nutrients in a calorie reduced diet in order to slow the aging process. There must also be a balance between the intake of proteins, carbohydrates and fats.

Walkers are usually not big eaters. Perhaps that fact combined with the life-extension benefits of walking is what accounts for the very long lifespans of walkers. *Eating less and walking more will give you a long-life for evermore!*

WALKERS WIN AS ORGANS THIN

As we age, many physiological changes occur within our bodies. These changes are what is commonly known as the aging process. Here's a brief list of what happens inside of our bodies as we get older:

- **Metabolism:** Your metabolic rate starts to slow down between 30-35 years of age. The number of calories needed to maintain your weight decreases by approximately 3% to 5% each 10 years after the age of 35. This means it's harder to lose weight as you grow older and much easier to get fat, even though you're eating the same number of calories you ate when you were younger. Also with the slow down in metabolism, you get more fatigued easier after physical activity.

- **Immune System:** The immune system also starts to slow down after the age of 35. As you get older it becomes more difficult to fight off infections and various illnesses. The body with aging produces less potent white blood cells that are used to fight viral and bacterial infections. The degenerative diseases of aging also are due in part to the decreased level of immunity.

- **The Senses:** Your sense of smell, taste, vision and hearing are notably affected after the age of 40. When you begin to lose your sense of smell you also lose your ability to distinguish between various taste sensations. With the loss of taste can come a loss of appetite, and the development of nutritional deficiencies. Hearing may also begin to gradually diminish after the age of 45. This usually begins with the inability to pick up sounds in the high-frequency range. Although these changes are all subtle, people start to lose parts of conversations as they become unable to pick up certain sounds.

- **Vision:** Visual loss varies in different age groups depending on a number of factors. In general, however, your vision begins to decrease after the age of 40. The ability of the pupil to dilate and contract regulates the amount of light reaching the retina. As we age this ability to dilate the pupil decreases, resulting in less light reaching the retina. Also the lens through which we see begins to cloud and harden as we get older, due to a decrease in the supply of blood reaching the lens. This condition pre-disposes towards cataract formation.

- **Respiratory System:** Your lungs lose approximately 5% of their maximum breathing capacity every decade after the age of 30. If you are a smoker they lose up to 10% of their capacity every 10 years. This results in the lungs' inability to pick up oxygen from the atmosphere and distribute it to the blood vessels for its ultimate destination—the body's cells. As we age we begin to lose lung elasticity which accounts for the inability of the lung to expand and contract completely. This results in oxygen being left in dead-spaces in the lung tissue, with no where to go but back out into the air again.

- **Bone and Muscle Mass:** Bone and muscle mass begin to decrease at a rate of 1-2% every year after the age of 30. As muscle mass shrinks, fat replaces it and you start to put on weight as you get older. As bone mass begins to decrease you become more prone to injuries and fractures, particularly in the post-menopausal woman. This condition is known as *osteoporosis* or thinning of the bones. Inactivity, obesity, a low calcium diet, excess caffeine, alcohol and tobacco all accelerate this process. As we age there is also a wearing-down of the cartilaginous pads that cushion our bones. This process leads to joint damage and degenerative changes in the bones. In some cases this may lead to arthritis.

- **Cardiovascular System:** Your blood vessels lose their elasticity as you age, causing a gradual rise in blood pressure. This leads to the heart having to work harder to pump blood throughout the body. If the heart has to work harder it can gradually enlarge. This enlargement can eventually lead to heart failure, if the heart's ability to pump blood effectively is impaired. With heart enlargement can come the possibility of erratic heart beats (arrhythmias) which can become dangerous if left untreated. As the blood vessels age, they become laden-down with deposits of cholesterol and calcium. These deposits eventually narrow down the artery's lumen (opening). This results in a decreased blood supply to the part of the body that these arteries supply—heart, brain, internal organs, legs, etc.

- **The Brain:** Your brain begins to shrink as you grow older, losing about 1% of its weight every two years after the age of 40. Slight impairment of memory and mental performance slows somewhat as a result of this brain shrinkage. Depression, which is often mistaken for senility, is one of the most ignored disorders in older people. Approximately 18% of the elderly suffer from this condition. Partly it may be related to shrinkage of brain tissue but mainly it is the result of stress, illness, death of loved ones, retirement, living alone, or just loneliness in general. Suicide is higher in older people than in any other age group.

- *The Internal Organs:*

  Kidney: The kidneys begin to lose 2-3% of their efficiency every 5 years after the age of 35. This can eventually result in kidney damage and the accumulation of waste products in the blood stream. This condition may be worsened in men as they age because of the gradual enlargement of the prostate gland. This enlargement closes down a portion of the urethra, making urination slow and difficult. If not treated, this condition can cause a back-up of urine, further damaging the kidneys.

  Liver: The liver loses some of its efficiency as we age. This can result in the inability of the liver to process many medications and drugs. In the elderly these drugs can accumulate and build up to toxic levels if the liver cannot metabolize them properly. Even alcohol cannot be eliminated properly because of the liver's and kidneys' inability to excrete it fast enough. So a single drink in the elderly may act as if they have had several drinks.

Pancreas: The pancreas also ages as we do, making it more likely that we develop diabetes as we get older. Once the insulin production of the pancreas slows down, then our blood sugar starts to rise, and if left unchecked then diabetes may result. Also, the pancreas' ability to produce digestive enzymes decreases as we get older, making the digestion and absorption of many foods difficult. Older people frequently complain of heartburn, indigestion and gas, which are frequently related to the aging pancreas.

Adrenal Glands: These glands also shrink as we get older. The adrenal gland hormones regulate many chemical reactions in the body and are responsible for the production of many important hormones that control the body's metabolism. They also produce the body's supply of cortisone-like chemicals which control many important body functions.

The Spleen: The spleen also shrinks as we age. The spleen's primary function is to act as a reservoir for the break-down of old red blood cells. When its ability is interfered with, the aging red blood cells disintegrate in the blood stream rather than in the spleen.

- **The Thyroid:** The aging thyroid causes a decrease in the production of the thyroid hormones. This accounts for the slowing of the metabolism in the elderly. If the thyroid function decreases too much (a condition known as hypothyroidism), then the person experiences drying of the skin, constipation, weight gain, fluid retention, anemia and heart disease. Heart failure may result if proper treatment is not given.

The Intestinal Tract: The intestinal tract consists of the digestive tube starting with the esophagus into the stomach, then to the small intestine and finally to the large intestine where your food's waste products are eliminated. As we age so does our intestinal tract. As the intestinal tract ages so does our ability to digest, absorb, and process food substances. If this digestive process is interfered with to any great extent, then we

may develop nutritional deficiencies and possibly mal-
nutrition. The slowing action of the intestinal tract
often leads to chronic constipation in the elderly.

Ovaries and Testicles: As we age so does the production
of both male and female hormones. Women experience
a multitude of symptoms as they reach menopause,
almost all of which are secondary to the decreased
production of estrogen. Many men as they age experience a decrease in libido or sex-drive because of the
decreased production of the male hormone—testosterone.

The Skin: As we age the epidermis or outer layer of the
skin starts to dry out and discolor (so-called age spots).
The next layer, the dermis, starts to thin making the
skin seem transparent (translucent), which reveals the
tiny blood vessels under the skin. The next layer is
called the subcutaneous layer and it is here that the fat
and connective tissue are found. As we age the fat layer
starts to shrink and the connective tissue layer begins
to lose its elasticity. All of these factors combine to
produce wrinkles and cause the skin to sag. The sweat
glands located in this subcutaneous tissue layer begin
to lose their ability to regulate the body temperature.
Combined with the decrease in fat content of this layer
of skin, the older person has difficulty staying warm in
winter and difficulty cooling-off the body in hot, humid
weather. As the skin ages, its protective pigment cells
decrease in number, increasing the skin's susceptibil-
ity to developing skin cancer.

* * * * * *

As all of the above mentioned organs and tissues of the
body age, they become susceptible to the ravages of disease,
illness, and cancer. The aging cells of these various organs
and tissues break-down gradually, losing the ability to operate their internal metabolic machinery properly. Viral infections, bacterial infections, degenerative diseases and cancer
cells can invade these weakened cells of your body, as these
cells go through the aging process.

So what do you think? Sounds like a horror story from a

creature double-feature monster movie, doesn't it? So what's a body to do? Lay down and die? Just sit there and take it like a man or woman? Not on your life! That list of degenerative changes that occurs in every living cell in your body as you age can be slowed down! Those decreases in body functions can be halted! That gradual decrease in both mental and physical faculties can be reversed! Those aging organs, tissues, and cells can be given new life again! No, you can't prevent the aging process from proceeding, but you certainly can slow down its progress to a snail's crawl.

You can stand up and take charge of your life and prevent the degenerative ravages of aging from crumbling your body like an old building. There is a way for you to *reverse the aging process and add 15, 20, 25, even 30 additional years to your life*. If you've been paying attention to this book, you know what it is. You know what it is even if you haven't been paying close attention to this book. Your body knows! Your brain knows! And certainly your mother knows. Yes, the answer is **WALKING**. Walking will add years to your life and life to your years. **Walk as if your life depended on it—It Does!**

Now you're saying to yourselves—"Is he kidding?" "Now, you've gone too far." "Nothing can stop the aging process." And I say to you, and you, and yes, even you—"Yes it can!" Walkers by and large live at least 15 years longer than sedentary folks. Walkers in every country in the world have been proven to be the longest-living segment of any population or civilization. From the Masii natives in Africa to the Russian tribes in Siberia; from the mountain climbers of Peru to the Bushman of New Guinea; from the train-men in London England to the mail-men of the United States. All of these people have one thing in common—*they're all walkers!* And for all intents and purposes they live longer than any other similar-age group of sedentary people in their respective cities or countries.

Dr. Alexander Leaf, chairman Dept. of Preventive Medicine, Massachusetts General Hospital, studied various populations throughout the world and concluded that the active segment of each population lived considerably longer than the inactive segment. He stated—*"It is apparent that an exercise like walking throughout life is an important factor promoting well-being and longevity. One is never too old to commence a regular program of exercise and once started, will never grow too old to continue it."* Walkers live longer and are illness-free longer than their sedentary counterparts anywhere in the world. This was the conclusion reached at the last national convention on *Clinical Research on Aging.*

WALK, DON'T SIT—LET'S MOVE IT!

A recent study at the State University of New York in Buffalo has now linked even **colon cancer** to lack of physical activity. This condition had been previously thought to be caused only by a *low-fiber, high-fat diet.* Now, however, it appears that men with sedentary jobs (bus drivers, book-keepers, accountants, computer operators, etc.) are 60 percent more likely to get cancer of the colon compared to more phys-ically active men (longshoremen, mailmen, auto mechanics, etc.).

In this study, the occupations of approximately 500 rectal and colon cancer patients were compared to the occupations of over 1,400 patients with other diseases. All of these patients were white males. Men who had spent more that 20 years in completely sedentary jobs had twice the incidence of colon cancer as compared to those men with active jobs. And men who worked at low-activity jobs had 1½ times the risk of colon cancer as active workers.

Physical activity, especially a regular *walking program,* appears to stimulate the movement of waste products through the colon, thus decreasing the time that the potential waste carcinogens are in contact with the wall of the colon. This is a similar theory to that which explains why a high-fiber, low-fat diet also helps to prevent colon cancer.

Walk, don't sit! Let's move it!

A WALK EVERY DAY KEEPS ARTHRITIS AWAY

Recent research suggests that walking may be the best exercise for most forms of arthritis. Most people with arthritis can benefit from a regular exercise program according to the majority of rheumatologists. And the exercise that most of the doctors recommended for their patients with arthritis was walking.

Walking strengthens the muscles and ligaments that are

attached to the arthritic joints. This helps to relieve the pain that occurs when the bones rub against each other. Walking also may prevent some of the joint inflammation and deformity that is associated with arthritis. The gentle joint motions of walking may relieve joint pain and swelling. Just make sure that you take it easy and rest frequently. Don't walk through pain.

The recurrent pain and joint swelling associated with arthritis acts as a depressant in the majority of patients with arthritis. Depression in turn leads to lethargy and inactivity. The inactivity instead of relieving the pain in most arthritics tends to lead to more joint involvement and greater immobility. Walking on the other hand with its biochemical and psychological mood-elevating effects, acts as a natural anti-depressant in the arthritic patient. Walking does wonders to improve the arthritic's feeling of well-being and it improves the vicious cycle of pain, depression and subsequent immobility.

Any patient who has some form of arthritis must be monitored closely by their personal physician. Each patient is an individual and will respond differently to various forms of exercise. Just as complete inactivity may lead to a worsening of arthritis, too much activity, especially strenuous exercises, may also have an adverse effect on arthritis. Listen to the advice of your own physician. Most doctors, however, will recommend a graduated walking program for the majority of their patients.

Don't let pain keep you in. Get out there and Walk to Win!

STAY YOUNGER LONGER

Modern medical research is constantly probing the mysteries of the aging process. Molecular biology and genetic engineering are two of the important tools being used by today's scientists in their effort to unravel the complex changes that accompany aging. Since The National Institute on Aging was founded in 1975, research funding has gone from approximately 15 million dollars to over 200 million dollars in 1987. Congress too, like most Americans, wants to live longer and look younger.

The average life expectancy for men is 70.5 years and for

women 75.2 years. Many scientists believe that the life span could easily be extended to well over 100 years if some of the mysteries of the aging process are decoded. After the age of 28-32 the aging process begins to "kick in." These changes first begin at the molecular level in all of the body's cells from the tiniest organs like the parathyroid and pituitary glands to the largest organs like the liver and skin. These changes begin to manifest themselves in a myriad of ways—graying or loss of hair and wrinkling of the skin; atrophy of the muscles and demineralization of the bones; diminished eyesight and hearing; slight to often imperceptible memory impairment caused by atrophy of brain cells; drooping and sagging skin and muscles; digestive and urinary tract disorders; cardiovascular and respiratory abnormalities; weakening of the immune system and thousands of other subtle changes that accompany the aging process.

Molecular genetics has found that each animal species has a different lifespan, including humans. So what's a body to do? Many people take the fatalistic attitude that their genes will determine when they are to die and that nothing whatsoever can be done to change their genetic code. Nothing could be further from the truth. There are a number of factors that effect the body's *immune system* which in turn effects the body's ability to repair damaged or degenerated genes. If, in fact, we can alter the genetic code in a somewhat similar fashion to what scientists do in genetic engineering, then we could conceivably alter life expectancy.

Well, you can do just that! You can *stay younger longer*. You can *live longer younger*. You can modify or alter your genetic code and beat the odds against dying an early death or a predetermined genetic-coded death for that matter. **The following secrets for breaking the genetic code and beefing up your immune system are:**

1. AVOID STRESS TO BREAK GENETIC CODE

Stress produces the release of the hormones *adrenalin* and *glucocorticoids* produced by the adrenal glands. High levels of these chemicals accelerate the aging process by speeding up the death of tiny brain cells and they damage nerve cells throughout the body. These two hormones also produce molecules called *free-radicals* which contain a very reactive form of oxygen. These free-radicals can damage the heart, blood vessels and the lining of the lung. They also have been implicated in the development of certain forms of cancer and arthritis.

Well, how do you avoid stress? It's not as easy as it sounds, is it? Actually it really is. The first thing you have to be aware of is that—*stress always wins—if you let it.* The way not to let stress win is to beat it at its own game. Stress has a lot of henchmen on its side—adrenalin, glucocorticoids and free-radicals. Well, who do you have on your side willing to back you up every step of the way. *Your feet*—that's who! Those two little fellows can beat any adrenalin, glucocorticoids and free radicals twice their size.

First of all when confronted with stress say the magic words—***feet retreat!*** No one alive or dead for that matter has ever beat stress standing toe-to-toe. If you make the mistaken decision to fight it out with stress, be prepared to go down for the count of ten and then some—maybe forever! Stress always wins when you confront it head on. The reason is that stress's henchmen—adrenalin, glucocorticoids and free-radicals have a 1-2-3 punch that's impossible to beat.

Adrenalin speeds up your heart rate and squeezes your blood vessels shut. It causes your pupils to dilate and your skin to become cold and clammy. It shuts down your kidneys and speeds up your intestinal tract. It elevates your blood pressure to dangerous levels making the possibility of a stroke or heart attack likely. Can you beat that 1st punch? Not if your life depended on it!

Glucocorticoids also narrow down your blood vessels and speed up your heart rate. They cause your body to retain fluid which can lead to heart failure. They also cause sodium retention from your kidneys which can further elevate your blood pressure to dangerous levels. They can also damage your kidneys and the adrenal glands themselves, which actually produced the glucocorticoids in the first place. And lastly, they have an adverse effect on your pancreas and can lead to an over-production of insulin which results in sharp rises and falls in your blood glucose levels—not a good thing at all for your overall health. Think you can duck that number two punch?—Not in a million years!

And what about that last punch—*free-radicals.* Do you think you can side-step it? Not if you were Joe Frazier. Free radicals are maverick atoms of oxygen that are produced by the stress reaction. They can cause the deterioration of blood vessels and the alveoli (tissues that line the lungs). They can damage the heart by causing degeneration of the heart tissue. These free radicals, and they really are radical, can cause a decrease in the regular oxygen supply to all of the body's cells and tissues including the heart muscle itself. Without oxygen, organs and tissues die. Without oxygen, heart muscle and brain cells die. These nutty hyped-up oxygen atoms can even cause glaucoma, arthritis and nerve damage. Don't even try to think about beating these crazy little atoms, you'd lose every time.

So what about that secret ingredient I spoke about earlier?—**FEET RETREAT!** The only way to beat these three criminal marauders is to turn on your heels and beat a quick retreat. *Walking away from stress* is your only defense against these dangerous-destroyers. And once you've literally and figuratively walked away from stress, these three gun-men have lost their bullets, so to speak. They've shot their load. They can't attack you if there's no you in sight. They can't shoot at a missing target.

Walking away actually dissipates these three killers from your blood stream. As you walk the levels of adrenalin, glucocorticoids and free-radicals start to decline. The relaxation hormones—beta-endorphines start to permeate your tissues and cells while the three killer chemicals are pushed out of your blood stream and eliminated from the body by your liver and kidneys.

Stress is actually a state of mind and if you're willing to succumb to it, you will. If you learn relaxation techniques, walking being the main one, you will learn to deal with stress effectively, rather than letting stress deal effectively with you. A refreshing walk not only dissipates the stress chemicals from the body but it also dissipates the negative thought processes from the brain. It clears the cobwebs and sweeps the dust out of the corners of your mind. It scrubs clean the walls of your aggressiveness and intolerance. It cleanses the windows of your intellect and it sharpens your mental awareness and understanding, so that you can deal with stress intellectually rather than emotionally. Yes, walking does all that and then some—try it! It works! Here's a prime example of walking to win, and winning here is more than just winning—it's your life. You can beat stress from within if you **WALK TO WIN!**

2. BEEF UP YOUR IMMUNE SYSTEM WITHOUT FAT OR SUGAR

It's important to select foods that are high in minerals and vitamins and low in fats and refined sugars. Eat more fruit, vegetables, fowl and fish and less meat and dairy products.

Foods high in saturated fats are particularly harmful to the immune system. These foods raise blood cholesterol levels which clog the arteries and subsequently slow down the flow of oxygen-rich blood and vital nutrients to the body's cells and tissues. This process actually shortens your life expectancy by allowing your vital organs and tissues to die a slow, painful death. No organ can live without adequate supplies of oxygen and nutrients. High-fat foods also take considerably longer than other foods to convert to energy. Eating a high fat meal diverts blood and oxygen from the brain to the digestive tract, leaving you feeling fatigued and light-headed.

Blood cholesterol levels can also be lowered by eating more fruits, vegetables, fowl and fish and reducing consumption of meats, dairy products and pastries, especially those made with palm or coconut oil. The fiber in beans, legumes and oat bran lowers cholesterol as well as the pectin in fruits such as apples, oranges and grapefruit.

Refined sugar plays havoc with the immune system by triggering sudden rises in insulin production which result in dramatic sharp drops in blood glucose levels. This condition known as hypoglycemia can result in fatigue, headaches, fainting spells, weakness and even convulsions. Not only is the body deprived of essential glucose for energy and metabolism, but the brain is also deprived of essential glucose which is necessary for brain function. If the brain cells are deprived of glucose for any length of time, then some of these brain cells may atrophy or die. Like oxygen, these brain cells need a constant infusion of glucose to enable the neurological network to function properly. Once deprived of glucose the brain exhibits memory loss, incoordination, speech impairment, generalized muscle weakness, and even convulsions if glucose deprivation persists for a long period of time.

3. ADEQUATE VITAMINS AND MINERALS

Remember when we spoke about the arch villains called the free-radicals? Well a diet high in yellow and dark green vegetables provides *Beta-carotene* which is a precursor to vitamin A. This chemical Beta-carotene breaks up free-radicals and protects the body against their harmful effects such as cancer and degenerative diseases. Likewise, vitamin E found in many cereal grains, fish and non-fat dairy products also protects against the villainous free-radicals.

An adequate supply of vitamins C and B-complex are essential to keep the immune system in good working order. These water-soluble vitamins are essential for good health and longevity. Fruits and vegetables provide an excellent source of these vitamins, however they must be continuously supplied to the body, because being water-soluble they are excreted rapidly by the body. A daily vitamin supplement of B complex and vitamin C is recommended to keep the body's cells and tissues constantly supplied with these essential vitamins. These vitamins are responsible for keeping the immune system in good working order and they help the body to repair its own DNA (material that makes up your genes).

4. BEAT FATIGUE AND INCREASE ENERGY

a. SLEEP

Most people require between 6-8 hours of sleep per night. Some individuals need less, others need more. If you wake refreshed in the AM and don't tire easily during the day, then you're probably getting enough sleep. The sleep/wake cycle is affected by many things, one in particular is the release of a hormone called cortisol. This hormone decreases before bedtime and starts to rise in the early AM hours before you awake. Travel and shift-work can effect your sleeping cycle by interfering with the cortisol blood levels. Your body usually will adjust to time changes after several days, by changing the rise and fall of cortisol production.

b. SMOKING

Smoking causes fatigue by impairing the uptake and delivery of oxygen to the cells of all of your body's organs. Smoking increases the level of carbon monoxide in your blood stream, which damages the heart and lungs leading to cardiovascular disease, pulmonary disorders and cancer. Smoking also destroys Vitamin C in the body which impairs the immune system and decreases your energy level. Also smoking causes premature wrinkling of the skin and a sallow complexion.

c. CAFFEINE

Excess caffeine consumption causes marked fatigue after the initial stimulating effect of the caffeine wears off. Caffeine also has an adverse effect on the cardiovascular and nervous systems. It causes a rapid heart beat, elevation of blood pressure and an irritation of all of the body's nerve endings. This can result in headaches, nervousness, sweats, shakes, mental confusion, anxiety and even paranoid behavior. Following these adverse effects comes marked lethargy, sapping the body of its vital energy.

d. SALT

Excess salt intake can cause a permanent elevation of blood pressure by interfering with the kidney's ability to eliminate salt from the body. This excess accumulation of sodium causes the body to retain more fluid and subsequently increases the volume of blood. This in turn makes the heart work harder causing a rise in blood pressure. In susceptible people this may result in permanent hypertension and premature death from strokes or heart attacks.

e. ALCOHOL

Excess alcohol causes liver disease, brain damage, nerve disorders, strokes, heart disease, hypertension, damage to the reproductive organs, spleen enlargement, hemorrhages of the esophagus, liver and pancreatic cancer and early death.

f. KEEP MENTALLY ACTIVE: THINK YOUNG!

As you age you can expect fatigue and a dulling of the mental senses unless you keep mentally active. Keeping mentally active requires that you continuously stimulate the brain cells by reading, doing puzzles, playing games such as checkers, chess or cards, keeping up with or learning a new hobby or skill or constantly interacting with other people. By keeping mentally alert you will stay younger longer and enjoy your years with less fatigue and more energy and pep. Remember, it's important to **think young!** Staying young is as much a state of mind as it is a state of body physiology.

5. STOP SEDENTARY SITTING

Inactivity is associated with obesity, diabetes, hypertension, heart disease, pulmonary and gastrointestinal disorders, arthritis, back problems, muscular and mental tension and premature death. Walking, on the other hand, increases the delivery of oxygen to the brain and body tissues which improves the circulation. This results in increased energy and mental alertness. Walking also decreases stress and tension thus producing muscular and mental relaxation. This in turn lowers the blood pressure and prevents cardiovascular disease. Walking also lowers the LDL-bad cholesterol and raises HDL-good cholesterol, protecting you from heart disease.

Walking burns calories and prevents or controls obesity and diabetes. Walking builds muscle and bone tissue and prevents osteoporosis, arthritis, and degenerative muscular and back disorders. Walking prevents the development of chronic lung disorders by keeping the lungs and respiratory muscles in good working order and by preventing the lung capacity from shrinking.

Walking boosts the immune system by producing chemicals known as *interferons* that do everything from warding off colds to preventing cancer. In fact, when you come right down to it, walking prevents almost every known disease and disability known to modern science. And above all, walking prevents premature death and even mature death. Walking will allow you to live years beyond your pre-determined genetic-code death. Population studies show that *walkers live at least 15-20 years longer* than their sedentary counterparts.

WINNING STEPS TO PREVENT YOUR DEATH

How long you live depends partly on your genetic code. Heredity does play an important role in your longevity factor. However, you can beat your genetic code if you eliminate most of the risk factors of heart disease, hypertension, vascular disease and cancer. The following simplified list is an outline of what you can do to eliminate many of the risk factors that are present in our everyday lives. **Here are 13 steps to prevent your death:**

1. Decrease salt in your diet to help prevent or lessen the risk of hypertension and stroke.
2. Maintain normal weight to prevent the risk of hypertension, heart disease, obesity, and diabetes.
3. Decrease cholesterol in the diet to lessen the chance of heart attacks, strokes, and blood clots.
4. Decrease saturated fat in the diet to lower blood cholesterol in order to prevent strokes and heart attacks, and to lessen the risk of breast, prostate, and colon cancer.
5. Increase the fiber in your diet to lower cholesterol and to prevent the development of hemorrhoids, varicose veins, diverticulosis and colon cancer.
6. Increase consumption of green and yellow vegetables which have high concentrations of vitamin A & C to prevent various types of intestinal cancer.
7. Avoid the use of smoked-meats and smoked-fishes which have high concentrations of nitrites that lead to stomach and esophageal cancer.
8. Avoid the use of excess caffeine which can lead to breast cysts, breast cancer, pancreatic cancer, prostate cancer, nervous disorders, heart disease, and high blood pressure.
9. Avoid the use of tobacco which can cause oral cancer, lung cancer, emphysema, hypertension and heart disease.
10. Avoid excess alcohol consumption which may contribute to liver cirrhosis, liver cancer, hepatitis, pancreatic tumors, heart disease and neurological disorders.
11. Avoid prolonged exposure to the sun to prevent the development of skin cancer.
12. Avoid stress whenever possible to prevent the body's stress hormones from raising your blood pressure and constricting your arteries.
13. *Walk every day to keep the grim-reaper away.*

In addition to these thirteen steps make sure that you have regular check-ups with your family physician. Be sure to carefully follow any recommendations that he has as to your diet, exercise, medications, etc. If you're ever in doubt as to your doctor's advice, don't hesitate to get a second opinion.

The worst thing that you can do is to ignore your doctor's recommendations. Also never be afraid to ask him questions about things that bother you. And never, ever ignore any unusual signs or symptoms that you develop. Check with your doctor immediately. Don't hide your head in the sand like an ostrich hoping that these symptoms or signs will go away by themselves.

There is no segment of the population that could benefit more from a walking program than the elderly. A younger person can increase his/her physical fitness 15-25% by exercising, an older person may be able to improve his or her physical fitness 35-50%. As our population gets older, more people are realizing the benefits of regular moderate exercise. In a recent national poll it was found that over 50% of people 65 and older walk regularly every day.

Walking can reverse or slow down the ravages of the aging process as we have previously seen. Walking helps to control weight, lower blood cholesterol and decrease body fat. Walking helps to build bone structure, strengthen ligaments and tendons, and increase muscle mass and strengthen muscle tissue. Walking helps to condition the lungs and respiratory muscles and improves the general overall breathing capacity. Walking also helps the cardio-vascular and circulatory systems by improving the efficiency of the heart's pumping action. Walking helps to keep the blood vessels elastic preventing the development of hypertension. Walking keeps the blood circulating and prevents the formation of blood clots by preventing the blood platelets from sticking together.

And finally, walking helps to improve the maximum oxygen uptake which increases the oxygen uptake from the atmosphere, its distribution through the blood stream and its final delivery to the cells of the body's organs and tissues. *This improved oxygenation at the cellular level is the basis for the life process itself.* If you can provide a constant infusion of oxygen on a regular basis at the cellular level, then you can slow-down the aging process. By providing this oxygen to the cells, your body can operate its cellular machinery more efficiently. The body's cells can utilize the nutrients they receive from the blood stream more efficiently when they are saturated with oxygen, and they can give up their waste-products easier for elimination from the body.

A WALK EVERY DAY
KEEPS THE DOCTOR AWAY
PROVIDES OXYGEN TO EACH TISSUE
AND THAT'S REALLY THE ISSUE
FOR WITHOUT IT YOUR CELLS DIE
AND THAT'S REASON ENOUGH TO CRY
SO GET OUT THERE AND WALK
DON'T JUST STAND THERE AND TALK
IF YOU WANT TO LIVE A LONG TIME
I'LL GIVE YOU SOME ADVICE OF MINE
WALK LIKE YOUR LIFE DEPENDED ON IT
AND YOU'LL SURELY PREVENT THE END OF IT.

"NOW HARRY, WHEN I TOLD YOU TO WALK EVERY DAY, I DIDN'T MEAN JUST FROM THE TV TO THE REFRIGERATOR!"

V. DR. WALK'S®
FITNESS &
DIET TIPS

"You know that Dr. Stutman has been given the honorary title of **Dr. Walk**® *by his patients, Holmes, since he has advocated walking as the ideal exercise for health and fitness, for nigh onto 25 years now."*

Dr. Watson to Sherlock Holmes
"The Mystery of The Walking Men" in
Walk To Win (Philadelphia: Medical Manor Books, 1989.)

"HOW ABOUT IT, MILDRED? SHOULD WE TAKE A CHANCE ON A WALK FOR FUN, FITNESS AND ROMANCE?"

CHAPTER 13

FITNESS FUN FOR EVERYONE

THEY CAN'T FOOL ALL OF US ALL OF THE TIME

According to the latest Roper Poll of October 1987, 50% of the United States population stated that walking was their favorite form of exercise. Surprised? Don't be. The fitness industry would like us to think otherwise. That's why hundreds of millions of dollars are spent each year on advertising health and fitness clubs, jogging apparel, aerobic centers, fitness machines and any other gimmicks that these advertisers can use to empty your wallets. Well, take heart America, they can fool some of the people some of the time, but not all of the people all of the time. They won't advertise walking because they can't make a dime from it.

THE PERCENTAGE OF ADULTS WHO REGULARLY ENGAGE IN VARIOUS FORMS OF EXERCISE

WALKING	50%
CALISTHENICS	19%
SWIMMING	18%
BICYCLING	16%
GOLF	15%
TENNIS + RACQUETBALL	14%
JOGGING	10%
BOWLING	9%

TAKE A HAPPY WALK

Americans are walking again like never before. According to the President's 1988 Council on Physical Fitness report, walking is the single most popular adult exercise in America. With over 44 million adherents, the numbers are steadily increasing as people of all ages are walking for health, fitness and fun. Walking is an exercise whose time has finally come. Why not? It's easy, safe, fun and it makes you feel and look great.

Walking is something that two people, no matter how different their physical conditions, can do together. It is a companionable exercise where you can enjoy each other's company and at the same time get all the benefits of exercising.

Walking is a great escape. You can get away from the phone, from the office, or from home a little while and take that needed time to relax. You can walk to think out a problem or walk to forget one. Walking acts as a tranquilizer to help us relax and it can work as a stimulant to give us energy. The late famous cardiologist Dr. Paul Dudley White said, *"A vigorous 5 mile walk will do more good for an unhappy but otherwise healthy adult than all the medicine and psychology in the world."*

Don't make the common mistake of thinking that walking is too easy to be a good exercise. On the contrary, walking is not only the safest but it's the best exercise in the world. If you're overweight, then walking is your best choice since you won't be putting excess stress on the ligaments, muscles, and joints.

How you walk also tells whether you're happy, sad, angry, ambitious or just plain lazy. Walkers with a long stride, a greater arm swing and a bounce to their step were happy, ambitious and self-assured whereas walkers with a short stride, a foot shuffle or drag and a short arm swing were often depressed, unhappy and angry.

Recent studies in women indicate that arm swing is the most indicative factor of their mood. The greater the arm swing the happier, more vigorous and less depressed the woman was. A short arm swing indicated that the woman was angry, frustrated and unhappy.

Stretch out your stride, swing you arm, and put a bounce

in your step whenever and wherever you walk. That's your road to good health, a successful career and a long happy life. Believe it! It works!

WALKING WITCHCRAFT

There is considerable agreement among most exercise physiologists that exercise on a moderate, even basis has a tranquilizing effect. A rhythmic exercise like walking for 20-30 minutes, seems to be the most effective method for producing this tranquilizing effect.

Several theories have been proposed to explain this tranquilizing effect. One current theory is that a slight increase in body temperature affects the brainstem and results in a rhythmic electrical activity in the cortex of the brain. This produces a more relaxed state and is the direct result of exercise. Other studies indicate that there is an increase in brain chemicals, particularly a group of chemicals called the endorphins. These appear to have a tranquilizing or sedative effect and result in relaxation.

In a recent study from Massachusetts General Hospital, reported in the *New England Journal of Medicine*, researchers suggested that regular exercise may increase the secretion of two chemicals called *beta-endorphin* and *beta-lipotropin*. These substances act as chemical pain killers or tranquilizers and thus can influence the body's metabolism and give a sense of tranquility and well being. This study noted that with exercise these levels of chemicals increased, and with more strenuous exercise this increase was even greater. This may, in part, explain the "runners' high" or "joggers' euphoria" that is reported with high-intensity exercise. They stated that this also may explain the withdrawal effect noted by runners after they stopped their running program and the frequency with which joggers sustain fractured bones while running without feeling any pain.

Walking, on the other hand, produces only a moderate rise in these brain chemicals. This results in a relaxed state of mind and produces a tranquilizing effect on the entire nervous system. Since walking is not a strenuous exercise, the level of these brain chemicals does not go too high, thus avoiding the analgesic or pain-killing effect produced with high-intensity exercises. This enables the walker to be aware of pain if he turns his ankle or foot while walking. The runner, on the other hand, because of the high analgesic levels of these brain chemicals, may not actually feel the chest pain from a heart attack and he may drop over dead before he becomes aware of the pain. The abnormally high levels of these brain chemicals in this case is another example of too much of a good thing—the devil's deadly death draught.

Walking witchcraft, on the other hand, is just the magic you need to fight the devil's sorcery and the voodoo of everyday stress and tension. The calm, serene enchantment of walking (moderate levels of the tranquilizing brain chemicals), fights off the black-arts of tension, nervousness, anxiety and stress. let the *wonderful wizard of walking lead you down the peaceful path of restful relaxation*. Now that's what I call a mouthful of tranquilizers!

HOW ABOUT A WALK
JUST FOR FUN!

Walk whenever you can, instead of driving. If you have to drive, park somewhere a few blocks from your destination and walk the difference. Take the stairs instead of the elevator whenever possible. Take a walk when you are in a new part of town or at a friend's home. Always walk when you are away from home to see the beauty of different surroundings. Enjoy your walk by exploring different areas around your home or office.

If the weather is bad you can go to an enclosed shopping mall and walk. You can stop and look in all the windows after you've completed your regular workout walk in the mall.

You don't have to time your pulse. You don't have to do warm up with stretching exercises before you walk. You don't have to do cool down exercises when you finish. You don't have to tire yourself or get overheated or out of breath. You don't need special clothing or equipment, just a good pair of comfortable walking shoes. You don't have to be an athlete or an acrobat. All you have to do is walk your feet for fun and you automatically, without trying, will stay fit and trim.

WALK TO WORK AND CARRY YOUR LUNCH

According to a recent report from the Census Bureau many Americans still walk to work and many even carry their lunch. Thirty years ago, more than three times the number of people walked to work. However, with today's increased ease of transportation most Americans have given up this safe easy way to stay in shape. Let's give a hand to the 12 states that haven't given in to today's ride-everywhere society.

STATES WITH THE HIGHEST PERCENTAGE OF PEOPLE WALKING TO WORK

(Rounded off to nearest decimal point)

State	Percentage
ALASKA	17.2%
NORTH DAKOTA	15.1%
MONTANA	14.6%
SOUTH DAKOTA	12.8%
WASHINGTON, D.C.	12.1%
VERMONT	11.4%
IOWA	9.5%
MAINE	9.3%
NEW YORK	8.7%
MASSACHUSETTS	7.8%
PENNSYLVANIA	7.6%
ILLINOIS	6.9%

TRAVEL FIT WITH THE FIT-STEP®

Whether you're taking a vacation or a business trip, you can still keep trim and fit with your walking program. Most major airlines, cruise ships and trains offer special diet menus. If you have to splurge on one meal a day, don't worry. You'll walk it off in no time at all.

Cruise ships and *trains* are ideal for short walks. Walk around the airport concourse while waiting for flights or during layovers. Most major *hotels* can give you a map of the area for a walking tour. Get up early before your meeting and take a brisk ½ hour walk and repeat it again before supper. Use the *stairs* whenever possible and walk around the hotel as much as possible if the weather is bad.

Many hotels have small *gyms* where you can swim or use a stationary bike—take advantage of them if the weather's bad instead of watching TV. Many business trips are associated with a lot of stress and walking can ease away the tension leaving you more relaxed and more efficient. Speakers always do better after they've had a walk—more brain oxygen and relaxing chemicals (endorphins) and less carbon dioxide result in sharp, clear, concise speech with no stage jitters.

You can keep fit and have lots of pep when you do the **FIT-STEP**®. Don't let a little trip, trip you up. Most people feel exhausted after a vacation or a business trip because they sit around all day and stuff their faces with food and drink. Make it a habit to walk at least ½ hour every day that you're away. You'll return from your travels fit, full of vigor, vim and pep.

WEATHER WARNINGS

I caution my patients against any kind of physical exertion when the weather is extremely hot and humid or cold and windy. There's no need, however, to stay indoors during mild to moderate changes in weather conditions, since very few of us have perfect weather all year. In fact, if you just wait for that warm, sunny, low humidity day to come along, forget it! You'll never walk. That type of day is never there when you want it. The most important consideration in your walking program is to continue it on a regular basis, day in and day out.

Consistency is the key word no matter what the weather is except in the extreme changes of weather that we will now discuss.

* * * * * * *

HOT, HUMID WEATHER

Hot and humid weather has its own special set of circumstances. Generally, you have the option in hot or humid weather of being able to avoid these weather extremes by just changing your walking times to early morning or after sunset to avoid the hazards associated with heat and humidity.

When the temperature is above 75°F or if the humidity is above 60%, there is the danger of not being able to cool the body off. As we exercise, we expend energy and produce heat. The only effective way to dissipate that heat is by the evaporation of sweat from the body surface. Since this process is impaired by **high temperatures** and **high humidity**, the body temperature will rise. **Radiant heat** from the sun will also increase the body temperature. Even with adequate fluid intake before and after exercise in hot weather, it is still a strain on the cardiovascular system. A walk in the early morning or late evening will avoid most of the problems associated with high temperatures and humidity, and radiant heat exposure.

Heat exhaustion with its rare complication of **heat stroke** can be avoided by these simple precautions. There is, however, on rare occasions that extremely hot or humid day when it is even unbearable to walk early in the AM or the late evening. High humidity presents many difficulties with any outdoor exercise program and should be avoided whenever possible.

This is the time to quietly and peacefully turn to Chapter 2 on the **indoor Fit-Step®** program and turn up the air conditioner and relax.

* * * * * * * *

HIGH ALTITUDE

High altitude can also affect your response to exercise, since there is a decrease in the oxygen content of the air. Fatigue sets in more rapidly during exercise since the blood will be transporting less oxygen to the muscles. Caution is advised, especially if you have a pre-existing lung or heart condition. If you fatigue easily or develop difficulty in breathing, then you should stop your walking program. For most people, however, a cautious and gradual approach to exercise here will have no adverse effects.

RAINY WEATHER

Rain presents another of life's little difficulties and nature's way of getting your walking program all wet. Well, a light rain should never prevent anyone (providing the weather is mild) from taking his or her daily walk. A raincoat, umbrella, and galoshes should be handily stored in the glove compartment, office or home so that they can do the job for which they were intended. You'll be surprised how fresh the air feels and smells after being cooped up indoors all day. If the weather is really bad, than an enclosed mall can be the perfect place to take your daily walk.

WALKING IN THE RAIN—NOT THE MOVIE!

How many times have you looked out of your window at the falling rain and said to yourself, "I wish it would stop raining so that I can get out for a breath of fresh air." Well keep looking, the air is still out there. It didn't go away because it started to rain. In fact, the air outside in the rain is actually fresher than it is at any other time. The rain washes away a lot of the air's impurities including pollutants, carbon monoxide and ozone.

So what are you waiting for? Find your umbrella and a pair of rain shoes and go outside and have yourself a truly refreshing walk in air that has been really washed clean. Walking in the rain can be an exciting experience. Look up at the changing patterns of the sky, watch the birds and ground animals, if you can. And above all, smell the air, the grass and the flowers, if they're around. It's a truly unique experience, because it's a time to see, feel and smell nature that I'll bet you've rarely done.

The only precautions that you need to take is to have an

umbrella or waterproof headgear, and waterproof leather shoes or rubber boots or shoes. Also remember to dress warmly if there is a chill in the air. A waterproof raincoat or slicker should be used if you want total body coverage. Be careful not to purchase nylon fabrics that have been coated with a waterproof chemical or plastic, since, although these fabrics keep rain out, they don't let heat and water-vapor (perspiration) out. If the garment doesn't breathe in order to let perspiration evaporate, then you could get chilled.

We're not talking about walking in a storm or when it's thundering and lightening. But a walk in a light or gentle rain can be fun and invigorating. If it starts to become a heavy downpour, seek shelter until it lets up a bit. Remember, don't let mild changes in the weather prevent you from your appointed walking rounds. It's not necessary to go out in all types of inclement weather, like the mail-man has to. But if walking in the rain was good enough for Gene Kelly, then it should be O.K. for the rest of us.

* * * * * * * * *

COLD, WINDY WEATHER

The most important consideration in any exercise program is to maintain it on a **regular** basis. However, when winter weather is extremely cold, one should avoid exercising outdoors when conditions are **hazardous**. Walking in the **snow** can be dangerous because you can never tell what type of terrain is underneath the snow cover and injuries are sustained quite easily. Also, **icy** conditions should be avoided since the danger of slipping and injury are always present. There are many good alternatives to continue your walking program on an indoor basis as you've seen in Chapter 2. If, however, the conditions are such that you feel that you would like to continue your walking program in cold weather there are several precautions that we must mention.

WINTER WALKING PRECAUTIONS

1. If you have any type of **medical condition** (heart, lung,

kidney, diabetes, high blood pressure, etc), you should avoid winter walking.

2. If you develop any **symptoms** such as shortness of breath, dizziness, fatigue, or pain and discomfort anywhere, promptly discontinue winter walking.

3. Follow **medical precautions** outlined at the end of Chapter 2.

4. **Dress properly** and make sure that you wear extra layers of clothing, heavy **sweatsocks** or **thermal socks**, a **face or ski mask** may be a good idea, and **mittens** or **ski gloves** are helpful. Mittens keep the fingers together and provide more warmth than regular gloves. Make sure that the **layered clothing** you wear is loose fitting and can be easily adjusted so that you have the ability to open all layers if necessary. If you begin to perspire, you should be able to partially open your clothing so that the perspiration can evaporate. It is interesting to note that you can get up to 100 times as cold in sweat-soaked clothing than in dry clothing.

   —**Shoes**—a lined shoe or boot will be particularly helpful in preventing numbness of the toes and feet and will help to preserve the circulation by preventing heat loss.

   —A **scarf** over your mouth will warm the air before it is inhaled.

   —A **hat** will also preserve body heat.

5. **Wind**—Take special precautions with winter wind. Start your walk into the wind, since you should face the worst part of the weather while you are still dry and relatively fresh. If you start your walk first with the wind at your back, you might get overheated and perspired and then when you return and walk into the wind, the perspiration could freeze on your skin with the possibility of developing **frostbite**. Cases of **hypothermia** (the body's inner temperature dropping below normal) have occurred in conditions such as this where the wind chill factor was such that its effect on a heated perspiring body produced hypothermia which is a dangerous condition.

6. **Visibility**—It is important to realize that in the winter visibility may be poor and the possibility of auto accidents are increased. Be sure that you wear highly colored clothing, especially if you are out after dark, and be sure that you pick a well-traveled route where the automobile traffic is limited.

WINTER WEIGHT-LOSS WALKING

Since winter is the time that most of us usually gain weight, a winter's walk can not only be fun but actually has an added **slimming effect** for you as a bonus.

Walking in cold weather has all the benefits of walking in warm weather with one basic plus — you don't have to walk as long or as far to get the same benefits, in particular the same weight-loss benefit. Since there is more exertion involved when you walk in cold weather, calories are expended more rapidly. Studies show that while a one hour walk at 3 miles per hour burns approximately 350 calories per hour, the same walk on a cold winter day expends close to **400 calories per hour**. Therefore, you can accomplish the same benefits and weight loss with only a ¾ **hour walk** as compared to the one hour walk in a temperate climate. The basic physiological facts behind this result from the added weight of your clothing necessitated by the cold weather and the subsequent extra effort needed in walking. The result: **MORE CALORIES BURNED PER MINUTE.**

TRIMSTEP® WALKING TIPS

1. Be alert. Be aware of your surroundings.
2. Look and listen carefully and observe who is behind and in front of you.
3. Avoid an area that is unpopulated—deserted parks, trails, streets, parking lots, open fields.
4. Vary your route and time of day that you walk. Stick to daylight hours.
5. Walk in familiar or well-populated areas. Plan your route beforehand.
6. If you feel uncomfortable in any area, turn back; follow your intuition.
7. Let someone know where and when you walk. Carry change for a phone call.
8. If possible, walk with a dog, a friend, or a stick (a walking cane or stick, an umbrella, or just a branch.)
9. Ignore strangers who ask you questions or call after you.
10. Don't wear radio earphones—they prevent you from hearing traffic or people coming up behind you.

11. Stay away from areas where people may hide—bushes, parked trucks, alleyways, parking lots, etc.
12. If you are threatened or are suspicious of anyone, run into a shopping center, apartment house, crowded street or just knock on someone's door.
13. Wear a whistle on a chain or carry a pocket noise alarm. Don't hesitate to use them even if you just suspect trouble.
14. Wear light-colored clothing, especially if walking at dawn or dusk so that you are easily seen by traffic. When clothing is wet it appears darker than when it's dry, so be careful in rainy weather.
15. Never trust a moving vehicle! They'll never give you the right-of-way. Don't argue with a car—you'll be the loser.
16. Avoid overgrown or wooded areas and dark streets.
17. Stay away from parked vehicles containing strangers.
18. If you become tired, stop and rest in a populated area (example: restaurant or a store).
19. If you're lost, call a friend or the police, never hitchhike.
20. Be bright at night. Wearing **reflective material** on clothing while walking after dark or at dusk can mean the difference between a safe walk or a trip to the hospital. Reflective strips or tape on clothing can increase visibility as much as 200 to 750 feet. According to the American Committee of Accident and Poison Prevention, this reflective material could reduce night-time pedestrian deaths by 30-40%. Be bright at night, don't risk your inner light.

TRIM-STEP®
WALKING AND HIKING
ORGANIZATIONS

Adirondac Mountain Club
172 Ridge Street
Glen Falls, NY 12801

American Forestry
  Association
1319 18th Street, N.W.
Washington, DC 20036

National Campers & Hikers
  Association
7172 Transit Road
Buffalo, NY 14221

National Park Service
North Atlantic Regional Office
15 State Street
Boston, MA 02109

American Hiking Society
1701 18th Street, N.W.
Washington, DC 20009

American Youth Hostels
75 Spring Street
New York, NY 10012

Appalachian Mountain Club
5 Joy Street
Boston, MA 02108

Appalachian Trail Conference
P.O. Box 236
Harpers Ferry, WV 25425

Dr. Walk's® Diet & Fitness
  Newsletter
3501 Newberry Road
Philadelphia, PA 19154

The Federation of Western
  Outdoor Clubs
512½ Boylston E. #106
Seattle, WA 98102

National Audobon Society
950 Third Avenue
New York, NY 10022

National Wildlife Federation
1412 16th Street, N.W.
Washington, DC 20036

The New England Trail
  Conference
P.O. Box 115
West Pawlet, VT 05775

Potomac Appalachian Trail Club
1718 N. Street, N.W.
Washington, DC 20036

Sierra Club
530 Bush Street
San Francisco, CA 94108

U.S. Forest Service
Box 3623
Information Office
Portland, OR 97208

U.S. Geological Survey
(Areas West of Mississippi)
P.O. Box 25286
Federal Center
Denver, CO 80255

"I'M GIVING UP—EXERCISE IS BORING"

How many times have you heard someone or even perhaps yourself say, *"I'm giving up. Exercise is boring"*. Over 65% of people who start an exercise program abandon it after 4-6 weeks. Surprising, isn't it? Not really! Initial enthusiasm is often quickly replaced by boredom. Most of the exercise equipment and athletic clothes quickly find their way into the recesses of the closet.

Walking fortunately is one of the only exercises that the majority of people stay with. The percentage of people who give up walking as a regular form of exercise is less than 25% of those who start on a walking program. Perhaps it's because walking doesn't require special equipment or clothing. Or perhaps it's because there are no clubs to join or dues to pay. Or perhaps it's just that most walkers are usually rugged individualists and are more determined than most to keep in good shape.

I think the real reason that walkers stay with their walking program is simply that *walking is fun!* And isn't that what an exercise should be? True, we all want physical fitness, good health, weight control and longevity. But we also want an escape from the stress of everyday living, and that's simply having fun. Walking provides a stress-free, fun-filled activity that we can do anyplace, anywhere, anytime whatsoever. Here are some tips to keep your walking program interesting, enjoyable and most of all, filled with fun.

1. Don't expect results too soon. Whether it's fitness or weight-control that you're looking for remember, *"Rome wasn't built in a day and neither were you"*. Give your body time to adapt to your regular walking program.

2. Make your walking program convenient and flexible. The more adaptable you are to when and where you walk, the more likely you are to do it on a regular basis.

3. Vary your walking program. One week walk 1/2 hour every day and the next week walk an hour every other day.

4. Change your walking route every week or two. If near home or work, walk a different way and observe, feel and smell new sights, sounds and odors on your new route.

5. Keep a record of your walking program. For example, how long did you walk today, and approximately how far did you walk? Record the time and location of your walk and your impressions of the area in which you walked. Maybe it's an area you'd like to stay away from or one you'd like to explore again.

6. Record your weight once every week to see if you are losing the amount of weight you'd like to or are just walking to maintain your present weight. Remember walkers who want to maintain their present weight usually can have a bonus snack everyday without gaining an ounce (see Chapter 4).

7. Either walk alone or with a friend or relative. Walking can be a social activity as well as an exercise. Spending time with someone you like or love can certainly add to the enjoyment of your walking program. Walking is one of the only exercises that lets you talk as you walk. If you are unable to talk because of shortness of breath then you're probably walking too fast.

8. *Talk a walk-break instead of a coffee-break.* Walking actually clears the mind and puts vitality and energy back into your body's walking machine. Coffee and a donut add caffeine and sugar to your body's sitting machine. Both the caffeine and sugar cause your insulin production to be increased, and following an initial rise in blood sugar, there is a sharp drop in your blood sugar from this excess insulin. So instead of coming back to work invigorated as you do from a walk-break, you come back fatigued, light-headed and dizzy from a coffee-donut-break.

9. *Buy or borrow a dog.* Studies show that dog-owners who actually walk their dogs have a built-in incentive to stay on a walking program. If you're not a dog person but need a hook to hang your walking program on, there are a number of shops that sell pedometers to keep track of the miles that you walk. Many stores now also carry walking sticks for dress or protection when you walk. These sticks can also help you climb hills if you are hiking and can act as a handy weapon if you have need to use one.

10. *Don't be afraid to take a break for a few days or even a week.* Any exercise program, even one as easy and fun-filled as walking can eventually become a little tiring. A few days break from your schedule will give you a short-breather so that you can return to your walking program with renewed interest and enthusiasm. Remember, you won't gain all of your weight back or get out of shape if you take an occasional break from your walking program.

11. *Never exercise if you are injured or ill.* Your body needs time to heal and recuperate from whatever ails you. Remember, you can't exercise through an injury or an illness. Many so-called fitness-nuts have tried this with disastrous results. For example, a strained muscle has been aggravated into a fractured bone or a simple cold has turned into pneumonia. Listen to your body. It's smarter than your brain.

12. *Promise yourself a treat when you stick to your walking program.* For example: a night at the theatre, a movie, a candle-light dinner, a new dress or a weekend away. Indulge yourself. You deserve it!

YOUR PERSONAL FITNESS CALENDAR

On a cold, crisp, clear January day,
A brisk walk keeps colds and flu away.

Avoid February's bitter, cold chill,
With a walk instead of a doctor's pill.

After deepest winter comes the March thaw,
Which makes walking fun and not a chore.

Don't be afraid of a light April shower,
Take your umbrella and walk for an hour.

Nothing can beat the lovely month of May,
A walk amongst the flowers makes you feel O.K.

You can feel just great in the days of June,
By walking happily and whistling a merry tune.

Even though there's heat and humidity in July,
Don't let an early morning or late evening walk go by.

Don't forget those hot steamy days of August,
An air-conditioned stationary bike is enough for us.

Oh how we love those beautiful days of September,
Those are the walks that we always remember.

Nothing can be more lovely than October's beautiful trees,
To walk amidst the colorful, spectacular falling leaves.

By the time we feel November's winds a' blowing,
Walkers know it's time to button up and get going.

As December's festive holiday season grows near,
Walk merrily along for good health and good cheer.

CHAPTER 14

FEARLESS FIBER VS. KILLER KOLESTEROL

AMERICA'S STARTING TO THINK LEAN

According to the U.S. Department of Agriculture, the dietary habits of Americans have changed significantly in the past 20 years. Although we are consuming more total calories, we are shifting our eating habits to more nutritious foods. The shift away from animal products has been motivated primarily by health concerns. Keep up the good work, America, and remember to **walk off those extra calories**.

AMERICA'S DIETARY HABITS — 1966 VS. 1986

CALORIES CONSUMED (per person, per day)

1966	3,180
1986	3,450

FOOD CONSUMED (per person, per year)

All Food

1966	1,368 lb.
1986	1,417 lb.

Meat

1966	154 lb.
1986	151 lb.

Fish

1966	11 lb.
1986	13 lb.

Poultry

1966	38 lb.
1986	66 lb.

Eggs

1966	309 eggs
1986	254 eggs

Vegetables
1966_____187 lb.
1986_____207 lb.

Fruits
1966_____120 lb.
1986_____143 lb.

Flour, Cereals
1966_____144 lb.
1986_____150 lb.

Coffee
1966_____38 gal.
1986_____26 gal.

Sweeteners
1966_____111 lb.
1986_____136 lb.

Milk
1966_____33 gal.
1986_____27 gal.

FIBER FACTS

What is fiber? In the first half of the 19th century the term **crude fiber** was the generally accepted term used in the food tables. This measurement, however, was not for human purposes. The definition of crude fiber was described as the plant food remaining after the food had been boiled first in acid and then in alkali. Crude fiber includes only a few of the actual fiber components of plants; however, it was the description used on most food packages until recently.

Dietary fiber is a newer measurement and refers to all fiber components of plants including crude fiber. It is therefore a more accurate measurement of the fiber content of foods. The dietary fiber content consequently has a higher numerical reading than grams of crude fiber. Fiber, commonly known as **bulk** or **roughage**, is the part of plant foods that cannot be digested completely, so that it passes through the digestive tract intact. Therefore, dietary fiber is the fiber content of food which is resistant to the human digestive enzymes.

The function of fiber: The most important function of dietary fiber is to **bind water** in the intestine in the form of a gel. This gel prevents over-absorption from the large intestine and insures that the stool content of the large bowel is both bulky and soft and consequently its passage through the intestine is not delayed. Another important function of fiber is its effect on the metabolism, absorption, and reabsorption of **bile acids and cholesterol**. Dietary fiber actually binds or attaches to both cholesterol and bile acids and consequently decreases their absorption from the bowel. It is now recognized that there are a number of diseases and disorders which are, at least in part, caused by a lack of dietary fiber (Burkitt, P.D., Trowell, H.C., eds. Refined Carbohydrate Foods and Disease, New York (London): Academic Press, 1975). These diet-related diseases can be classified as follows:

1. **Gastrointestinal disorders:** constipation, diverticulosis, appendicitis, hiatal hernia, hemorrhoids, cancer of the colon.
2. **Metabolic disorders:** Obesity, diabetes, gallstones.
3. **Cardiovascular disorders:** atherosclerosis (coronary artery disease) and varicose veins.

A recent study has shown that these diseases are now becoming prevalent in countries which have introduced western dietary customs. There is almost an inverse relationship between the amount of **fiber** consumed and the prevalence of these various diseases in different countries. The higher the intake of dietary fiber, the lower the incidence of the above named disorders.

* * * * * * *

The latest medical report on high fiber foods indicates that there may possibly be a *cancer-protecting substance* actually contained in some dark green and dark yellow vegetables and fruits. The substance known as **beta-carotene** (a nutrient that the body converts into Vitamin A) is found in high concentration in spinach, carrots, broccoli, brussel sprouts, cauliflower, winter squash, cabbage, oranges, grapefruit, apricots and peaches. These high fiber foods also contain large amounts of vitamin C. Both vitamins may possibly be protective against cancer of the lung, esophagus, stomach, large bowel and skin in some patients.

LOSE WEIGHT BY INCREASING FIBER IN THE DIET

Dietary fiber is the part of plants that is resistant to the breakdown by enzymes in our digestive tract. Many physicians believe that dietary fiber is an extremely important part of our diet and are advising their patients to increase the amount of fiber in their diet by eating more fruits, vegetables and whole grain cereals and breads.

Epidemiologic studies have shown that the western diet has become progressively **fiber deficient** over the past half-century, whereas the diet in under-developed countries is extremely high in fiber. This fact stems from the progressive elimination of fiber (the unabsorbable portion of the plant food) in western diets as a result of the **milling of flour** which removes the outer layer or covering (bran) of the wheat kernel. Bran is one of the most concentrated sources of food fiber.

High-fiber diets have been reported by a major medical university to be **excellent weight reduction diets**. Not only have these diets been effective in treating obese diabetic patients, but they have had marked effects on obese non-diabetics also. The following simplified high-fiber diet has been recommended for weight reduction:

1. **Whole grain products** (bran and whole grain cereals, and brown long grain rice)
2. **Whole grain bread** (stone ground or whole wheat)
3. **Garden vegetables** (carrots, celery, cabbage, green beans, lettuce, onion, corn, peas, tomatoes, potatoes)
4. **Fruits** (apples, oranges, pears, bananas, strawberries, blueberries, plums, peaches and cherries)
5. **Miller's bran:** Miller's bran is a dry wheat powder which is a convenient high dietary fiber. Each level teaspoon of miller's bran contains 2 grams of dietary fiber. Miller's bran may be sprinkled on cereal or other foods, or it may be mixed in with orange or tomato juice to improve its taste.
6. **Oat bran:** Oat bran is the newest entry into the fiber market. Recent evidence has indicated that oat bran has a more marked cholesterol-lowering effect than other types of dietary fiber.

A high-fiber diet is essentially a normal diet which has been changed to minimize or decrease the intake of refined foods. This encourages the consumption of fresh fruits, vegetables, whole grain cereals and breads. When the fiber is eaten from a variety of food sources, it produces its most beneficial effect, especially when it is eaten with each meal of the day.

Dietary fiber takes longer to chew and eat with the subsequent development of more saliva and a larger bulk swallowed with each mouthful. The larger bulk helps to fill the stomach and causes a decrease in hunger before more calories are consumed. High fiber diets help to provide bulk without energy, and may reduce the amount of energy absorbed from the food that is eaten. These high fiber diets are often referred to as having a low energy density and appear to prevent excessive caloric (energy) intake. Countries that consume high fiber diets rarely have obesity problems.

HIGH FIBER FOODS

FRUIT GROUP: Each serving of the below named fruits has approximately 2 grams of fiber.

apple	1 pear
banana	1 medium peach
½ cup of strawberries	2 small plums
1 small orange	10 large cherries

BREAD GROUP: Each serving has approximately 2 grams of fiber.

whole wheat bread	bran muffin
wheat bread (cracked)	stone ground bread

CEREAL GROUP: Each serving has approximately 2 grams of fiber.

shredded wheat - ½ biscuit	oatmeal 3 tbsps.
puffed wheat - 1 & ⅓ cups	wheat bran - 1 tsp.
corn flakes - ⅔ cup	grape nuts - 3 tbsps.

Cereals highest in fiber are 40% Bran, All Bran, Grape Nuts, Shredded Wheat, Whole Wheat Flakes, Raisin Bran, and all of the newer oat-bran cereals.

VEGETABLES GROUP: Each serving has approximately 2 grams of fiber.

celery - 1 cup	2 cups of lettuce
1 corn on the cob-2 inches	½ cup green beans
2 tbsps. baked beans	1 medium potato
1 medium raw tomato	4 brussels sprouts
½ stalk of broccoli	⅓ cup carrots

The following vegetables are highest in fiber: artichokes, green beans, cabbage, cauliflower, brussels sprouts, dried peas and beans, lima beans and peas.

MISCELLANEOUS GROUP: Each serving has approximately 1 gram of fiber.

2½ tsps. of peanut butter   10 peanuts
5 tbsps. of strawberry jam   1 large pickle

The following miscellaneous items also have higher than average fiber content: popcorn, chunky peanut butter, relishes, Miller's bran and wheat germ.

CHOLESTEROL: SINNER OR SAINT?

Cholesterol is a **fat-like substance** normally found in all living tissue and is an essential chemical for health. It is found in every cell and fluid in the body. Although it resembles fat in many ways, it has a completely different chemical structure called **steroid lipids**. Cholesterol also differs from fat in that it is not used by the body as food for the production of energy.

Cholesterol is extremely important, however, in the **metabolism of fat** and the production of **hormones** in the body. It is equally important in the formation of **bile salts** which aid in our digestion. **Cholesterol** also forms an important structural component of **membranes** (walls) of all the body's cells.

Since the body requires a certain amount of cholesterol all the time, it is manufactured naturally in our bodies, primarily in the liver. So, what's the problem? It looks as if cholesterol is pretty good for our health. Well it is, providing there's not too much of it. Unfortunately, we also get cholesterol into our bodies in the food we eat and that is where the problem begins.

Medical research has shown that when we take in **too much cholesterol** in our diets, the amount of cholesterol in our blood begins to rise. Once there is an excessive amount of cholesterol circulating in our blood stream, it starts to build up in the walls of the arteries. These yellow-rubbery deposits of cholesterol called **plaques** narrow the passageway of the artery (hardening of the arteries). This condition often leads to **heart attacks** and **strokes** since not enough blood can get through these narrowed blood vessels.

WHAT IS SATURATED FAT?

It is present in all products of **animal origin**—meat, fish, fowl, eggs, butter, milk, cream and cheese. Saturated fats are also found in **vegetable products** which are usually solid or semi-solid at room temperature. They include **shortenings** and **table spreads** which have been changed from liquid fats (usually cottonseed and soybean oils) into solids by a process called **hydrogenation**. This process makes the products more suitable for table use and prevents them from becoming rancid. However, this process converts polyunsaturated fats into **saturated fats.**

Other saturated fats in the vegetable kingdom include **cocoa butter, palm oil** and **coconut oil.** Most people are unaware of the fact that they consume considerable amounts of coconut and palm oil. It is used commercially in a wide variety of processed foods, baked goods and deep-fat fried products.

Saturated fats are dangerous because they can increase the amount of **cholesterol** in the blood. These fats can raise the level of blood cholesterol as much as, if not more than, the actual consumption of dietary cholesterol products.

WHAT ARE UNSATURATED FATS?

1. **Monosaturated fats** (neutral fats) are usually liquid at room temperature and tend to harden or cloud when refrigerated. They are the primary fats found in **olive oil, peanut oil** and most **nuts**. They are also present in small amounts in meats, dairy products and some vegetables. Olive oil has been found to have a cholesterol-lowering effect, according to recent medical evidence.

2. **Polyunsaturated fats** (essential fatty acids) are always of **vegetable origin** and are **liquid oils. Safflower oil** is the highest in polyunsaturates of all oils. Sunflower oil is second, followed by corn oil, sesame seed oil, soybean oil, cottonseed oil, walnut oil and linseed oil.

Polyunsaturated fats and monosaturated fats both help to **lower the blood cholesterol level** by assisting the body to eliminate excessive amounts of newly manufactured cholesterol. Don't just add polyunsaturated fats to your diet. It is essential that you substitute polyunsaturated fats for saturated fats to maximize their cholesterol-lowering effect.

It is interesting to note that we can manufacture saturated fat and most monosaturated fats in our bodies. However, polyunsaturated fats must be obtained from the diet and are, therefore, called **essential fatty acids**.

LOSE WEIGHT BY LIMITING INTAKE OF CHOLESTEROL AND SATURATED FAT

Controlling our weight by reducing the amount of cholesterol in our diet has a two-fold benefit. First of all it will help control and maintain our weight. Second, it will have a beneficial effect on the prevention of cardiovascular and cerebrovascular disease, since, as we have seen, these illnesses have been associated with high levels of blood cholesterol.

The typical **American diet** has a higher fat content than nearly any other country in the world. There is little doubt that this increased fat intake in our diet is responsible for the development of **obesity**, as well as many other disorders. **Fat** is the most concentrated source of calories, since a gram of dietary fat supplies your body with **9 calories**. This is compared to only 4 calories per gram of protein or carbohydrate. Since fat has this concentrated source of calories, it is the **most fattening** type of food that we consume and it stands to reason that cutting down on the fat intake is one of the best ways to cut down on the total amount of calories and maintain normal body weight.

Foods that are of **plant origin** do not contain cholesterol. These include fruits, vegetables, grains, cereals, nuts and vegetable oils (coconut oil and palm oil are two exceptions which incidentally are used in baked goods, snack foods and deep-fried foods). Always choose liquid or unsaturated vegetable oils, rather than solid or hydrogenated vegetable oil products, since these **polyunsaturated** liquid oils help to lower your blood cholesterol. Safflower oil, sunflower oil and corn oil are excellent choices. These polyunsaturated oils have no cholesterol in them. They also help to lower excessive amounts of cholesterol that the body itself manufactures.

Saturated fats, on the other hand, include products of **animal origin**. These fats are found in eggs, milk, butter, cheese, dairy products, meat, fowl and fish. These saturated fats are also found in some vegetable products which include table spreads (margarine) and shortenings which have been *hydrogenated* (changing liquid oils into solids or semi-solids). Although this hydrogenation process makes these products useful for table spreads and shortenings, it however changes them from polyunsaturated fats to saturated fats. Since these saturated fats raise both the total fat content and the cholesterol levels in our bodies, they should be avoided in our diets.

CHOLESTEROL CONTENT OF FOODS

MEAT, FISH AND POULTRY HIGH IN CHOLESTEROL

fatty cuts beef, pork, ham, veal and mutton

duck, goose

organ meats (kidney, liver, heart, sweetbread and brain)

luncheon meats and canned meats; sausage

sardines, herring

shell fish (shrimp, lobster, crab, clams, oyster, scallops)

MEAT, FISH AND POULTRY LOW IN CHOLESTEROL

chicken and turkey without skin

fresh fish (flounder, cod, bass sole, perch, haddock, halibut, salmon, trout, tuna, carp, pike)

tuna and salmon packed in water or with oil drained

lean ground meat and very lean cuts of beef, pork, ham and veal

DAIRY PRODUCTS HIGH IN CHOLESTEROL

whole milk, 2% low-fat milk still has 5 grams of fat

butter

cheeses

eggs

creams (sour, whipped, half & half, ice cream, cheeses made from whole milk or cream)

dairy and non-dairy coffee creamers

DAIRY PRODUCTS LOW IN CHOLESTEROL

non-fat or skimmed milk

low-fat buttermilk

yogurt (low-fat)

cocoa

LOW IN CHOLESTEROL
(Continued)

canned evaporated non-fat
milk
margarine high in poly-
unsaturates
egg substitutes

cheese made from
skimmed milk
egg white
low-fat cheeses
low-fat cottage cheese

BREAD AND CEREALS HIGH IN CHOLESTEROL

commercial muffins
biscuits
donuts
mixes containing whole
milk, butter and eggs

rolls and buns
coffee cakes
crackers
white bread
corn bread

BREAD AND CEREALS LOW IN CHOLESTEROL

whole wheat, French,
Italian, pumpernickel and
rye breads
homemade cookies, muffins
and biscuits, if made with
margarine or polyunsatur-
ated oil

cereals, hot and cold (whole
grain and bran type,
served with low-fat milk)
English muffins
bran muffins
matzo, soda crackers,
bread sticks

OTHER FOODS LOW IN CHOLESTEROL

most fish except shell fish
pastas, noodles and rice—
whole grain types
raw or cooked vegetables
without sauces or butter
or margarine
fruits and vegetables—
fresh, frozen or canned
with no sugar or syrup
added
beverages include tea, coffee
carbonated drinks

dried beans and peas,
including split peas,
chick peas, soybeans,
lentils, baked beans and
beans. (Since dried beans
and peas are high in
protein and low in
cholesterol, they can be
substituted for meat,
except for certain
essential amino acids)

DESSERTS & SNACKS HIGH IN CHOLESTEROL

commercial pies

pastries

cookies

cake

puddings

cocoa butter

whipped cream

ice cream

fried foods

snack foods

coconut

potato and corn chips

DESSERTS & SNACKS LOW IN CHOLESTEROL
(high in calories, however)

home baked pastries and
   pies (made with non-fat
   milk, liquid polyunsaturated
   oil and egg whites)
commercial gelatins
honey, marmalade
imitation ice cream (made with
   low-fat milk)
nuts

cookies, cakes and puddings
   made with unsaturated oil
   and non-fat milk
sherbet, ice milk
angel food cake, yellow
   cake (made with egg white
   only)
pure peanut butter

* * * * *

Boiling, baking, roasting and broiling are recommended so that the fat can be discarded. When frying, use only oil high in polyunsaturates like safflower, sunflower or corn oil and never reuse the oil, since it hardens and become partially saturated.

HOW CEREALS RATE IN FIBER, SUGAR, AND FAT

Adding fiber to the diet helps us reduce the risk of heart disease, colon disease and some cancers. But some high-fiber cereals contain heavy doses of sugar, while those low in sugar have little fiber. The Center for Science in the Public Interest groups 53 cereals by fiber and sugar content.

CEREAL	SERVING	FIBER	SUGAR
HOT CEREALS			
(Based on cooked cereal)			
MEDIUM FIBER			
Ralston High-fiber Cereal	⅔ c	5	0
Wheatena	⅚ c	4.5	0
Oat Bran[1]	⅔ c	4	0
Oatmeal, Quick[1]	⅔ c	3	0
LOW FIBER			
Cream of Wheat	¾ c	1	0
Cream of Rice	¾ c	0	0
COLD CEREALS			
HIGHEST FIBER			
All Bran w/Extra Fiber[2]	½ c	14	0
Fiber One[2]	½ c	13	0
100% Bran	½ c	10	18
All Bran	½ c	10	18
Bran Buds	½ c	10	25
MEDIUM FIBER, LOW SUGAR			
Shredded Wheat'n Bran	⅔ c	4	0
NutriGrain Nuggets	¼ c	4	3[3]
Wheat Chex	⅔ c	4	7
Wheat Germ	¼ c	3	0
Shredded Wheat	⅔ c	3	0
NutriGrain Corn	½ c	3	7[3]
NutriGrain Wheat	⅔ c	3	7[3]
Wheaties	1 c	2	11
Cheerios	1¼ c	2	3
Grape Nuts	¼ c	2	11[3]
MEDIUM FIBER, SWEETENED			
Nutrific Oatmeal Flakes	¾ c	6	32
Bran Chex	⅔ c	5	18
Bran Flakes	⅔ c	5	18
Mueslix Bran	⅓ c	4	39
Kellogg's Raisin Bran	½ c	4	32
Fruitful Bran	⅔ c	4	28
Fruit & Fibre	½ c	4	46
Post Raisin Bran	½ c	3	53
Fruit Wheats	½ c	3	18

Frosted Mini-Wheats	¾ c	3	21
Strawberry or Raisin Squares	½ c	3	18
Amazin' Raisin Bran	1 c	3	42
Raisin Nut Bran	½ c	3	25
Bran Muffin Crisp	⅔ c	3	32
Mueslix Five Grain	⅓ c	3	42
Grape Nuts Flakes	⅞ c	2	18
Just Right, Nugget & Flakes	⅔ c	2	18
Pro-Grain	¾ c	2	39

LOW-FIBER

Corn Chex	1 c	1	11
Rice Chex	1⅛ c	5	7
Kellogg's Corn Flakes	1 c	1	7
Product 19	1 c	1	11
Nut 'n Honey Crunch	⅔ c	0	32
Crispy Wheat n' Raisins	¾ c	0	35
Crispix	1 c	0	11
Rice Krispies	1 c	0	11
Special K	1 c	0	11
Honey Nut Cheerios	¾ c	0	35

HIGH FAT

Cracklin' Oat Bran	½ c	5	25
Quaker 100% Natural	¼ c	2	25
C.W. Post Family Style	¼ c	1	25
Nature Valley Granola	⅓ c	1.3	21

Note: All nutrient data comes from the manufacturers

[1]A good source of soluble fiber, which can help lower blood
cholesterol. Most other high-fiber cereals are rich in soluble
fiber, which helps prevent constipation, diverticulosis and
possibly colon cancer.
[2]Sweetened with aspartame (NutraSweet)
[3]Naturally occurring sugar in grains and malt flavoring
Source: Center for Science in the Public Interest.

GET THE FAT OUT OF YOUR FACE!

A recent report by the National Heart, Lung and Blood
Institute showed that over 100,000 lives could be saved every

year by lowering cholesterol to a level of 180-200 mg. It is estimated that more than 35 million Americans have high blood cholesterol. A related study by the American College of Cardiology (3/84) showed that arteries which were blocked with cholesterol could actually reopen again after people went on a low cholesterol diet. To lose weight on the outside of your body and fatty deposits inside your body, high-fiber, low-fat— is where's it's at!

The following are the new dietary recommendations for a *healthy heart and a trim diet start:*

A. **Limit fat to 25-30 percent of daily calories.**
    Most Americans consume more than 40 percent of their daily calories as fat. This amount should be reduced to 25-30 percent with only 10 percent of the fat calories coming from saturated fats (animal fats and whole milk dairy products, including cheeses, coconut and cocoa beans and solid vegetable oils).

B. **Limit cholesterol intake to 250-300 mg. daily.**
    Egg yolk is the most concentrated source of cholesterol in the American diet (274 mg in one egg yolk). Liver and other organ meats are very high. Shellfish, although low in saturated fat, is relatively high in cholesterol and should be limited to once every other week.

C. **Limiting protein to 20-25 percent of all calories daily.**
    Poultry without skin and fish are excellent sources of protein and are low in saturated fats.
    Plant protein such as beans, soybeans and legumes are also good sources of protein.

D. **Increasing complex carbohydrates to 45-50 percent of calories consumed daily.**
    Whole grain bread, cereal and pasta products, vegetables, legumes and fruits all provide excellent sources of vitamins, minerals and complex carbohydrates without fat.

E. A low cholesterol, low saturated fat diet will lower the **bad-**cholesterol (**LDL**) in the bloodstream, and prevent it from clogging up your arteries. **Walking** also helps to lower this bad-cholesterol (LDL) in your bloodstream.

F. **A regular walking program** will also raise the **good-cholesterol (HDL)** in your blood, which helps to remove the build-up of fat deposits in your blood vessels.

G. Follow the 10 Fabulous Foods that First start with an "F" For Fantastic Health:

1. Fruit
2. Fresh vegetables
3. Fish
4. Fowl
5. **Fettucini** (pastas, especially whole grain)
6. **Fiber** (whole grain breads and cereals, legumes and beans, seeds and nuts, and bran foods)
7. **Flour** (whole grain oat, wheat, corn, barley and bran)
8. **Fat-free** milk, cheeses, yogurt and mayonnaise
9. **Fabulous** fakes (artificial eggs, imitation butter, imitation mayonnaise, imitation cream cheeses, etc.)
10. **Fluids** (water, fruit juices, milk, decaffeinated teas, coffee and soda)

* * * * * * * * * * * *

Get the fat out of your face
And your big belly it will erase
A high-fiber, low-fat reducing diet
Will keep your brain's appestat quiet
As your body stays trim and lean
Your arteries will keep nice and clean
Combined with walking brisk and fast
This diet will make your lifetime last
And most of all you won't ever get obese
Nor will you develop any heart disease

"IF I CAN SOLVE DR. STUTMAN'S MYSTERY OF THE WALKING MEN, YOU WILL HAVE A VERY PRETTY CASE TO ADD TO YOUR COLLECTION, WATSON!"

CHAPTER 15

THE MYSTERY OF THE WALKING MEN

SHERLOCK HOLMES & DR. WATSON

As I awoke early one brisk Autumn morning to find Holmes in front of the window smoking his old briar feverishly while reading the Times, he looked up from his paper and asked, "Have you read the good news yet Watson."

"Well of course not Holmes as you've almost surely deduced, I've just awakened so how on earth could I have seen the morning papers."

"Just so my dear fellow. You invariably jump to the first conclusion that enters your mind. When I asked if you had read the good news yet, you instantly formed the conclusion that I was referring to this morning's paper. When in fact I meant the news that has appeared in the papers for the past two days, in addition to today's early edition of the *Times*."

"Forgive me Holmes for being so dense but as you can plainly see, I'm still half-asleep and haven't the foggiest idea of what news you're referring to, and besides you know that I have been quite busy for these past some days with patients at hospital."

"I realize that Watson, I'm just having my bit of fun. The good news that I am referring to involves your good friend from America."

"Now I'm more confused than ever", I said completely exasperated. "What friend are you now referring to Holmes. Out with it my dear fellow."

"Why your good friend and colleague Dr. Stutman from the United States Watson", he said matter-of-factly, "is setting sail for England at this very moment."

"Well why didn't you come straight out with it Holmes, instead of all this rigmarole. I do believe you delight in making a simple fact a confusing one. I really think you do it for the effect my good chap."

"You're right, Watson. You know there's always been a lot of the actor in me. *My turn that way is in my veins, and may have come with my grandmother who was the sister of Vernet, The French Artist. Art in the blood is liable to take the strangest forms.*"[1]

"What brings my old friend to England , Holmes? Does the paper or do the papers to be more specific, give the purpose of his visit?"

"Why yes Watson", Holmes shrugged. "They all give a similar account. It seems he is coming here to deliver a medical paper at the annual meeting of the National Association of Scientific Research in London next week. It also appears that the research is of a most secret nature and according to one reporter's account his medical research involves an extremely important formula which will revolutionize modern day medicine. Beyond that Watson, most of the accounts are speculative and are not specific as to the content of this so-called miracle formula. His research, the reports state, has been a closely guarded American secret and will only be revealed at this year's annual scientific meeting. I don't suppose you have any idea as to what the doctor is working on, since you do correspond with him from time to time?"

"I wish I knew what it all was about Holmes, but I haven't had a letter from the good doctor for over 6 months and he never discusses his research with me. He usually writes about his family, his medical practice and about the walking seminars that he conducts. You know that Dr. Stutman has been given the honorary title of Dr. Walk® by his patients, Holmes, since he has advocated walking as the ideal exercise for health and fitness, for nigh onto 25 years now. Aside from that he has never mentioned any specifics as to his research or any secret formula for that matter."

"That's too bad my dear fellow, for I fear that your friend may be in some grave danger."

"What's that Holmes? You mentioned nothing about reading any such thing in the papers. Let me have a look at

[1]Sir Arthur Conan Doyle, "The Greek Interpreter," in *The Memoirs of Sherlock Holmes* (London: George Newnes, 1892; New York: Harper & Bros., 1894).

those papers Holmes. Where does it say that he is in danger?" As I took the two editions of the *Times* from him, yesterday's and today's, he stared blankly out of the window at the early morning traffic on Baker Street. When I finished reading both accounts of Dr. Stutman's visit, I looked up from my papers. Holmes hadn't moved a muscle or said a single word all the time that I was reading. "I fear that you are keeping something from me Holmes. You seem to know far more about this matter than appears in the accounts mentioned in these two editions of the *Times*. What additional news did you receive and from what source pray tell?"

"Yes you are perfectly right my dear fellow," he remarked. "Come and have a look at this letter and see what you make of it. Surely you know the doctor far better than I do, since I have only heard you speak of him, never actually having met him myself. Perhaps you can possibly account for his strange behavior in this most singular affair. Come Watson, let's see if you can shed some light on this strange little problem."

Holmes slowly opened the side drawer of his desk and withdrew a long tan-colored envelope which he handed to me. As I inspected the envelope, I noticed the familiar American stamps in the upper right hand corner covered with the U. S. Postmark from Phila. PA, that I knew so well as coming from my good friend in America. The only difference that I noticed at once was that instead of the envelope being addressed to me, it bore the name of Mr. Sherlock Holmes, 221B Baker Street, London, England. Holmes then extracted several sheets of paper from inside the envelope and handed them to me. "See what you make of this strange affair Watson."

DR. WALK'S® STRANGE LETTER

I opened the sheets of paper carefully noting the familiar tan-colored stationary with the printed name and address of Dr. Stutman at the heading of the 1st page. The following is an exact duplication of the pages that I now have before me.

My Dear Mr. Holmes,

Although you do not know me personally, I'm sure Dr. Watson must have mentioned me to you at one time or another. We met some many years ago at a medical convention in Philadelphia and have continued to correspond, although infrequently, these many years. We have become great friends over the years and he has told me of your wonderful successes in the field of criminal investigation and of your remarkable powers in the most complex of problems. Not that I needed him to tell me of your extraordinary faculties, since your famous exploits are known throughout the world. In the United States in particular, we have many organizations which are devoted to the study of your methods. Please forgive me, for I am wandering far from the point of this letter. I feel that I can trust you with a most singular problem that I truly believe no one else in the world would be so qualified to undertake.

As you probably have already learned by now from the papers, I'm scheduled to deliver a medical paper of the utmost importance at the annual meeting of the National Association of Scientific Research. This meeting is scheduled in London next week and I am supposedly on the S.S. Philadelphia en-route for England at this very moment. In truth however, I will be in hiding somewhere in the United States, by the time you receive this letter. The reason for this little deception will become apparent as you will see momentarily. As I'm sure the newspapers have already mentioned, the scientific paper which I am supposed to deliver at this year's meeting contains startling discoveries which I have made in the fields of bio-chemistry and medical physiology. Suffice it to say that I cannot be any more specific on the matter, since these findings are of the utmost secrecy.

The reason for this little deception is that I fear that I am in grave danger. My life has been threatened on numerous occasions by several so-called scientists, in particular one evil-looking mathematician, who first offered to pay me handsomely for the results of my discoveries. Once having learned that I would not part with the results of my research, these men threatened my life if I would not yield to their demands. In order to stall for time I finally convinced them that I would consider their proposal on the ocean voyage to England. They intimated that I would be closely watched until I arrived in London and that if I did not reveal my findings to them, I would never reach the conference alive.

You may not be aware, but I'm sure Dr. Watson is, that I have a twin brother who is a rough sort of fellow and has served a fair amount of time in the state penitentiary for various crimes, armed robbery among them. It just so happened that he had recently been released from prison and was on parole at this very time. I explained the situation to him and he was quite willing to change places with me and spend a paid holiday vacation in England, at my expense. I arranged with his parole officer that he be released into my custody for the next 6 weeks, having given my word of honor that I would be responsible for his behavior. He certainly will be able to take care of himself with respect to these thugs who have threatened my life. They will have a sorry time if they try to tangle with him, since he holds the middle-weight prison boxing title for some many years now. When once they discover that he is not I, it will be too late to prevent the results of my research from being delivered at the scientific meeting. My brother has been apprised of the danger involved; however, he is quite willing and even ready, for that matter, to take the risk. He feels that he would finally like to be on the right side of the law, in our efforts to make public these important findings of my research.

Now then, enough of my story and more to the point, actually the first point of my letter. I would very much like my good friend, Dr. Watson, to represent me at this year's meeting and what's more I would appreciate immensely his reading my scientific paper at the convention. I truly believe that he will be in no danger, since these thugs will have no way of knowing that he will be acting in my behalf. Once the paper is read and its contents become public knowledge, they will be powerless to interfere.

The results of my research will have a profound effect on the lives of every man and woman on the face of the earth. I fear I can say no more, for even now I feel as if I am being watched. It is imperative that these findings reach the eyes and ears of the medical profession before they fall into the hands of these unscrupulous evil enemy agents, who will use these findings for their own personal gain. Please believe me when I say that if these findings fall into the wrong hands, the fate of the world will be held in the balance.

And now for my second point or request for that matter. I have coded the scientific formula of my findings in a cipher, should this letter be intercepted before it reaches you. This would surely prevent the formula from falling into the wrong hands. I got the idea of the cipher from one of your cases that Dr. Watson was good enough to share with me when he was visiting the states one summer a few years ago. Once having decoded the cipher, I pray that you'll give it promptly to Dr. Watson so that he may deliver it to the meeting henceforth. To further ensure secrecy, I have enclosed the cipher under separate cover, so as to further minimize the chance of two separate letters from being intercepted. I have devised what I feel is a most singular method of posting these envelopes, which I will go into in further detail at the end of this letter. If for some reason you receive the cipher without this explanatory letter, I believe that your extraordinary powers will still allow you to unravel the cipher and its meaning, by your deductive reasoning process. If on the other hand the letter and not the cipher reaches you, then no matter, I will have done all that could, using my limited powers, in an attempt to make my formula public knowledge.

I realize that by the time you receive the cipher you will probably only have a week before the meeting to decipher the code. But I and my American colleagues have great faith in your ability to do the impossible. We have read with great interest and awe your exploits as described by my dear friend, Dr. Watson. He has said on numerous occasions to me that your amazing deductive feats have never been equaled in the history of detection and criminal investigation. My esteemed colleague, the famous former Medical Examiner of Philadelphia, Dr. Aronson has said of you, that your deductive powers are the finest in the world and that once you set your mind upon a problem you would never rest until its solution was made apparent to you. The only way that mankind can be made safe, is if this secret formula is made public. For if in fact it falls into the hands of unscrupulous persons then I fear all is lost, for they will most certainly use these findings for evil purposes.

And so I must end my letter now, for as I have already said I am being watched closely. As I mentioned earlier in this letter, I have devised a method of posting this letter which I believe you would approve of hardily. Tonight, I will be attending the fall meeting of the *Sons of The Copper Beeches,* which is one of the numerous Sherlock Holmes organizations throughout the United States devoted to studying your methods. Once there, I will distribute a dozen similar envelopes bearing your name and address, to the twelve members in whom I have the utmost trust. Ten of the envelopes will contain nothing more than a blank sheet of paper. The eleventh envelope will contain this letter and the twelfth will contain the actual cipher. Since I will prepare the envelopes in advance, none of the twelve men will know which envelope they are carrying. I have asked each to post the letter at a different post office to further minimize the risk of any of these letters from being intercepted. I myself will post a thirteenth letter, also addressed to you which will contain only a personal message to Dr. Watson. These twelve men have not been given any of the particulars of this singular affair; however, being ardent followers of your exploits, they have consented to participate, because of my known friendship with Dr. Watson.

I feel that I have done everything humanly possible to ensure that you will receive both the letter and the cipher unopened and intact. Perhaps if I had had you to consult regarding this plan you might have been able to advise me of a more singular solution. However, I have had to devise this plan based on your deductive reasoning studies, using my own limited experience in such matters, without actually consulting the master. So be it!

I hope this letter finds you and Dr. Watson in good health. I look forward to hearing from you at your earliest convenience. Although I have left no forwarding address, my man Ekim will see that all correspondence reaches me. I realize that I have placed a heavy burden upon you, but unfortunately no one else in the world would be capable of performing so complicated and dangerous a feat. You have my deepest respect and admiration. My fellow colleagues of the *Sons of The Copper Beeches* also wish you well and send their very best regards.

Very truly yours,

Fred A. Stutman, M.D.
(Dr. Walk®)

"Well Watson, your friend has presented us with a very pretty little problem. Don't you think so, my good man?"

"I must confess Holmes, I can't understand the need for all of this secrecy. Why couldn't he just send the formula without resorting to ciphers and multiple envelopes with blank papers. I feel that the doctor has made a relatively simple problem a much more complicated one. I'm afraid my dear fellow that he has been reading too many of my accounts of your adventures and has by way of these stories imagined himself embroiled in a mystery plot that doesn't exist."

"I fear not, my dear fellow. You have heard the account of

his own experiences with these gangsters. How could you possibly think that he is exaggerating this affair? The doctor is not prone to delusions, is he Watson?"

"No, no," I protested. "I only meant that he may in fact have exaggerated the actual danger itself. I can't for the life of me believe that these thugs would murder the doctor for a formula. What possible use could they derive from such a thing? How on earth could they use new medical findings for evil purposes?"

"There, there, Watson," said my friend condescendingly. "You have the unique ability to see a romantic mystery when there is none and to see nothing whatsoever when one is actually staring you right in the face. And to answer your questions, Watson, you must know by this time that *It is a capital mistake to theorize before you have all the evidence.*[2] No my dear fellow, I believe we have before us a most singular problem, one that I hope will be reported one day in your accounts of my cases and I pray that you will be able to recount a successful conclusion to this interesting and surely complicated case."

"I'm not too sure that you're correct in this matter, for I know the doctor far better than you do Holmes and I think that he is exaggerating the details of this formula-cipher in order to impress you. You know Holmes, these American chaps are in effect besot with your deductive powers and have gone a bit too far, in my opinion, by forming these little clubs devoted to studying your methods. I should think that these fellows would have better things to do with their time."

"I quite agree with you there my dear fellow. I think that they take your accounts of my exploits far too seriously and should, in fact, put their free time towards more constructive hobbies and activities. Although, Watson, I must confess that these fellows have very little to stimulate their deductive reasoning thought processes, since most of the crime in America is done by thugs, mobsters and hoodlums. There is very little opportunity to study the feats of the great criminal minds as we do here in London, my dear fellow."

"But Holmes," I protested. "Many of these men who belong to these little clubs are doctors, lawyers and professional men of all sorts. I would think that they would have better things to do, than to study criminology."

[2]Sir Arthur Conan Doyle, *A Study in Scarlet* (London: Ward Lock, 1887).

"Not so my good man," Holmes insisted. "These fellows in all probability lead mundane, uneventful lives and feel that your little accounts of my deductive powers will bring excitement and stimulation into their daily bleak existences."

"Now Holmes, I think you are exaggerating a bit," I said, trying not to lose my temper.

"On the contrary Watson, it is you who have embellished your accounts of my cases and have exaggerated my deductive powers in your pretty little stories . . . *Detection is, or ought to be, an exact science, and should be treated in the same cold and unemotional manner. You have attempted to tinge it with romanticism, which produces much the same effect as if you worked a love-story or an elopement into the fifth proposition of Euclid.*"[3]

"I can't say that this is getting us anywhere Holmes. Why don't you concentrate on the problem at hand and leave the writing to me," I said indignantly. I felt that Holmes' ego being what it was, there was no sense in continuing this line of conversation any longer.

"I believe you're right, Watson. Let's see exactly what we have here. First here are twelve envelopes Watson. Ten contain nothing more than blank sheets of paper. The eleventh contained the letter that we have just read and the twelfth envelope contains a brief message to you Watson, which asks about your health and your medical practice. It also contains certain references to the doctor's children, two of whom have recently married and a third who is attending University. Here, come and have a look at it Watson and see if you can derive anything sinister out of this personal message."

After reading the letter carefully, I concluded that Holmes was correct. It was no more than a similar type of letter that I had been used to receiving from my friend. The only difference was that the envelope bore Holmes' name and not my own. "What about the thirteenth envelope, Holmes, and the cipher? Where is it my good man?"

"Patience Watson, if you read the explanatory letter carefully you would have remembered that the doctor said that each of the thirteen letters were sent by different people, from different post offices. The twelve envelopes that I have now before me were delivered over a period of four days. The

[3]Sir Arthur Conan Doyle, *The Sign of Four* (London: Ward Lock, 1890; Philadelphia: J.B. Lippincott, 1890).

thirteenth letter should be arriving shortly, my dear fellow. Ah, here is Mrs. Hudson with the mail Watson, and if I'm not much mistaken, here in fact is the thirteenth envelope which we have been waiting for. Mark well, Watson, today is the seventh day after the very first letter arrived. This fact in itself is a most singular occurrence."

THE MYSTERY OF THE WALKING MEN

As I watched Holmes' long thin fingers slit open the envelope with his letter opener, I could not but think that this whole affair was so completely uncharacteristic of my American friend. Although I knew him to be a man who possessed a great deal of scientific knowledge, I also knew that he was completely lacking in imagination. The idea of his conjuring-up a cipher was so very foreign to my knowledge of his personality. He was a man of few personal friends, yet to those who knew him, his sense of loyalty was unbounded. He was also known for his macabre sense of humor and he always enjoyed a good story or an amusing tale. But a cipher, I couldn't fathom such a thing as coming from my good friend. As I watched Holmes fingering the contents of the envelope, I became impatient and remarked rather loudly. "What have you got there Holmes? What is in that thirteenth envelope? Is it in fact a cipher? Well for God's sake Holmes, don't keep me in suspense any longer."

"Quite so my dear fellow," said Holmes quizzically. "Come and have a look at this and tell me what you make of it."

"I must confess that I can make very little of it Holmes," I said completely puzzled. "It just looks like a lot of nonsense to me. Why it's nothing more than an ordinary 4 x 6 index card with a child's drawing of what appears to be a string of cut-out dolls. I must confess, however, that these pictures vaguely remind me of something Holmes, but for the life of me I can't think of what."

"Why of course my good fellow," he said triumphantly. "It appears to be a series of pictures not unlike those in my case of *The Dancing Men,* that you were kind enough to chronicle for me, Watson. I fear, however, my good man that this case is what gave your friend the idea for his cipher. You really should be more careful, Watson, with whom you are discussing my cases. Although, I realize that the account of that sad affair has been fully published, you may have inadvertently given the doctor some confidential information concerning the case that we wished not to have made public knowledge."

"I beg your pardon, Holmes," I said crestfallen. " I did no such thing. Aside from a few minor details regarding the case, I told the doctor nothing more than what he had read in the published accounts. Besides Holmes, I resent the implication that I cannot be trusted in such matters."

"Don't disturb yourself my dear fellow, think no more of it. I fear that we have our work cut out for us in deciphering this cipher. As you can plainly see, Watson, these figures are not dancing men at all but are, in fact, small figures of men in various stages of walking. Some appear to be moving to the left and others to the right. Each you will notice, appears with varied combinations of either flexed arms and legs or extended arms and legs. It certainly is a pretty puzzle my dear fellow, and one at first glance that seems to be far more complicated than the cipher of *The Dancing Men*."

"Perhaps he has just used a similar cipher from your case and has applied it to these figures of the walking men."

"I rather doubt it Watson, for as you must certainly remember, the cipher in the case of *The Dancing Men* was one in which the symbols of the various figures of dancing men stood for letters of the alphabet. *And as you are aware, E is the most common letter in the English alphabet. Speaking roughly the letters T, A, O, I, N, S, H, R, D and L are the numerical order in which the other common letters occur.*[4] Once having matched these commonly appearing letters to the appropriate commonly occurring figures, the cipher was easily decoded. As you must already know Watson, *I am fairly familiar with all forms of secret writing, and am myself the author of a trifling monograph upon the subject, in which I analyze one hundred and sixty separate ciphers, but I must confess that this is entirely new to me.*[5] I fear that I am completely at sea regarding this most unusual, singular cipher."

"I beg your pardon Holmes, but you underestimate yourself my dear fellow. Your monograph is anything but trifling.

[4]Sir Arthur Conan Doyle, "The Dancing Men," in *The Return of Sherlock Holmes* (London: George Newnes, 1905; New York: McClure, Phillips, 1905).
[5]Ibid

Why, as you must surely know, Scotland Yard uses it almost exclusively as the standard textbook for deciphering secret messages of the utmost international significance."

"Yes, you're perfectly right Watson,"said my friend boastfully. "In fact, now that you mention it, I have even been asked to act in a consulting capacity for the American Secret Service, in decoding secret messages and difficult ciphers used in international espionage. I believe that I have not given this problem my fullest attention Watson, so that if you'll forgive me, my dear fellow, I must sit quietly without interruption in order to study this most singular cipher. *It is quite a three-pipe problem, and I beg that you won't speak to me for fifty minutes.*"[6]

I continued to watch Holmes deep in thought as he labored over the cipher. This went on not for fifty minutes, but hour upon hour, long into the night. I must have dozed off sometime before midnight when I suddenly awoke with a start, seeing that the room was filled with smoke. *In the dim light of the lamp I saw him sitting there, an old brier pipe between his lips, his eyes fixed vacantly upon the corner of the ceiling, the blue smoke curling up from him, silent, motionless, with the light shining upon his strong-set aquiline features.*[7] One good look into the ash tray led me to the deduction that this had been at least a seven or eight-pipe problem. Choking and coughing as I finally awoke, I exclaimed, "good God Holmes, what time is it already? I must have dozed off for some little time now. It must be the middle of the night already."

"Just one little moment pray tell, and I'll be with you presently," said my friend huskily. He then turned slowly to face me with a somber face and exclaimed, *"You have a grand gift of silence, Watson. It makes you quite invaluable as a companion."*[8] This cipher appears to be much more difficult than I had originally thought it to be. It has a few singular points that I have been able to unravel; however, the main body of the cipher is either so extraordinarily complicated or so incredibly simple that I am missing the point altogether."

"I still think that my friend has used some variation of

[6]Sir Arthur Conan Doyle, "The Red-Headed League," in *The Adventures of Sherlock Holmes* (London: George Newnes, 1892; New York: Harper & Bros., 1892).
[7]Sir Arthur Conan Doyle, "The Man with the Twisted Lip" in *The Adventures of Sherlock Holmes* (London: George Newnes 1892; New York: Harper & Bros., 1892).
[8]Ibid.

your code from *The Dancing Men,* Holmes. I can't believe that the doctor is ingenious enough to invent an entirely different code. I may not have mentioned it before Holmes, but although my friend possesses a great deal of scientific knowledge, I fear that he is a man of very little imagination. I firmly believe that a cipher is the last thing in the world that he would be able to devise. I can see him writing about medicine, health, fitness, dieting and, particularly, walking; but a cipher — preposterous! What ineffable twaddle!"

Holmes slowly turned towards me and exclaimed excitedly, *"I never get your limits, Watson . . . there are unexplored possibilities about you.*[9] You have done it again my good fellow."

"Done what," I said, feeling more than slightly puzzled.

"Why my good man, you've just pointed me towards the very clue that I've been seeking. You are like a beacon from a lighthouse Watson, steering a lost ship towards the very safety of the shore. What would I do without my Watson?"

"Well, I can't imagine what it was that I've actually said Holmes, but I'm gratified that I've been of some small assistance in this matter," trying not to look too pleased with myself. Feeling that I had scored handsomely, I thought that I might as well try to introduce another significant point that had been troubling me from the first about this affair. "Holmes," I said hesitatingly. "Why did the doctor not send the cipher and the letter in one envelope instead of resorting to this complicated multiple envelope charade?"

Holmes turned slowly towards me and smiled as he said, *"Your native shrewdness, my dear Watson, that innate cunning which is the delight of your friends, would surely prevent you from enclosing cipher and message in the same envelope."*[10]

Frankly, I couldn't be sure from Holmes' manner whether he was praising or mocking my question. I quickly changed the subject and stated matter of factly, "how much longer now do you think that it will take you to solve the riddle of the cipher Holmes, and pray tell what was the clue that I gave you that pointed you towards the solution?"

"By morning my dear fellow, if I know my ciphers, I

[9]Sir Arthur Conan Doyle, "The Sussex Vampire," in *The Case-Book of Sherlock Holmes* (London: John Murray, 1927; New York: Charles H. Doran 1927).
[10]Sir Arthur Conan Doyle, *The Valley of Fear* (London: Smith, Elder, 1915; New York: George H. Doran, 1915).

should have this little problem solved. I pray tell, Watson, you should now retire to your bedroom, for you are looking quite the worst for this affair. A good night's rest will do wonders for you. When you awaken I hope to have the answers to all of your little questions. Now leave me so that I may get on with my work."

I slowly dragged myself to my bed and sank into the down pillows without even removing my clothes. I remember before nodding off, that Holmes rarely ever needed sleep when he was embroiled in a case. He seemed more alert when I left him than most men are at the beginning of their workday.

THE THREE PART SOLUTION

I awoke shortly before dawn and observed a light glowing from the sitting room. I quietly entered the room and observed a few rays of light, sprinkled with dust particles, filtering through a crack in the window shade. I sat down in my easy chair and exclaimed, "My God Holmes, it's morning already. You are courting disaster with the hours that you keep. Your health will invariably suffer, my dear fellow, since even detectives must sleep from time to time." Although he said nothing. . . . *I observed that Holmes's eyes were shining and his cheeks tinged with color. Only at a crisis have I seen those battle-signals flying.*[11]

He turned slowly in my direction after he had finished lighting his pipe and sent a wreath of blue-gray smoke up towards the ceiling. "I'm glad to say Watson, that you have put me back on the right scent. *I had come to an entirely erroneous conclusion, which shows my dear Watson, how dangerous it always is to reason from insufficient data.*[12] You realize Watson, that when you off-handedly said that the doctor was a man of very little imagination, that you indeed unknowingly pointed me towards the correct solution to this little problem we have before us. You inadvertently said that

[11]Sir Arthur Conan Doyle, "The Golden Pince-nez", in *The Return of Sherlock Holmes* (London: George Newnes, 1905; New York: McClure, Phillips 1905).
[12]Sir Arthur Conan Doyle, "The Speckled Band," in *The Adventures of Sherlock Holmes* (London: George Newnes, 1892; New York: Harper and Brothers, 1892)

you could see your friend writing about and I quote . . . *'medicine, health, fitness, dieting and particularly walking; but a cipher—preposterous!'* That was it my good man. He wrote about what he knew."

"I'm afraid that I've lost you Holmes. What has that to do with decoding the cipher," said I, even more puzzled than before.

"Oh Watson, dear Watson, how many times have I told you to use your brain instead of you heart. You must carefully reason through a problem, although I must admit that *You have really done very well indeed.* Even though . . . *it is true that you have missed everything of importance.*[13] However, that is of no significant matter since you have acted as a lightening rod, diverting my bolt of genius towards the correct solution. *Some people without possessing genius have a remarkable power of stimulating it.*"[14]

"Yes, Yes Holmes, I quite agree that I have pointed you towards the solution. Now if you would be so kind as to explain the matter to me, perhaps we can get on with the case," said I, fully exasperated by this time.

"Quite so my dear fellow. You will remember Watson, when first I had studied the cipher, I stated that there were a few singular points about it which I was able to unravel; however, I was completely mystified by the main body of the cipher. As you have undoubtedly heard me often say Watson, *It is a capital mistake to theorize before one has data. Insensibly, one begins to twist facts to suit theories, instead of theories to suit facts.*[15] But enough of theory and now to the facts at hand. Mark well Watson, this whole affair can be explained simply in three separate parts. Each one, however, intertwined immeasurably with the others. I believe I can elucidate these three essential points before Mrs. Hudson arrives with our breakfast, my dear fellow."

"Please do Holmes, for I must confess that you are confusing me more than I was before you started this long-winded preface to your solution of the cipher."

[13]Sir Arthur Conan Doyle, "A Case of Identity," in *The Adventures of Sherlock Holmes* (London: George Newnes, 1892; New York: Harper and Brothers; 1892).

[14]Sir Arthur Conan Doyle, *The Hound of the Baskervilles* (London: George Newnes, 1902; New York: McClure Phillips, 1902).

[15]Sir Arthur Conan Doyle, "A Scandal in Bohemia," in *The Adventures of Sherlock Holmes* (London: George Newnes, 1892; New York: Harper & Bros., 1892).

PART 1: THE SECRET CIPHER FORMULA

"Forgive me my dear fellow. Now to the facts of the case. Part one involves the actual cipher itself. You were completely correct when you said that the doctor was incapable of devising a cipher by himself. Your friend, when faced with imminent danger, thought of the idea of sending the formula to us in code. Having remembered your story of *The Dancing Men,* he decided to make a similar code of his own. Realizing that your story was public record, he felt that these enemy agents, as he likes to call them, could also decode the cipher if he made it identical to the one in your story. He then decided to change the cipher by making it more difficult. But as you have previously stated, he certainly was a man of very little imagination. So he added a twist to the cipher, which in fact made it almost impossible to decode, were it not for your off-handed comment about his only being able to write about health, fitness, dieting and walking."

"Yes, I fully remember my words, Holmes, but pray tell how does that fit into the cipher itself?"

"Well my dear fellow, you will remember that I said there were a few singular points of the cipher that I was initially able to unravel. I noted from the first that every other line of the cipher contained three separate groups, each consisting of figures of seven walking men. Each of the three groups of seven figures was different from the others; however, these three separate groups appeared in the same order on every other line. It was as if he was repeating three seven-lettered words over and over again on alternate lines. Well, at first the significance of this singular finding meant nothing, but upon hearing your description of the doctor, the pieces began to fall into place. *You know my method. It is founded upon the observation of trifles. . . . Singularity is almost invariable a clue.*[16] I reasoned that no message could have three different seven-lettered words repeated by themselves on every other line. But then I placed myself in the doctor's limited experience in cipher-making and asked myself what it was that he was knowledgeable about. And your words again rang true, Watson—medicine, health, fitness, dieting and walking. Well the word *medicine* consists of eight letters and the word *health* has

---

[16]Sir Arthur Conan Doyle, "The Boscombe Valley Mystery," in *The Adventures of Sherlock Holmes* (London: George Newnes, 1892; New York: Harper and Bros., 1892).

only six letters. But the other three Watson—*fitness, dieting and walking,* all have seven letters, my dear fellow. Well the cipher then became decodable, since almost all of the most commonly occurring letters in the English alphabet are present in these three words. These letters as you know from our previous case *The Dancing Men,* are E, T, A, O, I, N, S, H, R, D and L. You will notice that except for the letters O, H and R, all of the other common letters occur in these three words. Once having deduced by trial and error, and by applying the simple principles of cryptogram solving, which of the three words were which, the entire cipher became child's play. The three words that appeared on every other line were: *Walking—Dieting—Fitness,* in that order."

Holmes then passed the cipher bearing the drawings of the tiny figures of the walking men to me. Each of the figures had a letter written above it and each set of figures formed a series of words. "Why Holmes," I exclaimed. "This appears to be amazingly simple."

"Elementary my dear Watson," Holmes cried out with a smug look upon his countenance. *"Every problem becomes very childish when once it is explained to you.*[17] But what make you of the meaning of the message, my dear fellow? I'm sure that you'll agree that it is a most singular formula, if we can actually call it that. How do you account for it my dear fellow, for you surely know the doctor far better than I do."

I stared with amazement and wonder at the cipher before me. At first I had not grasped the meaning of the message that now lay before me. I had only seen it as a series of unconnected words. But now reading it aloud, I must confess that it made no sense at all, knowing the doctor as I did, and knowing his stand on the subjects of health and fitness. I have set down the cipher exactly as Holmes had decoded it on that cold October morning.

NEVER WALK ½ HOUR EVERY DAY OR ONE HOUR EVERY OTHER DAY
WALKING - DIETING - FITNESS
NEVER EAT LOW FAT, LOW-CHOLESTEROL, LOW SUGAR, HIGH FIBER FOODS
WALKING - DIETING - FITNESS
NEVER AVOID STRENUOUS EXERCISES, CALISTHENICS, WEIGHT LIFTING & JOGGING
WALKING - DIETING - FITNESS
NEVER AVOID SMOKING, ALCOHOL, DRUGS, CAFFEINE, AND SALT
WALKING - DIETING - FITNESS

---

[17]Sir Arthur Conan Doyle, "The Dancing Men," in *The Return of Sherlock Holmes* (London: George Newnes, 1905; New York: McClure, Phillips, 1905).

"There must be some mistake Holmes. I can't deliver this message to the National Association of Scientific Research. Why it stands for everything that my friend has been against all of these years. I can't believe that he has changed his findings this drastically. Do you actually think that this message represents his new research formula, Holmes? I shudder to think what turn of events will follow, should I read these findings at the Scientific Research meeting. And yet if I do not present his findings, I should be betraying a trust. For God's sake Holmes, what am I to do? Could you possibly have decoded the cipher incorrectly?"

"There, there Watson, don't excite yourself so. Calm yourself, my dear fellow. Do not distress yourself any further. *There is a delightful freshness about you, Watson, which makes it a pleasure to exercise any small powers which I may possess at your expense.*[18] You will plainly see the significance of the meaning of this very unusual cipher, as I now begin to explain the second part of the singular affair of the *Walking Men.*"

"Pray do so, Holmes, for I feel that I'm all at sea with regards to this most uncharacteristic message from my friend. I certainly do not desire to make a mess of this affair at the Scientific Meeting."

PART 2: PROFESSOR MORIARTY & THE SHERLOCK HOLMES CLUB

"Think carefully, Watson. Isn't it particularly strange that of all the thirteen envelopes, the cipher was the very last to arrive. The first twelve envelopes arrived randomly over a 4-day period and yet the cipher straggled in on the seventh day. The odds of that happening Watson, would be better than 13 to 1, and yet it has occurred. A most singular point to make note of my dear fellow. After decoding the cipher Watson, I began to seriously ponder this little oddity. *How often have I said to you that when you have eliminated the impossible, whatever remains, however improbable, must be the truth?*"[19]

"How difficult indeed would it be, Watson, for anyone of

[18]Sir Arthur Conan Doyle, *The Hound of the Baskervilles* (London: George Newnes, 1902; New York: McClure, Phillips, 1902).
[19]Sir Arthur Conan Doyle, *The Sign of Four* (London: Ward Lock 1890; Philadelphia: J.B. Lippincott, 1890).

the twelve so-called friends of Dr. Stutman, from his little Sherlock Holmes club called *The Sons of the Copper Beeches,* to hold his own and the other eleven envelopes up to a strong light, on some pretense mind you, and make a switch when he saw the one containing the 4 x 6 index card and the one with the written letter through the light. It would certainly be easy enough to recognize an index card and a hand-written letter from blank sheets of paper. He, in turn, would be able to keep the envelope with the 4 x 6 index card for himself and follow the other chap with the actual letter to the post office, and somehow or other effect the interception before or after it was posted. Or failing to do this, Watson, he could have arranged to have each letter intercepted, by having each of these chaps followed and their letters taken from them by force, before they were posted. Even if the letters themselves were mailed, I'm sure that these criminal scientists have connections in the U.S. post offices, since as you realize Watson, crime in the States is commonplace. Whatever the actual method of the interception Watson, that is in effect what happened."

"Granted that you're correct, Holmes. I don't quite see what purpose all this serves."

"My dear fellow, *Perhaps there are points which have escaped your Machiavellian intellect,*[20] but no matter. It goes without saying Watson, that there must be a traitor infiltrated in that little club who no doubt is under some grave compulsion from these criminals, to leak vital information to them. Who knows Watson, it may be some unfortunate barrister or medical-man who because of some personal or legal indiscretion, would in turn be the ideal blackmail candidate. For example, *When a doctor does go wrong he is the first of criminals. He has nerve and he has knowledge.*[21] Whatever the reason, he in turn either delivered the cipher and the letter to these criminals or directed them to their prey. I fear, however, that your friend outsmarted himself, Watson, by making his plan so elaborate. The simplest plan is often the one which invariably escapes detection. *The more featureless and commonplace a crime is, the more difficult it is to bring*

[20]Sir Arthur Conan Doyle, *The Valley of Fear* (London: Smith, Elder, 1915; New York: George H. Doran, 1915).
[21]Sir Arthur Conan Doyle, "The Speckled Band" in *The Adventures of Sherlock Holmes* (London: George Newnes, 1892; New York: Harper & Bros., 1892).

home.[22] In this particular case, the more complicated a plan becomes, the more tails it grows, so that the law or as in this case the criminals, to be more precise, have to grab on to."

"Yes, yes Holmes, I see that the doctor was remiss in his plans. But what of it? Where is all this getting us towards your second point, my dear fellow?"

"Patience Watson. You may well remember, that your friend mentioned so-called unscrupulous scientists who were trying to steal his formula. And, in particular, he alluded to an 'evil-looking mathematician.' We must ask your friend for details about this particular person, if and when we ever see him. However, I have no doubt that this mathematician is none other than our old arch-enemy, Professor James Moriarty."

"You can't mean that Holmes. You, better than anyone should know that Moriarty was killed at the Reichenbach Falls several years ago. I believe that it is you who is making this case more complicated than it really is and not the doctor, my good man."

"I'm afraid not my dear fellow. I know that I saw Moriarty fall into the Falls at Reichenbach, Watson, but somehow or other I'm sure that he survived. As you already are aware, I myself barely managed to escape death at those very falls. It is not only this case which has brought this possibility into my mind, Watson, but several other singular occurrences over the past few years which have firmly convinced me that Moriarty is still alive. *There is no one who knows the higher criminal world of London so well as I do. For years past, I have continually been conscious of some power behind the malefactor , some deep organizing power which forever stands in the way of the law, and throws its shield over the wrong-doer.*[23] That power, that force, Watson, can be none other than our old antagonist, Professor Moriarty. Somehow, someway, my dear fellow, our evil friend survived the falls and has resumed his place at the center of his giant spider's web, extending his filaments not only throughout the entire underworld of London, but through the criminal elements of America also. *From the point of view of the criminal expert, London has become a singularly uninteresting city since the (supposed) death of the*

[22]Sir Arthur Conan Doyle, "The Boscombe Valley Mystery" in *The Adventures of Sherlock Holmes* (London: George Newnes, 1892; New York: Harper & Bros., 1892).
[23]Sir Arthur Conan Doyle, "The Final Problem" in *The Memoirs of Sherlock Holmes* (London: George Newnes, 1894; New York: Harper and Brothers 1894).

late lamented Professor Moriarty.[24] However, now Watson, I will once more have the unique opportunity to match wits with the world's foremost criminal mind. I have become lethargic of late, as you well know, my dear fellow. Without adequate stimulation, my mental faculties have grown steadily duller. *To let the brain work without sufficient material is like racing an engine. It racks itself to pieces.*[25] Now pray tell, I can make use of the great genius that the good God gave me to work with. All my brain needed was some oil to lubricate its rusty hinges. Between here, and there and nowhere Watson, lies its endless train of thought."

"I fear that you are straying far from the second point in your explanation of the affair of the walking men, Holmes," said I, attempting not to pay any particular notice to the superior, pompous attitude that my friend was affecting. As I have said on numerous occasions, modesty was not among Holmes' virtues. He could be as vain about his 'superior brain,' as any school-girl was about her beauty.

"Yes, you are quite right, my dear fellow. I digress from the facts of the case. As I have already said, Watson, I feel certain that Moriarty was behind this entire affair. For I'm sure it was he who received both the cipher and the letter from one or more of the *Sherlock Holmes Society's* members, turned traitor or traitors, whatever the case may be. Once determining that the letter held nothing of importance for him, he sent it on to us. He then, I'm sure, sat down with the cipher and decoded it. How long it took him I have no way of knowing, but it must have taken him some few days because of the lateness of its arrival here. The mathematical mind Watson, can sometimes grasp theoretical problems with a much quicker response than the non-mathematician. In any event once having decoded it, he re-coded it, changing the message ever so slightly, just enough, however, to change its meaning entirely; thus rendering an extremely beneficial health and fitness formula into a highly toxic and dangerous one."

"But what of the personal note to me, that the doctor posted himself, Holmes? Why wasn't that intercepted? And how did the criminals know that he wasn't sending the cipher himself?"

[24]Sir Arthur Conan Doyle, The Norwood Builder" in *The Return of Sherlock Holmes* (London: George Newnes, 1905; New York: McClure, Phillips 1905).
[25]Sir Arthur Conan Doyle, "The Devil's Foot" in *His Last Bow* (London: John Murray, 1917; New York: George H. Doran, 1917).

"A good point, Watson. They didn't know! That we can be sure of, my dear fellow. So they must in some way or another have gotten hold of his letter also, either before or after he posted it. Moriarty has evil connections in every sphere, Watson. I'm sure that he has criminal connections also in the U. S. postal offices among other places. Quite an easy job to open and re-seal an envelope without detection. So you see, my dear fellow, one cannot put anything beyond Moriarty's grasp. He invades the atmosphere like a poisonous gas. He is ubiquitous, Watson, being everywhere at once but nowhere to be found. His giant spiders's web with all of its filaments has extended across this very ocean from our grand-old England to the shores of America. And note well Watson, that in America there is fertile criminal soil for Moriarty to sow his deadly evil seeds. So you see my dear fellow, once having discerned that the letter posted by your friend was just a personal message to you—he re-sealed the envelope as he did with the other twelve envelopes (the ten which contained the blank sheets of paper, the one which contained the doctor's long explanatory letter to me, and the one with the cipher) and then sent them all along to us. However, as I have pointed out, he delayed sending the cipher until he had changed it."

"You know Watson, now that I think of it, I must confess that an even simpler explanation of these envelopes comes to mind at this particular time. All thirteen letters could, in fact, have been sent quite innocently from America and then intercepted here in London before they reached us. I have no way of knowing that fact. In any event the results are the same. If in fact the actual deed was done here in London Watson, then I have done these American chaps of the *Sherlock Holmes Society* called *The Sons of the Copper Beeches* a grave disservice by suspecting them of betraying their friend. *One should always look for a possible alternative and provide against it. It is the first rule of criminal investigation.*[26] If once we have determined that the letters were in fact tampered with here in London, I shall personally send a letter of apology to your friend's colleagues in America, for suspecting them of so heinous a crime. Whether Moriarty re-coded the cipher in America or here in London, however, in no way effects the final

[26]Sir Arthur Conan Doyle, "Black Peter" in *The Return of Sherlock Holmes* (London: George Newnes, 1905; New York: McClure, Phillips, 1905).

results of this affair, since I have correctly deduced the mystery of the cipher and the two blunders of Moriarty."

"What blunders," I exclaimed, trying not to lose my patience altogether. "You have certainly taken a complex circuitous route for this so-called simple explanation, of the mystery of *The Walking Men*, Holmes."

"You are perfectly correct in you admonition, Watson. *Perhaps, when a man has special knowledge and special powers like my own, it rather encourages him to seek a complex explanation when a simpler one is at hand.*[27] Mark well this final point of the second part of the mystery, Watson. You will note that I have taken pains to remark on the lateness of the delivery of the cipher and of the odds of that late arrival being greater than 13 to 1. This is where Moriarty made his first blunder, Watson. The reason for its being delivered so late, was that Moriarty need extra time to decode the cipher and once having done this, to then alter the code ever so slightly, so as to change its meaning entirely. Had he but waited to send all of the envelopes at the same time, after decoding and re-coding the cipher, no one would have been the wiser. But he sent out the first twelve envelopes immediately, and waited several days to send out the altered cipher. His mental faculties must still be a little rusty after his fall at Reichenbach, or perhaps he actually sustained a head injury which has jangled the neurons and synapses in his brain."

"In what manner did he change the cipher, Holmes?" I asked, trying not to appear too dull-witted.

"I thought that was obvious, my dear fellow. Of course, by just adding the word *"never"* to the beginning of every other line, Watson. As you no doubt have noticed yourself, without the words *"never"* we have the basis of Dr. Stutman's formula for good health, fitness and longevity. With the word *"never"* added to each sentence, we have the formula for disease, disability and death. So there, my good fellow is the solution to the second part of the riddle of *The Walking Men*. And one further point which you will undoubtedly find as incontrovertible proof that the cipher was altered imperceptibly. You will notice, Watson, that the figures of the walking men which represent the words *"never"* on every other line are a little smaller than the rest of the figures, so that they may comfort-

[27]Sir Arthur Conan Doyle, "The Abbey Grange" in *The Return of Sherlock Holmes* (London: George Newnes, 1905; New York: McClure Phillips, 1905).

ably fit into the margins of the 4 x 6 index card. *You may not be aware that the deduction of a man's age from his writing is one which has been brought to considerable accuracy by experts.*[28] This principle applies to drawings as well as to writing, and this alteration was evidently drawn by a much older man and one with a special knowledge of higher mathematics, Watson. The figures you will note are neatly-drawn and smaller than the rest, almost like a mathematical formula. *You can tell an old master by the sweep of his brush. I can tell a Moriarty when I see one. This crime is from London, not from America.*[29] This was his second and final blunder, Watson."

"Why on earth he didn't re-draw the entire cipher to make it appear uniform, Watson, is however a complete mystery to me. It would then have been impossible to detect any alteration whatsoever in the cipher and this whole affair might have ended quite badly. It must, as I've said before, have been due to the dulling of Moriarty's faculties, for in his hey-day, he would never have made such a blunder, let alone two blatant errors in judgement. No Watson, I fear that we are no longer dealing with the same master criminal brain as we did in our earlier cases. Well, no matter, we have solved the mystery of the cipher of *The Walking Men* and you can now present Dr. Stutman's true findings to the National Scientific Research Meeting, which incidentally, from the date on the calendar is the day after tomorrow. Not a moment too soon, my dear fellow, otherwise general chaos would soon have erupted both in America and here in England."

"Once again, you have made a complex problem appear to be surprisingly easy, Holmes. Yes, I know you don't have to say it again that—*Every problem becomes very childish when once it is explained to you.*[30] I grant that you have made the explanation relatively simple. But what of the third part that you mentioned of this singular problem, Holmes? Surely you have readily solved the riddle of the cipher, so that I may present the true findings of the doctor's research at the Scientific meeting. What then is there left to explain regarding this most unusual affair, Holmes?"

[28]Sir Arthur Conan Doyle, "The Reigate Squires" in *The Memoirs of Sherlock Holmes* (London: George Newnes, 1894; New York: Harper and Brothers, 1894).

[29]Sir Arthur Conan Doyle, *The Valley of Fear* (London: Smith, Elder, 1915; New York: George H. Doran, 1915).

[30]Sir Arthur Conan Doyle, " The Dancing Men" in *The Return of Sherlock Holmes* (London: George Newnes, 1905; New York: McClure, Phillips 1905).

PART 3: FAST FOOD AND
FITNESS FACTORIES

"My dear fellow, you never cease to amaze me. Once having the solution to a particular problem, you are content to look no further. *Crime is common. Logic is rare. Therefore, it is upon the logic rather than upon the crime that you should dwell.*[31] Deduction my dear fellow involves more than just solving a cipher. It is the logical step by step analysis of each phase of a complex problem that invariably leads to its successful solution. In this particular case we have first decoded the cipher. Next we have deduced the method of the cipher's interception and its subsequent alteration. But my dear fellow, you have not even considered the most elementary question in this whole affair. Why, Watson? Why did Moriarty and his henchmen go through all of these elaborate measures to intercept and re-code the cipher? Surely not for the sport of it my dear fellow, for Moriarty has never expended energy for sport. Remember Watson, he is a mathematician and everything that he does is calculated to bring him money and power. Think man, think!"

"I fail to see the point of it Holmes. I must confess that it's as much a mystery to me now as it was when we first received the cipher. Pray tell, please continue with the third part of your solution Holmes. What essential points have I overlooked?"

"Why Watson, have you forgotten who owned the largest chain of fast-food pubs in England before his feigned demise? And who, my dear fellow, was the principle investor in all of the so-called health and fitness centers in London? Why Moriarty of course! These are not well known facts Watson, but— *It is my business to know things. Perhaps I have trained myself to see what others overlook.*[32] In his absence these establishments were run by his henchmen, but now with Moriarty at the helm again, these dens of disease, disability and death will proliferate rapidly. These centers and pubs, my dear fellow, require huge numbers of members and customers in order to turn a pretty profit. It is also not well known, Watson,

---

[31]Sir Arthur Conan Doyle, "The Copper Beeches", in *The Adventures of Sherlock Holmes* (London: George Newnes 1892; New York: Harper & Bros., 1892).

[32]Sir Arthur Conan Doyle, "A Case of Identity in *The Adventures of Sherlock Holmes* (London: George Newnes 1892; New York: Harper Bros., 1892).

that many of his disciples in America are building similar centers and pubs in an effort to fleece the purses of the gullible American public. These Americans also, are ripe pickings for Moriarty and his henchmen, Watson."

"I still don't quite see what you're driving at Holmes. How might Moriarty's establishments profit from this affair?" I asked, trying not to appear utterly confused.

"With the release of the *bogus cipher,* Watson, the public would flock to these establishments like ducks to water. What better news could Moriarty hope for, than to have a world-renowned expert on health and fitness, extol the false virtues of strenuous exercises and a fatty diet. Once the counterfeit message was made public at the Scientific meeting, these so-called fitness-centers would be mobbed with clientele clamoring to be punished with strenuous exercises. These worthy citizens would pay dearly to join these denizens of death, in order to strain and stress themselves towards elusive mythical fitness goals. And the fast-food pubs, Watson, which until recently had suffered a decline in customers for apparent health reasons, would now enjoy a plethora of gluttonous people stuffing their faces with fatty foods and drink. These tawdry taverns would become remarkable wealthy, feeding off of the carcasses of their cholesterol-clogged customers."

"My God Holmes, I never realized the seriousness of the situation. Had I but delivered that deceptive message at the meeting, I would in effect be indirectly responsible for more than a fair number of deaths both here in England and in America."

"Do not distress yourself so, my dear fellow. As you see, all's well that ends well. Now you will be able to present the true findings of your friend's formula at this year's Scientific meeting. And in effect Watson, you will be assisting the good doctor in his fight against sedentary life-styles, strenuous exercises, fatty meals and excessive drink."

"Holmes I can't say that we have ever encountered such a case as this. The entire world will inevitably owe you a debt of gratitude Holmes, not to mention the doctor and myself personally. You have in effect saved both of our reputations, in addition to hundreds of thousands of lives both here and in America. You are truly a genius Holmes to have solved so intricate a problem as this." I said proudly to my friend.

"You are aware Watson that . . . *They say that genius is*

*an infinite capacity for taking pains. It's a very bad definition,
but it does apply to detective work.*[33] You know, my dear fellow,
all this talk about the mystery of the *Walking Men,* puts me in
need of a nice refreshing walk along Baker Street."

A WALK TO WIN

I stared at my friend in amazement upon hearing his very
words. For . . . *Sherlock Holmes was a man who seldom took
exercise for exercise's sake . . . he looked upon aimless bodily
exertion as a waste of energy and he seldom bestirred himself,
save where there was some professional object to be served.*[34]
"To be sure Holmes," I said incredulously. "You really should
get more regular exercise, especially with the erratic hours
that you keep."

"A capital idea, Watson. You are right, *I get so little active
exercise that it is always a treat*[35] to get outdoors and stretch
my legs in a brisk walk. You know Watson, I think that I
might regularly set aside some time every day for a brisk
walk as your friend suggests. It is apparently as good for the
brain as it is for the body, my good man, and it will therefore
aid me in honing more acutely my deductive reasoning powers. For as you readily know . . . *I am a brain, Watson. The rest
of me is a mere appendix. Therefore, it is the brain I must
consider.*[36] Walking will act as nourishment for my brain,
Watson."

As I had previously remarked on many an occasion, modesty was certainly not one of Holmes' strongest suits. "Yes
Holmes, I am quite aware of your superior brain, but I had
quite a different idea in mind so far as our walk was concerned. Have you ever thought of just taking some form of
regular exercise just for fun? Just to feel the fresh air in your
face and to feel and smell nature at your heels. To be at peace
with the world, Holmes, and to be able to relax a little in this
hectic, stress-filled existence of ours. Shouldn't that be the

[33]Sir Arthur Conan Doyle, *A Study in Scarlet,* (London: Ward Lock, 1887).
[34]Sir Arthur Conan Doyle, "The Yellow Face" in *The Memoirs of Sherlock Holmes*
(London: George Newnes, 1894; New York: Harper & Bros., 1894).
[35]Sir Arthur Conan Doyle, "The Solitary Cyclist" in *The Return of Sherlock Holmes*
(London: George Newnes, 1905; New York: McClure, Phillips, 1905).
[36]Sir Arthur Conan Doyle, "The Adventures of the Marazin Stone" in *The Case Book
of Sherlock Holmes* (London: John Murray, 1927; New York: Charles H. Doran,
1927).

primary goal of so blissful and relaxing an exercise like walking? There's more to life than just detective work, Holmes!"

"You know there may be some truth in what so say, Watson, but I rather doubt it. Perhaps, I can combine what you feel are the psychological and healthful benefits of walking with my own singular interpretation of the elements of traveling by foot. *There is no branch of detective science which is so important and so much neglected as the art of tracing footsteps.*[37] This way Watson, I can combine exercise with detective work."

"You are incorrigible Holmes, yet I must admit that your deductive reasoning powers are truly amazing."

"Elementary my dear Watson. We have won my dear fellow, so let us celebrate and call our little victory walk, a *WALK TO WIN.* You know, that has a nice ring to it, Watson. You should mention it to your friend when you see him, as being a good title for one of his little walking books. If he doesn't use it, I may consider writing a small monograph on it myself. *Come, Watson, come!" he cried. "The game is afoot.*[38] Let us begin our walking program."

I smiled as I watched Holmes put on his Inverness cape and his Deer-Stalkers cap. As I waited patiently as he dressed, I again picked up the card with the figures of the *Walking Men* and once again marvelled at the true meaning of Doctor Stutman's secret formula for good health, physical fitness and longevity.

Walk ½ Hour Every Day or One Hour Every Other Day

Eat Low-Fat, Low-Cholesterol, Low-Sugar, High Fiber Foods

Avoid Strenuous Exercises, Calisthenics, Weight Lifting & Jogging

Avoid Smoking, Alcohol, Drugs, Caffeine and Salt

As I put the card with the walking men aside, I exclaimed rather excitedly. "You know Holmes, I think you've really put your finger upon the very essence of the thing. The phrase, *Walk to Win,* not only is a very catchy phrase, but it has a loud ring of truth in it. From my friend's studies, I've learned that

---

[37]Sir Arthur Conan Doyle, *A Study in Scarlet,* (London: Ward Lock, 1887).
[38]Sir Arthur Conan Doyle, "The Abbey Grange" in *The Return of Sherlock Holmes* (London: George Newnes, 1905; New York: McClure Phillips, 1905).

walking is at the core of the very moral fiber and biological structure of our minds and our bodies. In essence, it is at the center of our very existence, Holmes. And I truly believe that you actually do win when you walk regularly every day. You win the war against disease, disability and death. And winning thusly, affords you the bounty of good health, physical fitness, weight-control and above all—longevity. I'll certainly mention the phrase *WALK TO WIN* to the doctor, Holmes, for I feel certain that he will justly be able to use it as an excellent title for his next book."

As we opened the front door and stepped out onto Baker Street, Holmes exclaimed . . . *"How sweet the morning air is! See how that one little cloud floats like a pink feather from some gigantic flamingo. Now the red rim of the sun pushes itself over the London cloud-bank. It shines on a good many folk, but on none, I dare bet, who are on a stranger errand than you and I.*[39] Instead of our usual quest for evil criminals, we are on a walking quest for good health, physical fitness and longevity. Truly a **WALK TO WIN**,[40] Watson."

"Yes it certainly is amazing Holmes."

"Elementary, my dear Watson."

---

[39]Sir Arthur Conan Doyle, *The Sign of Four* (London: Ward Lock, 1890; Philadelphia: J.B. Lippincott, 1890).

[40]Stutman, M.D., Fred A., *Walk to Win* (Philadelphia: Medical Manor Books, 1989.)

"ELEMENTARY, MY DEAR WATSON. TO GET IN SHAPE WE'LL FOLLOW IN DOCTOR STUTMAN'S FOOTSTEPS!"

APPENDIX

CALORIE, SALT & CHOLESTEROL COUNTER

For a quick reference convenience, this listing of commonly consumed foods is indexed alphabetically by main food category, then alphabetically within each category. The sodium, cholesterol, and calorie values are based on data provided by the US Department of Agriculture and by manufacturers and processors of prepared food items. The values listed represent averages obtained from a representative sampling of products within category. Though the actual amount of sodium, cholesterol, and calories may vary between different brands, this index will serve as a useful working guide for record keeping.

ABBREVIATIONS AND SYMBOLS

dia = diameter
fl = fluid
mg = milligram
lb = pound

oz. = ounce

qt. = quart

T = tablespoon
Tr = trace
tsp = teaspoon

" = inch
> = more than
< = less than
+ = values do not include amount of sodium found in the local water used in preparation

- = accurate data unavailable

The following charts are printed with the permission of ICI Pharmaceutical.

FOOD CONTENT GUIDE

FOOD/ITEM	AMOUNT	SODIUM (MG)	CHOLESTEROL (MG)	CALORIES
BEVERAGES				
Bitter Lemon	6 fl. oz.	20+	0	80
Cherry	6 fl. oz.	14+	0	91
Chocolate	6 fl. oz.	12+	0	108
Cola	6 fl. oz.	5+	0	75
Cream Soda	6 fl. oz.	14+	0	86
Ginger Ale	6 fl. oz.	6+	0	66
Grape	6 fl. oz.	12+	0	90
Lemon-lime	6 fl. oz.	32+	0	69
Orange	6 fl. oz.	18+	0	90
Quinine (tonic water)	6 fl. oz.	5+	0	68
Root Beer	6 fl. oz.	7+	0	80
Strawberry	6 fl. oz.	15+	0	89
Carbonated - Low Calorie				
Cherry	6 fl. oz.	49+	0	1
Chocolate	6 fl. oz.	40+	0	2
Cola	6 fl. oz.	33+	0	Tr
Cream Soda	6 fl. oz.	40+	0	<1
Ginger Ale	6 fl. oz.	19+	0	1
Grape	6 fl. oz.	59+	0	1
Lemon-Lime	6 fl. oz.	57+	0	Tr
Orange	6 fl. oz.	39+	0	Tr
Root Beer	6 fl. oz.	37+	0	<1
Noncarbonated				
Cocoa	8.8 fl. oz.	128	35	242
Coffee - Ground	6 fl. oz.	1	0	2
Decaffeinated	6 fl. oz.	<1	0	3
Freeze-dried	6 fl. oz.	<1	0	4
Coffee - Instant	6 fl. oz.	1	0	2
Instant-flavored	6 fl. oz.	2	0	56
Juices - Apple	6 fl. oz.	1	0	90
Cranberry	6 fl. oz.	5	0	103
Grapefruit	4.4 fl. oz.	2	0	104
Orange -				
fresh	4.4 fl. oz.	1	0	60
canned	4.4 fl. oz.	1	0	66
crystals	4.4 fl. oz.	1	0	57
frozen	4.4 fl. oz.	1	0	56
Prune	4.5 fl. oz.	2	0	99
Tomato	4.3 fl. oz.	244	0	23
Lemonade (frozen)	4.4 fl. oz.	1	0	55
Tea (slightly sweetened)	8.4 fl. oz.	0	0	5
Alcoholic Beverages				
Beer - canned, regular	12 fl. oz.	25	0	150
canned, low-cal.	12 fl. oz.	Tr	0	110
Distilled Liquor*				
80 Proof	1 fl. oz.	<1	0	65
86 Proof	1 fl. oz.	<1	0	70
90 Proof	1 fl. oz.	<1	0	74

FOOD CONTENT GUIDE

FOOD/ITEM	AMOUNT	SODIUM (MG)	CHOLESTEROL (MG)	CALORIES
94 Proof	1 fl. oz.	<1	0	77
100 Proof	1 fl. oz.	<1	0	83
Manhattan Cocktail (can)	3 fl. oz.	Tr	0	123
Martini Cocktail (canned)	3 fl. oz.	Tr	0	100
Tom Collins Cocktail (can)	3 fl. oz.	Tr	0	105
Whiskey Sour Cocktail	3 fl. oz.	Tr	0	120
Wine - Burgundy	3 fl. oz.	3	0	73
Chablis	3 fl. oz.	3	0	62
Champagne	3 fl. oz.	3	0	75
Cooking	4 fl. oz.	657	0	2
Dessert	3 fl. oz.	4	0	122
Table	3 fl. oz.	4	0	75

FOOD CONTENT GUIDE

FOOD/ITEM	AMOUNT	SODIUM (MG)	CHOLESTEROL (MG)	CALORIES
BREADS/CRACKERS				
Cornbread	4 oz.	449	0	231
Cracked-wheat	1 slice	136	0	60
Date-nut	½" slice	150	26	80
French	1 slice	133	1	67
Italian	1 slice	135	1	63
Pumpernickel	1 slice	131	1	75
Raisin	1 slice	91	4	75
Rye	1 slice	139	1	70
Vienna	1 slice	133	1	70
Wheat	1 slice	140	0	73
White	1 slice	117	4	62
Whole-wheat	1 slice	132	1	56
Crackers				
Butter	1 oz.	310	3	130
Cheese-flavored	1 oz.	295	1	136
Cheese & Peanut Butter	1 oz.	281	3	139
Corn Chips	1 oz.	160	1	160
Graham	2½" square	47	0	30
Melba Toast	1 piece	30	2	10
Oyster	1 cup	312	0	124
Saltine	1 cracker	35	1	12
Soda	2½" square	60	0	24
Cracker crumbs, Graham	1 cup	576	0	330
Cracker meal	1 T	110	0	44
CEREALS				
Bran Flakes	½ cup	172	0	84
Bran Flakes - raisin	½ cup	154	0	100
Corn Flakes	1 cup	291	0	112

FOOD CONTENT GUIDE

FOOD/ITEM	AMOUNT	SODIUM (MG)	CHOLESTEROL (MG)	CALORIES
Hominy Grits	1 cup	502	0	112
Oatmeal (cooked w/o salt)	1 cup	2	0	132
Oat Flakes	⅔ cup	198	0	107
Rice (cooked w/o salt)	⅔ cup	1	0	120
Shredded Wheat (w/o salt)	1 cup	1	0	146
Wheat Flakes	1 cup	722	0	248
CONDIMENTS/CONDIMENT-TYPE SAUCES				
Barbecue Sauce	1 T	130	0	19
Catsup	1 T	188	0	19
Chili Sauce	1 T	201	0	16
Hollandaise Sauce	1 T	83	0	15
Lemon Juice	1 T	<1	0	4
Mustard	1 T	118	0	8
Pickle Relish - Sweet	1 T	107	0	21
Sour	1 T	110	0	3
Seafood Cocktail	1 T	261	0	22
Soy Sauce	1 oz.	2077	0	10
Steak Sauce	1 T	276	0	20
Tartar Sauce	1 T	136	4	81
Tabasco	½ tsp	6	0	0
Vinegar - Cider	½ cup	1	0	17
Distilled	½ cup	1	0	14
Red or White Wine	2 T	10	0	1

FOOD CONTENT GUIDE

FOOD/ITEM	AMOUNT	SODIUM (MG)	CHOLESTEROL (MG)	CALORIES
DAIRY PRODUCTS/EGGS				
Butter				
Salted	¼ lb. (1 stk)	1119	284	812
Salted	1 T	138	35	100
Unsalted	¼ lb. (1 stk)	11	284	812
Unsalted	1 T	1	35	100
Whipped, salted	1 T	89	22	67
Whipped, unsalted	1 T	<1	22	67
Cheese				
American or Cheddar Natural	1 oz.	198	28	68
Diced	1 cup (4.6 oz)	917	130	521
Grated	1 cup (3.9 oz)	777	110	442
Process, regular	1 slice	322	25	85
Process, reduced sodium	1 slice	184	25	63
Bleu or Blue	1 oz.	390	24	64
Colby	1 oz.	169	27	110
Cottage Cheese - Reg	4 oz.	260	20	120
Dietetic (low-fat)	4 oz.	499	<2	88

FOOD CONTENT GUIDE

FOOD/ITEM	AMOUNT	SODIUM (MG)	CHOLESTEROL (MG)	CALORIES
Flavored	4 oz.	360	<3	128
Cream Cheese - Plain, unwhipped	1 oz.(2 T)	70	113	100
Plain, whipped	1 oz.	25	32	98
Farmer	1 oz.	111	6	91
Limburger	1 oz.	227	28	93
Muenster	1 oz.	204	25	104
Parmesan, grated	1 T	78	10	23
Swiss	1 oz.	201	28	102
Cheese, American	1 slice	337	20	90
Cheese Spread	1 T (.05 oz.)	228	9	50
Cream				
Half & Half	8 fl. oz.	111	104	320
Light table or coffee	1 T (.05 oz.)	6	10	32
Whipping	8.5 fl. oz.	76	317	838
Sour	8 fl. oz.	99	152	485
Dip	2 T	203	13	111
Margarine (no animal or vegetable fats)				
Salted - (1 stk)	¼ lb.	1119	0	817
Salted	1 T	138	0	101
Unsalted - (1 stk)	¼ lb.	11	0	817
Unsalted	1 T	1	0	101
Whipped, salted	½ cup	750	0	578
Whipped, unsalted	1 T	70	0	70
Milk				
Condensed	1 cup	343	105	982
Dry, whole	1 cup	587	158	728
Nonfat, instant	⅞ cup	484	20	82
Evaporated	1 cup	297	79	345
Fresh - Whole	1 cup	122	34	150
Whole 2%	1 cup	150	22	120
Skim	1 cup	127	5	90
Ice Cream, 10% fat, Regular	1 cup	84	53	257
Ice Milk, hardened	1 cup	89	26	199
Yogurt - Regular	½ cup	62	10	68
Low-calorie	½ cup	62	4	45
Eggs				
Chicken - white only	1 large	48	0	17
yolk only	1 large	9	250	59
Boiled, no salt	1 large	61	250	81
Fried in butter	1 large	155	284	99
Poached	1 large	130	242	78
Scrambled, with milk & cooked in fat	1 large	164	263	111
Egg substitute	¼ cup	0	<1	40
DESSERTS/PASTRIES				
Cakes, home recipe with icing - Angel Food	1" wedge	132	0	126
Chocolate, 2-layer	1" wedge	253	46	394
Devil's Food	1" wedge	253	46	394
Sponge	1" wedge	128	189	229
Cookies - Brownie	1 oz.	57	16	126

FOOD CONTENT GUIDE

FOOD/ITEM	AMOUNT	SODIUM (MG)	CHOLESTEROL (MG)	CALORIES
Butter	1 oz.	119	15	23
Chocolate	1 oz.	39	5	28
Chocolate Chip	1 oz.	114	10	53
Coconut Bar	1 oz.	42	10	43
Fig Bar	1 oz.	71	5	74
Gingersnap	1 oz.	162	5	30
Macaroon	1 oz.	10	5	95
Molasses	1 oz.	109	15	60
Oatmeal	1 oz.	46	10	83
Peanut Butter	1 oz.	49	10	35
Raisin	1 oz.	15	1	60
Sandwich, creme	1 oz.	137	15	70
Shortbread	1 oz.	17	10	40
Sugar Wafer	1 oz.	54	20	19
Cupcake, with icing	2¾″	114	10	184
Doughnut - Cake Type	1	160	30	125
Powdered	1	38	30	117
Sugared	1	34	30	150
Pastry - Danish	2.3 oz.	238	20	161
Pie, home recipe, 2 crust - Apple - wedge	1½″	476	7	404
Blueberry	1½″	423	10	382
Cherry	1½″	480	10	412
Peach	1½″	423	10	405
Pecan (1 crust)	1½″	305	30	577
Pumpkin	1½″	325	93	321

FOOD CONTENT GUIDE

FOOD/ITEM	AMOUNT	SODIUM (MG)	CHOLESTEROL (MG)	CALORIES
FISH/SHELLFISH				
Bass - freshwater, baked, stuffed fillet	4 oz.	30	75	294
Bass - striped, oven-fried fillet	4 oz.	30	75	222
Catfish - freshwater fillet	4 oz.	68	80	117
Crab - drained solids	1 cup	1600	162	200
Crab Imperial	1 cup	1602	308	323
Fish Sticks, frozen	4 oz.	80	30	200
Flounder, baked	4 oz.	269	65	229
Frog Legs, meat only	4 oz.	0	57	83
Grouper, meat only	4 oz.	-	70	99
Haddock, fried in batter	3½ oz.	177	66	165
Perch - yellow, meat only	4 oz.	77	64	103
Pompano, meat only	4 oz.	53	70	188
Salmon, canned, no salt	4 oz.	73	40	238
Sardine, canned	3½ oz.	541	127	330
Scallops, steamed	4 oz.	301	60	127
Shrimp, meat only	4 oz.	159	170	103
Shrimp, french-fried	4 oz.	211	250	255

FOOD CONTENT GUIDE

FOOD/ITEM	AMOUNT	SODIUM (MG)	CHOLESTEROL (MG)	CALORIES
Trout - rainbow, dressed	4 oz.	-	62	221
Tuna, canned in water, no salt	6½ oz.	75	116	234
Walleye, meat only	4 oz.	58	75	105
Whitefish, meat only	4 oz.	59	21	176

FOOD CONTENT GUIDE

FOOD/ITEM	AMOUNT	SODIUM (MG)	CHOLESTEROL (MG)	CALORIES
FRUITS				
Fresh				
Apple, with skin (any variety)	2½" dia.	1	0	61
Avocado, peeled, cubed	1 cup	6	0	251
Banana, peeled, med.	6 oz.	1	0	101
Blueberries, canned, water pack	½ cup	1	0	47
Cantalope, fresh, cubed	½ cup	10	Tr	24
Cherries - sour, pitted	½ cup	2	0	45
sweet, peeled	½ cup	2	0	57
Cranberries	1 cup	2	0	52
Date, without pit	4 oz.	1	0	311
Grapefruit	½ medium	1	0	50
Grapes	½ cup	4	0	33
Lemon	1 medium	3	0	20
Lime	1 medium	1	0	15
Orange	1 medium	2	0	73
Peach, no skin	1 medium	1	0	38
Pear	1 medium	3	0	101
Plum	1 medium	2	0	75
Prune, dried	1 medium	<1	0	43
Raisin	4 oz.	31	0	205
Strawberries	1 cup	1	0	53
Watermelon	4" wedge	4	0	111
Canned				
Applesauce, sweetened	½ cup	3	0	97
Blueberries*	½ cup	1	0	126
Cherries*	½ cup	1	0	109
Cranberry Sauce	½ cup	1	0	202
Grapefruit*	½ cup	1	0	74
Grapes*	4 oz.	5	0	65
Olives, green, pitted	4 med.	384	0	134
Peaches*	4 oz.	2	0	79
Pears*	4 oz.	1	0	87
Plums*	4 oz.	1	0	107
Prunes, stewed	1 cup	3	0	262
Raisins, cooked	½ cup	16	0	260
Frozen				
Apples	4 oz.	16	0	158
Blueberries	4 oz.	1	0	120
Cherries, sour	4 oz.	3	0	146
Peaches	4 oz.	2	0	104
Strawberries	4 oz.	1	0	97

FOOD CONTENT GUIDE

FOOD/ITEM	AMOUNT	SODIUM (MG)	CHOLESTEROL (MG)	CALORIES
MEAT				
Bacon, sliced	1 piece	193	20	189
Beef - Brisket	4 oz.	68	107	467
Chuck	4 oz.	68	107	371
Flank	4 oz.	68	103	222
Ground	4 oz.	53	107	248
Rib Roast	4 oz.	68	107	499
Round	4 oz.	68	107	296
Rump	4 oz.	68	107	393
Steak, Club	4 oz.	68	107	515
Steak, Porterhouse	4 oz.	68	107	527
Steak, Ribeye	4 oz.	68	107	450
Steak, Sirloin	4 oz.	68	107	463
Steak, T-bone	4 oz.	68	107	536
Beef Hash	7½ oz.	1327	62	396
Bologna	1 slice	245	13	84
Braunschweiger	1 oz.	300	55	101
Corned Beef	4 oz.	1313	75	220
Frankfurter	1 weiner	499	29	140
Ham	4 oz.	174	101	424
Lamb, leg	4 oz.	79	111	316
Liver - Beef	4 oz.	209	497	260
Calf	4 oz.	134	497	296
Chicken	4 oz.	69	846	187
Turkey	4 oz.	62	679	157
Pork - Boston Butt Roast	4 oz.	74	100	400
Chop	4 oz.	49	67	332
Spareribs	4 oz.	74	101	499
Sausage, pork	1 oz.	240	18	115
Veal	4 oz.	91	115	266
POULTRY				
Chicken - light meat	4 oz.	75	99	206
dark meat	4 oz.	100	99	209
skin, fried	1 oz.	-	21	119
Duck	4 oz.	84	198	172
Turkey - light meat	4 oz.	58	68	132
dark meat	4 oz.	92	85	145
skin only	1 oz.	-	41	128
SPREADS/OILS/SALAD DRESSINGS				
Spreads				
Honey	1 T	1	0	61
Jam	1 T	2	0	54
Jelly	1 T	3	0	49
Marmalade	1 T	3	0	51
Mayonnaise	1 T	84	0	104
Peanut Butter	1 T	97	0	101
Sandwich Spread	1 T	94	4	57

FOOD CONTENT GUIDE

FOOD/ITEM	AMOUNT	SODIUM (MG)	CHOLESTEROL (MG)	CALORIES
Oils, Salads & Cooking				
All types, including olive	1 T	0	0	124
Salad Dressings				
Blue Cheese	1 T	164	6	66
French	1 T	219	3	101
Italian	1 T	314	Tr	65
Roquefort	1 T	164	9	65
Russian	1 T	130	4	65
Thousand Island	1 T	112	Tr	61
Salad Dressings - Dietetic				
Blue Cheese	1 T	229	4	20
French	1 T	153	0	21
Italian	1 T	216	0	15
Russian	1 T	162	0	18
Thousand Island	1 T	140	6	29
SNACKS				
Candy Corn	1 oz.	60	0	103
Cheese Crackers	1 piece	20	0	10
Nuts, mixed - dry roasted, salted	1 oz.	189	0	170
oil roasted	1 oz.	220	0	189
Peanuts, roasted - salted, no skins	1 oz.	119	0	163
unsalted, with skins	1 oz.	1	0	163
Popcorn - butter and salt	1 oz.	550	110	129
plain	1 oz.	<1	0	109
Potato Chips	1 oz.	284	90	161
Pretzels	1 oz.	476	0	110
SOUPS				
Bean	1 cup	1049	22	168
Beef Noodle	1 cup	949	5	100
Chicken Noodle	1 cup	959	7	72
Clam Chowder, New England	1 cup	1954	50	160
Mushroom, creamed	1 cup	1082	1	216
Onion	1 cup	992	0	65
Pea - green, with water	1 cup	899	8	130
split, with water	1 cup	941	8	130
Potato, creamed	1 cup	1049	5	112
Tomato, with milk	1 cup	1055	23	172
Vegetable	1 cup	830	2	78

FOOD CONTENT GUIDE

FOOD/ITEM	AMOUNT	SODIUM (MG)	CHOLESTEROL (MG)	CALORIES
SALT/SPICED (PACKAGED)				
Garlic Salt	1 tsp	1850	0	2
Onion Salt	1 tsp	1620	0	4
Seasoning Salt	1 tsp	1620	0	1
Substitute Salt	1 tsp	<1	0	Tr
Table Salt	1 tsp	2325	0	0
Basil	1 tsp	TR	0	3
Bay Leaf	1 med.	TR	0	5
Nutmeg	1 tsp	<1	0	11
Oregano	1 tsp	<1	0	6
Parsley	1 tsp	5	0	4
Pepper, black	1 tsp	<1	0	9
Tarragon	1 tsp	<1	0	5
Thyme	1 tsp	<1	0	5
SUGAR/CANDY				
Sugar				
Brown	1 T	4	0	48
Brown	1 cup	64	0	791
Confectioners'	1 T	<1	0	30
Confectioners'	1 cup	1	0	474
Granulated	1 T	<1	0	46
Granulated	1 cup	2	0	751
Maple	1 oz.	4	0	99
Sugar Substitute	1 tsp	Tr	0	2

"WALKERS: BY JASON MELISH, FOURTH GRADE. MY DAD SAYS THE BEST WALKER IS JOHNNY WALKER. THE END."

INDEX

Rockwell

"I NEVER SAW A JOGGER SMILE. IT HURTS TOO MUCH!"

A WINNING COMBINATION
THE BEST WALKING BOOKS &
A 30-DAY MONEY-BACK GUARANTEE

Please send me the following books. It is my understanding that if I am not completely satisfied with any book, I may return it within 30 days for a full refund. Thank you.

QUANTITY	TITLE OF BOOK	PRICE	TOTAL AMOUNT
	Walk, Don't Run Medical Manor Press (ISBN 0-934232-00-8)	$6.95	
	The Doctor's Walking Book Ballantine Books (ISBN 0-345-28764-9)	$5.95	
	DietWalk® Pocket Books (ISBN 0-671-61450-9)	$3.95	
	Walk, Don't Die (Hardcover) Medical Manor Books (ISBN 0-934232-06-7)	$18.95	
	Walk, Don't Die (Paperback) Medical Manor Books (ISBN 0-934232-05-9)	$9.95	
	Walk to Win (Hardcover) Medical Manor Books (ISBN 0-934232-08-3)	$19.95	
	Walk to Win (Paperback) Medical Manor Books (ISBN 0-934232-07-5)	$10.95	
	Dr. Walk's® Diet & Fitness Newsletter Medical Manor Books (4 issues/year)	$9.95	
	TOTAL NUMBER OF BOOKS ORDERED	Sub-total	
☐ Check enclosed with order. ☐ Please charge to my credit card number: ☐ American Express ☐ Visa ☐ MasterCard		Postage $1.25/ book	
		TOTAL ORDER	

Number _____ Exp. Date_____

Name_____ Signature _____

Address_____ Company Name_____

_____ Phone Number _____

Medical Manor Books, 3501 Newberry Road, Phila., PA 19154   (800) DIETING

In Pa. (215) 637-WALK

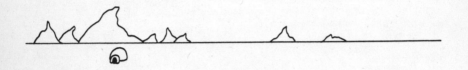

"YOU'RE THE ONE WHO WANTED TO GO FOR A WALK IN HIGH-HEELS!"